Institut International de Philosophie
International Institute of Philosophy

Philosophy of Education
Philosophie de l'éducation
Pädagogische Philosophie

edited by/édité par/herausgegeben von

Prof. Dr. Peter Kemp
(Institut International de Philosophie &
School of Education, Aarhus University)

Volume/Band 1

LIT

Peter Kemp (ed./éd./Hg.)

COMMITMENT IN EDUCATION

LIT

Cover Illustration copyright Nyoman Nuarta: **Horizon** 2000
(Polester resin 83 × 30 × 40).
The illustration is taken from the book : Nyoman Nuarta, edited by
Jim Supangkat, published by The Garuda Wisnu Kencana Foundation,
Jakarta, 2001

Gedruckt auf alterungsbeständigem Werkdruckpapier entsprechend
ANSI Z3948 DIN ISO 9706

Bibliographic information published by the Deutsche Nationalbibliothek
The Deutsche Nationalbibliothek lists this publication in the Deutsche
Nationalbibliografie; detailed bibliographic data are available in the Internet at
http://dnb.d-nb.de.

ISBN 978-3-8258-1713-8

A catalogue record for this book is available from the British Library

©LIT VERLAG Dr. W. Hopf Berlin 2009
Fresnostr. 2 D-48159 Münster
Tel. +49 (0) 2 51-620 32 22   Fax +49 (0) 2 51-922 60 99
e-Mail: lit@lit-verlag.de   http://www.lit-verlag.de

Distribution:
In Germany: LIT Verlag Fresnostr. 2, D-48159 Münster
Tel. +49 (0) 2 51-620 32 22, Fax +49 (0) 2 51-922 60 99, e-Mail: vertrieb@lit-verlag.de

In Austria: Medienlogistik Pichler-ÖBZ GmbH & Co KG
IZ-NÖ, Süd, Straße 1, Objekt 34, A-2355 Wiener Neudorf
Tel. +43 (0) 22 36-63 53 52 90, Fax +43 (0) 22 36-63 53 52 43, e-Mail: mlo@medien-logistik.at

In Switzerland: B + M Buch- und Medienvertriebs AG
Hochstr. 357, CH-8200 Schaffhausen
Tel. +41 (0) 52-643 54 85, Fax +41 (0) 52-643 54 35, e-Mail: order@buch-medien.ch

Distributed in the UK by: Global Book Marketing, 99B Wallis Rd, London, E9 5LN
Phone: +44 (0) 20 8533 5800 – Fax: +44 (0) 1600 775 663
http://www.centralbooks.co.uk/html

Distributed in North America by:

Transaction Publishers
New Brunswick (U.S.A.) and London (U.K.)

Transaction Publishers
Rutgers University
35 Berrue Circle
Piscataway, NJ 08854

Phone: +1 (732) 445 - 2280
Fax: + 1 (732) 445 - 3138
for orders (U. S. only):
toll free (888) 999 - 6778
e-mail: orders@transactionpub.com

THE I.I.P. COLLECTION ON PHILOSOPHY OF EDUCATION

EDITORIAL

"Philosophy of Education" is a philosophy focusing on education. Specifically, how is education possible in a multicultural world, where new problems raised by new technologies in communication and production challenge traditional thinking across all national and regional borders? They challenge the role of the teacher, the educational relationship, the social and institutional conditions of education and the importance of education for the future of society: for ethical and social justice, for cosmopolitan upbringing and for the climate and the environment in general.

These are the main problems considered in the Collection on "Philosophy of Education" sponsored by the International Institute of Philosophy.

Peter KEMP,
Professor Emeritus at the School of
Education, Aarhus/Copenhagen,
President of the XXIInd World Congress
of Philosophy,
General Treasurer of the
International Institute of Philosophy.

TABLE OF CONTENTS

Peter KEMP, *Introduction* 9
Evandro AGAZZI, *Must Education be Committed?* 21
Alexander VON OETTINGEN, *Philosophy of Education and Educational Antinomies* 35
Henrik VASE FRANDSEN, *The Concept of Freedom between Religious Interpretation and Political Application* 57
Irene SVITZOU, *Education and Pleasure in Plato's* Laws 69
Evanghélos MOUTSOPOULOS, *Education – A Lasting Value* 79
Guttorm FLØISTAD, *Value-Based Leadership in Education* 93
Hans LENK, *Achievement Motivation and Enthusiasm. Authentic Commitment and Enthusing Participation in Sport and Education*... 121
Vladislav A. LEKTORSKY, *Education as Creativity* 147
Lars-Henrik SCHMIDT, *Untraditional Education* 159
Kurt NIELSEN & Anne-Marie EGGERT OLSEN, *Educating for Democracy: Adaptation or Political Awareness?* 177
Peter KEMP, *Cosmopolitan Commitment in Education* 195
About the Authors 215
Index 219

INTRODUCTION

Peter KEMP
(School of Education, Aarhus University,
Campus: Copenhagen, Denmark)

It is not easy to be an educator in a post-modern world. On the one hand, communication systems have developed in such a way with the invention of the computer and the internet that it seems we can find all the knowledge we need there and that the personal teacher becomes superfluous as mediator of knowledge and even distracting for the pupil or the student. On the other hand the human being has more and more acquired an idea of the importance of its own subjectivity and its right to be free in its appropriation of knowledge and norms that committed teaching is often considered as an intrusion into its personal life. From this point of view the committed teacher seems superfluous as mediator of norms and even offensive to the pupil or the student.

The authors of this book agree that education as transmission of scientific knowledge is totally insufficient for human beings today in a technological society, because wisdom about the good life between people and about norms in general cannot be deduced from "neutral" scientific and technological knowledge about world and life. They also agree that education as upbringing and formation of the human being cannot dispense with the commitment of the educator who must stand for what he or she teaches. Thus, a school with a teacher that educates as a machine is like a school without a teacher, a nightmare of an inhuman system of education.

It follows that the crucial questions for the philosophy of education in our time are: What is commitment? What is a committed educator? How is it possible to be committed in education?

As Evandro Agazzi points out in this book, commitment according to *The Concise Oxford Dictionary* means "engagement or involvement that restricts freedom of action". It is a restricting action. Restriction by what? By the cause one is committed to. This can be said in English. But it is remarkable that the dictionary uses the French term *"engagement"* in order to define commitment. Therefore the question: "What is commitment?" can be equated with the question: "What is engagement?"

1. THE MEANING OF ENGAGEMENT

Let us briefly recall the development of the meaning of this word and its concept[1].

The verb *"engager"* in French means *"mettre en gage"* or *"donner en gage"* (to give something as security). The word *"gage"* comes through the German word *"wadi"* from latin *vas, vadis*. The verb *"vado"* means "I am approaching someone". The noun *"vas"* then get the meaning: what I put into the hands of someone as security for my debt. And in law a *vasimodium* becomes a gesture which guarantees that a defendant will present him- or herself before a court. Finally it simply means the legal process itself.

At the end of the 11th Century, at the time of the birth of French culture, the word *"wadi"* was replaced by the word *"gage"*. In the following century the verb *"engager"* appears in *La geste des Lotharains* for the first time. And the noun *"engagement"* appears simultaneously in *La Charte d'Abbéville*. But *"engager"* has in the beginning only a legal sense indicating the debtor's giving of a deposit to his lender as security for his debt.

Thus, originally engagement is an attachment, an action by which a human being binds itself. This explains that the meaning of *"engagement"* could lose its pure legal sense and acquire a more ethical sense. Being a bond of oneself by something no matter what, *"engagement"* does not require a material guarantee, giving one's word is sufficient. By giving one's word one has committed one's honour in a promise. And one loses the esteem of others if one betrays one's word and does not keep one's promise.

Thereby the intransitive verb *"s'engager"* is created in the sense of to commit oneself to something. Engagement becomes an act of putting at stake: I tie myself, my action for the future. This existential meaning appears in Montaigne and Pascal. And the opposite to engagement appears as *"dégagement"* that means the act by which one withdraws from the play.

---

[1] Cf. Peter KEMP, *Théorie de l'engagement*, tome I, *Pathétique de l'engagment*, Éditions du Seuil, Paris 1973, pp. 16-17.

However, in French *engagement* loses often its strong existential meaning and becomes identical with hiring a person. It can also designate the mutual promise (in English: an engagement) of a couple, an investment, a recruitment, the beginning of a battle, an encounter between enemies, etc.

But *engagement* has still preserved its existential meaning in other contexts, so that, as we have seen, it can enter into the definition of the English word, commitment. And in French philosophy of the first half of the 20th Century some important figures such as Gabriel Marcel, Emmanuel Mounier and Jean-Paul Sartre have revitalized the existential concept of *engagement*. To Marcel *"engager"* is putting one's own reality at stake[2]. To Mounier in his early writings engagement is the incarnation of the human spirit in action, and in his main work, *Traité du caractère* published in 1946, it is the person's reaction in responsibility to the appeals of the world[3]. To J-P. Sartre, inspired by Marcel, Mounier et Paul-Louis Landsberg[4], engagement means taking action in the world in order to shape its future, and after World War II he presented his whole thinking as a philosophy of engagement[5].

The existential sense of the concept of engagement or commitment is the background of all the essays in this book. It is the unspoken presupposition of the question about what education might be, how education is possible today where the educator has to practise in a world that seems to be able to do without a teacher as a person committed to a culture, to an idea of humanity and an idea of a globalized ethics.

2. IDEAS OF COMMITTED EDUCATION

Let us take a look at the different suggestions about what committed education might be in our time and the problems that the educator has to consider in the present world where he or she seems to be more and more superfluous as a mediator of knowledge and norms, and where the pupil and the student seem to have no other role than being a transformer of knowledge into technical functions at the same time as he or she paradoxically believes that the only lasting value is one's own individuality or inner life.

---

[2] Gabriel MARCEL, *Journal Métaphysique* (1928), Gallimard, Paris 1935, p. 183.
[3] Emmanuel MOUNIER, "Révolution personnaliste" (1934), in *Œuvres*, I, Seuil, Paris 1961, p. 179; "Traité du caractère" (1946), in *Œuvres*, II, p. 422.
[4] Cf. Peter KEMP, *Pathétique de l'engagment*, pp. 19-33.
[5] Jean-Paul SARTRE, *L'être et le néant,* Gallimard, Paris 1943, pp. 352 et 558; *L'existentialisme est un humanisme* (1946), Nagel, Paris 1982, p. 101.

In his essay "Must Education be Committed?" *Evandro Agazzi* focuses on the possibility of education facing the claim of being free, i.e. free from indoctrination, from ideas imposed as valuable without the possibility of free consent. Is the educator not limiting him- or herself by being committed to certain values, and is his or her teaching not an effort to limit the freedom of others to the same values? The answer is that the educator certainly limits him- or herself by being committed, but that the commitment if it is authentic is freely contracted. It follows that the limit of freedom of action is not a limit of freedom of choice. Our choice of commitment might have been otherwise, but if it is a true engagement, nothing has forced this choice, and nobody can oblige anybody to a certain commitment. Moreover, for the pupil and student a committed education should be a help offered to him or her for filling his or her freedom of choice with a concrete presentation of possible ultimate ends that can be chosen as guidelines for action and a good life. Thus, Agazzi claims that the commitment in education not only can, but must be an orientation of action and not a limitation of freedom. Indeed, values as ultimate ends have a force of attraction and not of coercion. They play a fundamental role as articulations of certain more general values such as human dignity, equality, justice and solidarity.

In his chapter on "Philosophy of Education and Educational Antinomies" *Alexander von Oettingen* considers the same problem by considering the need for education in relation to respect for the freedom of the other as the root of a series of antinomies in educational theory and practice. According to Oettingen, these antinomies have different forms: one of them consists in anticipating the future of the child by telling him or her about what to do and not knowing which standards and values will be the best for the child. And already in *Émile* (1762) by Jean-Jacques Rousseau he finds a paradigmatic antinomy in the contrast between an upbringing in view of life in the city and the idea of the free individual. According to Wilhelm von Humboldt (1767-1838) education must focus on both the individual and the world and relate them to each other. But the world is very differentiated having financial, political, normative, social, scientific and technical conditions. Therefore there must be public education where the child and the student learn to discuss the relationships to the world. However, theory is not enough as stressed by Humboldt's contemporary, Johann Friedrich Herbart. He developed a philosophy of education in which he launched an idea of educational tact that implies that individual decisions and educational experience cannot be totally captured by theory. He claimed that the object of educational practice is the methodical and intentional transmission from the educator to the educated, all the while philosophy of education is the reflection on the conditions of realizing this transmission. Oettingen consider that we still need such a philosophy of education in order to clarify the antinomies we have to handle in educational practise. He pleads for such a philosophy that is neither anti-empirical nor normatively neutral and least of all unscientific, but may contribute to the discussion of what constitutes educational normativity.

Whereas Oettingen scutinizes the antinomies in education, *Henrik Vase Frandsen* in his chapter on "The Concept of Freedom between Religious Interpretation and Political Application", focuses on the ambivalent experience of freedom that is the ground of the antinomies we encounter as educators. How can the freedom to which I educate people and myself be the result of my freedom to choose and begin an education? And to the extent that this freedom restricts the freedom of the other, how can we justify this restriction that I have chosen freely to provoke? Frandsen reminds us that according to Immanuel Kant and Hannah Arendt freedom is a new begining, it consists in the act of beginning something. But how to educate to this freedom? Frandsen answers that this happens by appeal. The true teacher does not indoctrinate, but makes an appeal in the way he teaches his material. For the student this appeal comes from another, but this fact in itself is not an indoctrination, since the student only hears it and is influenced by it when he responds to it. And if the urgency and pressing character of the appeal is a pressure of a nearly religious character, it is a pressure to freedom, to beginning, to engagement. So the appeal not only presupposes committment of the educator, but intends to arouse the commitment of the student.

Now the question of the ultimate end of education can be raised. Why do human beings need education? What is the highest goal of all the educational activities? This question was considered already from the very beginning of western philosophy, by Plato and Aristotle. As *Irene Svitzou* shows in her essay on "Education and Pleasure in Plato's *Laws*", two goals of education are combined in the classical Greek view: persons' *eudaemonia* or pleasure and the preservation of the City State as a whole. In his dialogue on *Laws* the elder Plato claims that the laws of the society have to serve these two goals. Although he recognizes that we might only be puppets in the hands of God, he considers that we cannot do without commitment to an education that brings harmony not only to the individual soul but also to society as a whole. And Plato stressed that true education aims at that kind of pleasure that people feel by adapting their life to the laws of the community. In other words, good education yields knowledge about justice in the social life and about the rules of the City whereby we can obtain a happy life. Moral evil is ignorance about the good; it makes us unhappy and gives us pain. But the knowledge that is at stake here is not only about moral theory and good literature; it is also capacity in dance and music that cultivates the whole body.

Evanghélos Moutsopoulos sees also in his presentation of "Education – A Lasting Value", a connection in the classical view between education to independent action of the individual and education to democracy in social life. They are connected because education must be learning about values. A value is born in the human consciousness and slowly is progressively justified as universal at some level of intersubjectivity. It is originally an individual creation and has nevertheless force only as commonly accepted. This is the reason why education could not remain a private task. And from Plato and Aristotle on the idea was developed that education should be institutionalized. It includes schooling, instruction and culture. Schooling uses constraint, instruction gives technical competence and culture enriches both the group and individual consciousness with new value dimensions. Thus, its aim is not only to accumulate knowledge but to let human beings learn to use it for the good life. Education was also about norms. This idea of institutionalization of education became reality with the creation of the *Bibliotheca Alexandrina* followed by many medieval schools and universities, first under religious guardianship, then taken over by the States. Finally education has been claimed as a universal human right, which should be respected in every society. But without commitment to the values traditionally conveyed by the teaching of humanities education will fail. These values have shown themselves as indispensable for moulding a democratic and humanist character for the human being and encourage the questioning spirit that belongs to education since Socrates. And among the values education has shown itself as a lasting value.

Guttorm Fløistad who writes about "Value-Based Leadership in Education" emphasizes that to values belongs a commitment to them. And this commitment in itself cannot be taught as a simple transmission of knowledge about values, because it is a very personal affair that supposes a feeling of common commitment. The individual must be turned into a participatory subject, not isolated from others but also not dominated by them. Therefore the students' attachment to institutions and subjects of study is crucial for the learning process. If they are alienated in relationship to their schools and universities, their motivation and attentiveness to education are blocked. It follows that a teacher who stands for the content of the teaching is indispensable. Referring to different practical experiences Fløistad shows that rational justification of values does not bring forth commitment, but a long process of interpersonal exercise including care of the child and interest for the student is needed. In schools a class culture based on general values must be developed. But how it should be done depends on many things: the teacher's personality, his pedagogical and social creativity, his knowledge of the local history, its manner and customs, its songs and celebrations, etc. However, when the teacher succeeds in committing the children or the students to one field, the commitment is often translated into other fields as well.

In his chapter about "Achievement, Motivation and Enthusiasm" *Hans Lenk* calls attention to another classical Greek idea that is still important for education when he portrays the commitment to sport as a model for commitment in other activities. In sport, training and workouts require a kind of devotion, enthusiasm and personal authentic engagement that makes sport an exemplary realm for proper accomplishments in all human action. And Lenk considers the most outstanding personal achievements as those that are nowadays performed by athletes at the top-level where the intensity and cardio-muscular burdens of training and competition are the highest and in particular wherever no financial interest is at stake. Together with other creative achievements such as those in dance, music and play, in writing and savouring literature, and even in science and philosophy sport offers opportunities for one's own achievement in our generally conformist and equalizing society. And this is what education must be about; it must focus on meaningful, authentic achievement that has to be learned and exercised again and again. Yet enthusiasm for the task as such and personal achievement does not exclude teamwork. On the contrary. Competition must be combined with cooperation and team achievement, and prototypes and paragon examples of excellent achievements must be considered as highly important for the motivation of the commitment in education. Lenk claims that the philosophy of education should be developed according to these practical experiences, and that a philosophical interpretation of the human being as the authentically personal achieving being should be integrated into philosophical anthropology at the basis of norm and criteria in education.

But commitment includes not only enthusiasm; it also has to do with creative and critical thinking. In his contribution about "Education as Creativity" *Vladislav A. Lektorsky* takes up the question how to learn this kind of thinking. This learning is more needed than ever. Since the Enlightenment the ideal of education has been to give a lot of knowledge about natural and social dependencies to the younger generation. Today this ideal is contested. The use of scientific knowledge has not only brought material wellbeing but has also created a lot of problems in areas from ecology to inter-human relations. Nowadays we must face these problems. We must be able to doubt and to create new solutions. But how can doubt be taught? In most systems of education today the main aim of education is the appropriation of knowledge and skills and there are always ready answers to the different questions. But a new type of question not having such answers are needed. One must be allowed to doubt about norms and criteria, not only those of others but also one's own ideas. It follows that traditional education cannot help creative thinking and form a learning motivation. Pupils and teachers must be involved in discussions of problems that have no generally accepted solutions, and the questions of participants in these discussions can help them to clarify together their own presuppositions. Finally, critical dialogue should be used not only for teaching creative and critical thinking, but also for moral and aesthetic education, because moral relations suppose critical self-reflection and creative transformation of oneself. Also, art is a means of achieving new perspectives and joining an experience of other people, social groups and cultures. Therefore art belongs to the dialogue with other people and cultures. It follows that dialogue is a key to education as creativity and indispensable for the education of mankind in the future.

Likewise *Lars-Henrik Schmidt* focuses on a new way of education in his essay on "Untraditional Education". He points out that educational formation (in German: *Bildung*) is not tied to formation in crafts or arts, but concerns what the educator does to the doings of others. That does not mean that it is not esthetical. Educational formation is cultivation of taste. But traditional education is training in the understanding of the works of others instead of training in making images and texts in creative collaboration with others. The latter is difficult, because there is no longer a ready written script, some given classical works to teach about and to promote in front of an audience. The educator is no more an actor, on a scene in a theatre, but he must assert himself in an arena where he has to play with others according to his taste and distaste. The idea of education as developed by the Enlightenment is still traditional education, because it implies that some people know the direction that others must take. Their knowledge has universal validity and the Enlightener can say: "follow me!" This idea was already contested by the Romantic philosophy of education claiming that education should be based on a particular culture and its development. More recently, in the post-war period enlightenment has been replaced by criticism, and a new opposition has appeared between self-enlightenment and self-cultivation. Self-enlightenment is an Apollonian self-critique by which we become part of something larger than ourselves, whereas self-cultivation is a Dionysian extension of the self. But in education we must ask: how is it possible to develop a sense of community in a context of self-cultivation? We must give up the idea that we can "elevate" others by claiming: "Follow me!" But we can promote cultivation by promoting culture, not simple as a given legacy, but as a cultural life including an experimental way of living. Untraditional education assumes this cultivation. It is not anti-traditional, but different from traditional education. It is still a cultivation of taste, but rather as distaste, formation by declining of what is perceived as unacceptable. This demands a new professionalism that includes skills in other disciplines than those we usually take into account: for instance discourse analysis, psychoanalysis and social anthropology. Through these disciplines we can learn to experience a powerlessness in which everyone else is also powerless, but in this common experience each of us can become less powerless. Untraditional education is therefore education of powerlessness as a gateway to the other.

The essay of *Kurt Nielsen and Anne-Marie Eggert Olsen* extends the problem of commitment in education in our time into the political sphere. They ask: "Education for Democracy: Adaptation or Political Awareness?" They reject the system-theoretical position that observes politics without any normative expectations. And their question is: How can we educate with the best intention or commitment to give raise to democratic citizens without constraining the students to adapt to all preconceived ideas and institutions? Upbringing for democracy has often been such an adaptation. Contrary to this adjustment of education to the dominant political system some people speak about democratic formation, but since "formation" has a conservative accent, others prefer to speak about learning and developing competence. However, according to Nielsen and Eggert Olsen, formation cannot be avoided if one wants a political upbringing that is not imposed by an external authority but acquired and accepted by the individual itself. Formation is such a process.

It cannot be intentionally directed from outside, and therefore political formation is normally not thought of as imposed by legislation. Moreover, democratic upbringing and formation must allow dissent if it would be really democratic. Therefore it cannot be instrumentalised or subordinated to an authority or be upbringing for particular political norms or systems. For instance, upbringing becomes adaptation to a given social order if it presupposes that democratic society is already realized and democracy indisputable, so that criticism of the way that democracy is imposed is excluded from political formation. In such a society democracy becomes extremely vulnerable. It is true that a democratic state that guarantees civic rights is different from a democratic society characterised by democratic virtues such as freedom, equality in welfare, tolerance, solidarity, etc. But both the democratic state and democratic society can be criticized for not being democratic enough, and they are not democratic at all if such a criticism is not allowed.

In the last essay on "Cosmopolitan Commitment in Education" I argue that educational commitment in our time must be cosmopolitan. I try to show that the defence of the freedom of the individual does not exclude a cosmopolitan engagement, but on the contrary that cosmopolitanism includes an opposition against a total subordination of the individual under the state: as cosmopolitan the citizen keeps the right to criticize its own state in the name of its double citizenship both as national and global citizen.

CONCLUDING REMARKS

The contents of this book show a predominance of Danish authors. This is not only because they have all been colleagues of the editor who knows their competences in the field of philosophy of education. It is also because special historical, cultural and political conditions permitted the creation, in the year 2000, of a unique Institute of Philosophy of Education at the Danish University of Education. Lars-Henrik Schmidt was the first Rector until its integration in 2007 as a School of Education in the University of Aarhus. The Institute of Philosophy of Education that I built up during its first five years became a hotbed for new ideas in philosophy of education and a renewal of the whole discipline; it remains today a strong unity of philosophy of Education in the transformed institutional context. I am happy that I have been able to give some of my collaborators from this institute an occasion to prove their capacity in this book together with internationally recognized philosophers from other parts of the world.

The theme commitment in education was chosen for this volume. But many other themes could have been taken up such as justice in education, learning as mimesis, cosmopolitanism in education and environmental education. I hope some of these projects can be realized in the future thanks to the commitment of other philosophers from different part of the globe in the domain of education that grows so promising in our time.

MUST EDUCATION BE COMMITTED?

Evandro AGAZZI
(University of Genoa, Italy)

FREEDOM OF ACTION AND FREEDOM OF CHOICE

What does it mean "commitment"? The *Concise Oxford Dictionary* contains the following short definition: "engagement that restricts freedom of action". More articulated definitions of the meaning of this concept are not only possible, but also available in other dictionaries. In its simplicity, however, the one we have just quoted is particularly useful to start our reflections, for it is probably this link with the limitation of freedom that could explain why, in contemporary doctrines regarding education, it is often maintained that education must remain "neutral" or "not committed". Avoiding commitment in education seems to be the consequence of an imperative that has become a kind of fundamental principle of present ethics (at least for those cultures that have been influenced by the "progressive spirit" of modernity), the absolute respect for anyone's *freedom*. We must note, however, that even in the short definition of the *Concise Oxford Dictionary* mention is made of freedom of *action*, and it is by no means legitimate to equate the *whole meaning* of freedom with freedom of action. This identification or reduction is certainly a tacit and almost implicit feature of "modern" philosophy started in the seventeenth century, but one cannot ignore that in the long tradition of Western thought it was customary to distinguish at least two kinds of freedom, *freedom of choice* and *freedom of action*, and the primacy was attributed to the first, since freedom of choice has been considered as the essential characterization of *human will*, that is different from any other impulses to action (that we find, e.g. in animals) because it is *free*, that is, *free to choose* a course of action, independently of the concrete possibility of actually realizing that action.

At first sight this distinction seems rather abstract and of little significance since what matters, after all, is that human individuals can enjoy the largest freedom of action because their freedom of choice would remain frustrated if the chosen course of action could not be realized. This is in part true, but cannot discard the primacy of freedom of choice that is a necessary *prerequisite* of freedom of action. Indeed it is often said that freedom of choice cannot be submitted to limitations since the individual remains always free to *want* something even when this something is out of his possibility of realization (as Occam once said – in order to stress the intangibility of *free will* – even someone who threw oneself from a bridge can want not to fall down though he is no longer free not to fall down). This is true but people who are willing to induce other person to *act* in a certain way without using more or less clear forms of coercion, know that a rather efficacious way is that of influencing their freedom of choice. The most widespread use of this technique is represented by advertising (especially subliminal advertising): persons who receive this kind of "invitation" to buy or to do something remain certainly *free* not to follow these suggestions, but very often they make their free choice according to the suggestions received. At a much deeper level this occurs in the case of the variety of "indoctrinations" that are present in domains such as those of religions, social and political ideologies, moral prescriptions. These reflections show that the most fundamental issue, when we are concerned with the protection and promotion of human freedom (even if we are convinced that what "concretely" matters is freedom of action) is to take care of a *substantial* freedom of choice. By *substantial* we mean a freedom of choice that is not only safeguarded "in principle" (as we have seen, this is always the case and we shall call *formal* such a basic freedom), but that is also realizable "in practice". How to secure a correct link between substantial freedom of choice and substantial freedom of action is a complex problem and we are convinced that the concept of *commitment* offers a viable solution for it.

COMMITMENT AS ENGAGEMENT

In the short definition of the *Concise Oxford Dictionary* commitment is presented as an *engagement* but the notion of engagement is itself not univocal and we can at least distinguish a moral and a legal sense of this concept. According to its *legal* sense (or other similar meanings), engagement is equivalent to a *constraint* that limits our freedom of action, in the sense that we are *obliged* to do or not to do something because failing to respect this engagement would imply a certain *sanction*. From a legal point of view the circumstance that the engagement was *freely chosen* is rather immaterial, and only in certain cases it could entail that the engagement is not valid (practically, in those cases in which it could be proved that the person was "forced" to *take* the engagement and this would amount to recognizing a not complete freedom of *action*). In a *moral* sense, the engagement is freely chosen and, though still entailing a limitation of our freedom of action, it concerns a freely chosen limitation that morally bounds our moral conscience in the form of a *duty* that we must respect independently of any sanction and that we are even free (at the level of a freedom of action) not to respect but that we *ought to respect* if we want to be consistent with the *free will* that has guided us in the adoption of the engagement. This is why it seems reasonable to equate the concept of commitment with the concept of a *moral engagement* that provides us with a reasonable link between freedom of choice and freedom of action. But now one can see that freedom of choice clearly appears as the fundamental value in the name of which we defend the principle of the absolute respect for one's freedom, essentially because we are convinced that *free will* is the core of *human dignity*. As is well known, the elaboration of this doctrine is especially due to Kant and has become a cornerstone of our modern Western culture.

Put in these terms, the thesis of avoiding commitment in education could seem justified by the idea that only in this way we can respect the freedom of choice of the persons who are receiving this education. But is this thesis really sound? Not really, because freedom of choice remains an *empty* box, a pure potentiality, if there are no elements among which one can choose. Therefore, a responsible education must be conceived as the task of helping people to *fill* their freedom of choice, that is, to transform the abstract intangible but *formal* freedom of choice in what we have called a *substantial* freedom of choice. How this could be done, that is, how this necessary task could be fulfilled without falling into the abuse of subliminar persuasion or indoctrination can emerge from a careful analysis of freedom of choice

AN ANALYSIS OF FREEDOM OF CHOICE

Freedom of choice takes place at different levels. The most elementary is represented by the great variety of everyday situations in which people can choose among different *means* available for attaining a delimited and well determined *goal* (or set of goals) under a set of *given conditions*. This procedure has relations also with the moral sphere and, in particular, is studied in the Aristotelian concept of *phronesis* (or *prudence*) that is fundamental in the *Nicomachean Ethics* of this philosopher. A modern version of this perspective is somehow mirrored in what is commonly known as *rational choice theory* that, however, represents a not negligible restriction of the ancient conception. To put it briefly, rational choice theory assumes that human behaviour is guided by *instrumental reason*. Accordingly, individuals always choose what they believe to be the best means to achieve their given ends and therefore they are normally regarded as maximizing *utility* (a general notion used to denote everything they cherish, such as money, long life, but also moral standards). In spite of its seemingly general features, this theory is implicitly inspired by a specific moral doctrine, utilitarianism, and the limitation of its scope appears also from the concrete domains where it has been applied: it has become part of the foundational theory of *economics* and has gradually extended more recently to a few other *social sciences*. Another fundamental aspect of this theory is that it adopts *methodological individualism* (it conceives of social situations or collective behaviours as the exclusive result of individual actions). The ambition of this theory is that of offering a mathematical treatment of human choices but, to approximate this goal, a certain number of assumptions is introduced in order to specify when a choice is "rational", and even more unrealistic assumptions are made in order to simplify calculations and allow for predictions. We are not interested here in those technicalities that, by the way, have sparkled criticism from several fields against rational choice theory. We want simply to note that this approach, seemingly suggested by the idea that individuals act according to their free will, ends up, paradoxically, by imposing to their free choice such a bundle of constraints in the name of rationality, that freedom of choice is practically reduced to arbitrariness: a rational choice is actually almost fully determined. Such an approach is understandable as an effort for introducing a "scientific" treatment of human actions, and every science has to be as much deterministic as possible (and resort to statistical evaluations when rigid determinism is out of reach), but this cannot imply that such a scientific treatment is proportionate to the understanding of human freedom in general and of freedom of choice in particular.

The limitations of rational choice theory consist in its being restricted to the consideration of "instrumental" reason, and this can be an obstacle in the full understanding of free will. Indeed, even in the case of Aristotelian ethics, scholars often recognize an insufficient analysis of human will, though the "computational" flavour of the *phronesis* is integrated there with the doctrine of the s*ophia* or wisdom. The limited scope of the computational or instrumentalist approach becomes patent when one considers that, for the rational choice theory, the ends are *given* and not chosen. This already means that the freedom of choice that this theory allegedly tries to make formally rigorous does not regard the ends, and this is certainly puzzling from the point of view of a characterization free will since the most salient characteristic of a freely chosen action obviously should be that of freely choosing the *ends* of the action. We shall come again to this point a little later and for the moment we want to stress that we are not denying the importance of making people accustomed to use a refined form of instrumental rationality, to elaborate certain guidelines for finding the best solutions for the great variety of problems occurring in the "elementary" situations of everyday life. The solutions of such problems are essentially based on *factual knowledge* and an acceptable degree of *reasoning ability*. That which can be called "standard education" (in order to distinguish it from "committed education") is expected to offer as much as possible in the domain of this knowledge and ability and, in such a way, to prepare people to solve in an optimal way the problems they meet in their everyday life (including professional life). The question, however, is whether such an education can be expected to prepare people to solve problems arising within situations that are not "elementary", but "complex", not in the trivial sense of being "complicated", but in the deeper sense of requiring also a choice among different ends. In order to find an answer to this question we come back to the analysis of instrumental reason.

It is obvious that the *goals* usually aimed at in the concrete situations of everyday life are not pursued *as such* but because they are in turn *means* for achieving goals of a higher degree (e.g., one does a certain work with the goal of getting some money, but this in turn is looked for in order, let us say, to buy food, and food is looked for in order to survive, and so on). This process cannot continue indefinitely and ends up with certain goals that a given person considers *desirable in themselves* (as one can see, we are not rejecting methodological individualism at this stage). These goals (that we shall call *primary goals*) *justify* the chain of choices (and the consequent actions) that the concerned person actually performs. Very often people admit such primary goals without *critical assessment* but simply because they are in keeping with personal tastes, or implicitly vehiculated by social contexts, by a certain tradition, by momentary fashions, and the like. All this, however, is not really worthy of human persons who are endowed with *reason* and, as such, should ask themselves whether these *primary goals* are really worthy of being pursued *in themselves* or whether they cannot be considered as *ul-*

timate ends. At this juncture one can see that a *free choice* for intelligent beings cannot avoid being a free choice arrived at after a mature *rational reflection* on these ultimate ends, a reflection that can no longer follow the path of instrumental reasoning since these ends are not pursued "in view of" something else, and if a choice among them must remain possible (otherwise we should not have a free choice) the spectrum of these ends, though being rationally analyzed, must have the characteristic of something that is *proposed to the free will*.

A *committed education* must be seen as an help offered to people for *filling* their freedom of choice with a concrete presentation of possible *ultimate ends*, and as an exercise of *rational reflection* capable of putting people in the condition of a responsible exercise of their *free will*. This education will obviously not present *matters of fact* (and in particular must refrain from presenting such ultimate ends as a matter of fact) but help people to develop their capability of forming *value judgements*. This is entailed by the fact that such ends must appear as *worthy* of being pursued and this adjective clearly oversteps the level of factual ascertainment. Therefore, a committed education must concern itself with *values*, and this is precisely the opposite of the "neutral" education that is typically conceived as "value free".

THE DISCOVERY OF VALUES WITHIN FREEDOM

We have come now to the hard core of our problem, that is, to the legitimacy of a value-oriented education once it has been admitted that the respect of people's *freedom* is an absolute imperative in any interaction with other persons. Indeed a frequent objection raised against a value-oriented education is that it would undermine the free will or freedom of choice of people by a subtle form of indoctrination, through which the teacher tries to bring his pupils to share his own values. This position seems even supported by a thesis advocated by such a famous scholar as Max Weber who, speaking of the social sciences (that is, a domain in which consideration of values is methodologically unavoidable), prescribes that such sciences must be *value-free* in this precise sense, that the social scientist must carefully avoid to express value judgments on the social phenomena he studies because this would jeopardize the *objectivity* of his inquiry. This obligation becomes even more strict in the teaching of these sciences: the professor must refrain from permitting that his own values (particularly of moral, social and political nature) inspire his teaching or gleam from it, and this for simple intellectual honesty, since his authority and power as teacher put him on an unequal footing with regard to his students. Of course, he has full right, as a free human being, to have his values, to fight for them, but he is entitle to do this within other contexts, such as the political arena and public debates where, in addition, he is not entitled (so at least Weber says) to bring his "scientific" competence as a support of his arguments, that must remain bound to the specific features of the value controversies that cannot be "objective" and simply mirror one's personal convictions ("polytheism of values", to use his expression, is fundamental in a free society).

These remarks are certainly serious and call our attention on a real *risk* of a value-oriented education, a risk, however, that has to do not with the "physiology" but with a "pathology" of this education, a pathology that can be equated with an insufficient intellectual honesty of the teacher. The step that lacks in the pathological way of realizing this education is the essential ingredient of a *critical reflection* on the presented values. But was this not precisely something Weber considered intrinsically hopeless? It is, but only if one limits rationality to the model of *scientific rationality* that Weber defended. Yet the forms of rationality are fortunately broader than the restricted form of scientific rationality and can be very profitably applied to the inquiry on values, though they might not attain the degree of "objectivity" that this rationality can (at least to a certain extent) provide. We shall now try to propose a way for discovering values that remains far from indoctrination since it takes its moves from an analysis of the notion of freedom itself, starting not from abstract definitions, but from the most concrete ways of conceiving freedom emerging in the intuitive perception we have of our personal freedom.

This means that we shall not embark in certain sophisticated distinctions that have been elaborated in the large literature devoted to this theme (such as "freedom of", "freedom from", "freedom to" and so on). It is sufficient to consider a few "concretizations" of individual freedom that have been singled out from the beginning of the "libertarian" tradition of modern culture and have then become universally recognized at least within our Western civilization, but have also been more widely accepted as expressing certain fundamental *human rights.* The most significant of them are freedom of thought, freedom of religion, freedom of conscience, freedom of speech, freedom of assembly, freedom of trade, freedom from coercion, freedom from bodily injury, to which we should also add the right to life and the right to property. These different forms of freedom are not unrestricted and can even come to conflict sometimes, but we shall consider this point later. It is not an abuse of language to call *values* these rights, because they are considered as *worthy* of being respected, promoted and defended, so that we are convinced that the respect of *our* individual freedom entails the respect of these values when other people's *actions* affect us. We are also convinced, however, that these rights are not just our personal rights, but are *universal*, that is, *valid in themselves*, so that they necessarily entail for us corresponding *duties,* that is, that also other persons enjoy the same rights and, as a consequence, our *freedom of action* is limited by the duty of respecting these values when we have to do with other persons.

This sketchy analysis has shown that an elementary examination of freedom brings to light a certain number of rights that generate duties once they are also considered as values. This detail must not be overlooked: when we speak of *duty* we use a *moral* concept, that is different from the *legal* concept o*f obligation*. It is true that in modern civilized societies efforts have been made in order to translate these rights and duties into legal norms, but this has happened because of the historical tendency to give legal force to moral principles, that is, to secure a level of public protection to these rights. But without a reference to the underlying moral foundation legal norms may easily appear as simple expression of coercion, and this is one of the reasons for the decreasing sense of respect for legal ordering we often find in our societies. We have also noted that these duties often entail a limitation of our *freedom of action*, but this is not implicit in the pure and simple link between rights and duties, it depends on the consideration of the *social* context. Only because other persons enjoy the same rights as myself I have the duty of limiting my freedom of action in order not to violate their rights. This patently shows a limit of methodological individualism and, as a matter of fact, scholars who accept to be qualified as "libertarians" normally admit that the maximization of individual freedom must be pursued in the presence of certain *constraints*, the most important of which are precisely the above mentioned *rights*, and this is an implicit *de facto* broadening of the perspective of strict methodological individualism.

This example is useful because it shows that there are fundamental values that are not imposed through indoctrination, but are uncovered by rational reflection on fundamental personal convictions and proposed as a reasonable "filling" of our freedom of choice, though by being *committed* to such values we are also rationally bound to accept certain limitations of our freedom of action. We have intentionally said "proposed" to our freedom of choice and, more precisely, we could say proposed by reason and not by other persons, though one or more persons might have helped us in developing our reflection. Moreover, everyone remains free not to accept these values (at least in part) because not even the force of our reason can *compel* our free will: as is normal in moral decisions, we remain free not to accept principles or norms in spite of being rationally convinced that we *ought to* accept them. The awareness of these facts is very important for a correct understanding of freedom, since it shows that the exercise of freedom always occurs within a context of *constraints* that cannot be equated with *coercion* but are the consequence of the articulation of freedom itself, and this is true also of freedom of choice and not only freedom of action where this is very obvious.

FROM RIGHTS TO NEEDS, A FURTHER STEP IN THE UNDERSTANDING OF FREEDOM

Another class of constraints that surround the exercise of our freedom is represented by the variety of *human needs* that can limit more or less seriously our freedom of action. It is obvious that we cannot realize certain intended actions if, for instance, we have not enough money, health, education, social status, and the like. This is why the adequate satisfaction of these needs has been gradually recognized as a precondition for the actual exercise of human freedom and this explains why many of them have been promoted to the status of *human rights* and included in the list of what is implicit in the respect for human *dignity*. One must be aware, however, that the recognition of these needs, and especially of the adequate *measure* of their satisfaction, has been and still is much more subject to historical and cultural determination. Therefore, it is relatively easy to admit that the rights to sufficient food, medical care, shelter, education count among the fundamental human rights, but it is also undeniable that what could be considered "sufficient" one century ago for people living in a pre-industrial society could be insufficient for people living in industrialized countries today, and the same can be repeated considering people living today in countries of very different economic development. This is why it is not so easy to propose a list of such needs-rights as it was in the case of the fundamental rights perceived as concrete articulation of the general notion of individual freedom. The determination of this list, however, is of secondary importance for the sake of our discourse, for it is sufficient for us to recognize that persons seriously affected by the lack of "sufficient" satisfaction of these needs are concretely deprived of a large spectrum of their freedom of action. Still it remains rather unclear how the respect for these rights could impose limits to *our* individual freedom of action (except in those trivial cases in which our action could directly deprive another person of her food, or put at risk her health, and so on).

This seems to be a weakness of the consideration of these rights but, on the contrary, it is of great importance since it opens the perspective of a *positive* exercise of freedom, that is, an exercise not limited to the "negative" care of avoiding to infringe other people's rights, but engaged in *promoting* (through individual actions but especially at the social and political level) the adequate satisfaction of these needs-rights also for people who are affected by a lack of this satisfaction. It is also rather clear that methodological individualism is inadequate for the treatment of these issues, because we all are conscious that the real promotion of such rights requires a collective engagement and concrete actions of considerable size that cannot result from the scattered addition of single individual actions of persons of good will. Yet a grain of truth of methodological individualism remains untouched, because the social and political *choices* necessary for the promotion of such collective actions cannot take place if they are not the expression (though not literally the result) of many individual choices that converge toward the formation of the necessary political decision.

We could express the spirit of this new perspective on freedom by saying that the analysis of certain constraints of freedom has produced the emergence of a commitment to *liberation*, and this gives us the opportunity of reconsidering the concept of commitment and seeing how it can really amount to a "filling" of freedom.

COMMITMENT AS ORIENTATION
AND NOT AS LIMITATION OF FREEDOM

We have intentionally begun our discussion on committed education by quoting a short definition of commitment that underscores its being a *limitation* of our freedom of action, and we have done this in order to face up directly to the most usual objections levelled against committed education, that see in it a subtle threat not only to freedom of action but also to freedom of choice or freedom of conscience. But now we want to consider other not less significant meanings that we normally associate with the concept of commitment. Without disturbing dictionaries we can express such meanings in different almost synonymous ways such as "putting one's heart into something", "undertaking something with enthusiasm", "firm intention to do something in the future", "honesty of mind or intention in feeling bound to a course of action or to the realization of some goal". This list could be easily broadened but is sufficient in order to bring to light the "positive" meaning of commitment, consisting in the fact that it does no longer express what one should *refrain from doing*, but what one should *endeavour to do*. This is the deep reason for which commitment, as we have repeatedly maintained, offers the possibility of "filling" our freedom of choice, transforming it from a purely *formal* freedom into a *substantial* freedom, into a freedom that actually has at its disposal a variety of *goals* among which to choose and, for reasons already discussed, this is of paramount importance when such goals are the *ultimate ends* of a person. Therefore, it is the most fundamental *interest* of a person (in a profound sense of "interest" concerning the whole of her existence) to make her existential choices among ultimate ends that really deserve being pursued. This is why *conscious* persons devote serious *reflection* to the determination of these ultimate ends, simply because the result of this reflection will determine their *sense of life* and the global *orientation* of their life. The *existential* advantage (that cannot be trivialized as a simple psychological advantage, though being also this) of having duly attended to this reflection is a security in action, an alacrity, a capability of engaging in serious projects, a force of resistance against adverse conditions and obstacles, in short the capability of "fully living" instead of "scraping a living", of "getting along" as so many people do.

These considerations reinforce our previous thesis, that such ultimate ends deserve being called *values*, because they are ends *worthy of being pursued as such* and for this reason they have such a great "propulsive force", this is a force of *attraction* and not of *coercion,* and this is the reason why they do not entail limitations of our freedom of choice and of action. We can also call these values *ideals*, not because they have just a mental existence, but because they are not something physical, something that could have the force of concretely blocking or compelling our actions. They are the values that have been *intentionally* promoted to the role of guidelines for our life. Therefore, a life without reference to values is a life without ideals, and this is actually a sub-human life. Of course, this is true only if they are accepted *freely*, and this condition can be satisfied only when they have been determined through a *rational reflection*, as we have already stressed. This reflection cannot have the traits of a logical demonstration, even less those of an empirical recognition, but it can and must avail itself of a variety of tools for conceptual analysis and rational argumentation that we use in everyday life and in philosophy, though they could not attain the (alleged) cogency of scientific proofs. But this is not accidental for at least two reasons. First, because scientific investigations achieve their objectivity thanks to a great simplification and *delimitation* of their field of inquiry and their methods of investigation, whereas the issues at stake in our case regard *the whole of life*, including numberless questions that overstep the interests and methods of the sciences. Second, because the result of the rational reflection must still leave space for *freedom*. It would be ridiculous that someone said "I do not accept the theorem of Pythagoras" in Euclidean geometry, or "I do not accept the law of gravitation" in Newtonian mechanics, whereas it is possible that one refuses to accept a certain value in spite of having found no mistakes in the rational reflection that should induce him to accept it.

FINAL CONSIDERATIONS REGARDING COMMITTED EDUCATION

We have already hinted at this situation above and shall not repeat here those considerations. They are of relevance, however, in order to understand why and how a committed education is legitimate. The purpose of this education must be only that of helping pupils to "fill" their freedom of choice, that is, to elaborate their table of values and their ideals for life and, from what we have said, it should be clear that such a goal cannot be considered alien to education. In fulfilling this delicate task the teacher must first try to show to his pupils how important it is for any person to have her values and ideals, and to recognize them in a *critical* way. This critical examination cannot avoid the concrete presentation of such values, and intellectual honesty imposes to the teacher that he present and submit to real discussion not only his own personal ideals, but also those that he does not share. In particular, he could follow a methodology more or less similar to the one presented here, taking as starting points certain commonly accepted principles emerging from an analysis of freedom. But he could as well begin by taking seriously and analyzing conceptually other elements, such as the spontaneous sense of revolt against injustice naturally present in the conscience of his pupils. At the same time, he should make clear that, without falling into relativism, the results of their common reflection are offered to the conscience of every person and are left up to her responsible choice and further reflection, since the maturation of one's personality is an endless task for every human being, that can always revise his/her even most fundamental convictions if his/her conscience induces him/her to do so. The risk of relativism, however, is not really very serious because the great majority (perhaps even the totality) of fundamental values are universally recognized. The difficulty consists in the fact that in concrete existential situations some of them can enter into conflict, and in these cases different solutions may appear reasonable and morally correct to different persons. This depends not only on the different "hierarchy of values" one person has formed, but also on the interpretation of the different degree of involvement of single values in the concrete situation concerned. This explains why two persons sharing the same spectrum of values, and perhaps even sharing the same hierarchy, diverge in the value-judgment over a concrete situation, and this is why, in the last analysis, it is the personal conscience of every person that must indicate the correct choice in a context where matters of fact and questions of value are simultaneously implied.

It is certainly not difficult to recognize that the list of values we have exemplified can be, so to speak, "summarized" by presenting them as articulations of certain more general (if not more fundamental) values, such as human dignity, equality, justice, solidarity, and it may be profitable also to show how they are related with such general values. It is also rather clear, however, that these general values are in some way a little "abstract" and difficult to be proposed without a certain vein of indoctrination. Indeed their determination is far from unproblematic and requires additional precisions usually very complex. For example, if we define justice as "giving to everyone what is his own" this seemingly obvious statement leaves totally in the dark what is "what is his own" in the case of single concrete persons. Similarly, it is easy to admit the value of equality in the treatment of persons, but then one can feel difficult to understand why it is not right to treat in an equal way persons that are not equal from several points of view that can be relevant in concrete situations. Or, to give a last example, it is rather easy to share the moral norm that one should "give what is superfluous to people in need", but then we have to face the difficulty of making precise the concept of superfluous. On the contrary, if we focus our attention on those more concrete values that we have exemplified we can easily extend our reflection to other fundamental issues such as tolerance, peaceful coexistence, mutual understanding among people belonging to different cultures, solidarity, that have not been promoted yet into the official list of values, but are among the most urgent needs of our present globalized world and are fully worthy of being present in a committed education.

PHILOSOPHY OF EDUCATION AND EDUCATIONAL ANTINOMIES

Alexander VON OETTINGEN
(School of Education, Aarhus University,
Campus: Copenhagen, Denmark)

In the following I will attempt to define philosophy of education in times like the present which are characterised by a great interest in philosophy as well as pedagogy[1].

This attempt being far from unproblematic is at the same time an incalculable undertaking. You may even claim that the enterprise – due to the complexity of the matter – is slightly naïve. Pedagogy and philosophy are not well-defined provinces which can merely be brought into play with the intention of discovering the relation between the two of them. It is the other way round. The limits of both of these provinces are vague, undefined and open in the sense that they can only be defined to a certain extent. It is equally difficult to define philosophy or pedagogy and philosophy of education. In addition, it is only to a small extent that one can ally oneself with the vocational tradition, which has only contemplated the latent interfaces of pedagogy and philosophy, sporadically. Vocational philosophy has rarely taken pedagogy seriously, and has much too often rendered it commonplace, at times employing a senior teacher's tone of voice. Pedagogy, on the other hand, has ignored its philosophical implications, imagining that it could manage without philosophy.

This dissociation, however, is on the retreat. Not only due to the fact that, by founding the Department of Philosophy of Education at the Danish University of Education, the subject is now officially taught, but also due to a more general, philosophical interest in pedagogy. Peter Kemp points to two reasons for this tendency: "It is partly the result of a

---

[1] The following draws from my dissertation of the same title *Pædagogisk filosofi som reflekteret omgang med pædagogiske antinomier* (Educational Philosophy as a Reflected Handling of Educational Antinomies), Klim, Århus 2006.

more intensive debate on the influence of pedagogy on human life in an unstable world ... and partly it is a counterstroke to the displacement of pedagogy from certain new forms of vocational philosophy[2]."

Another plausible explanation is that, in the aftermath of the realistic and linguistic turns of the 1970s and the 1980s respectively, we now experience a philosophical turn within pedagogy. A partly philosophical, partly educational interest which does not confine itself to education but which increasingly affects all human spheres. On one hand, this development can be seen as a manifestation of the aspect that we live in an *educationalised era* in which not only the individual but rather the entire society is learning. On the other hand, you may interpret the present development as a recognition that you need to consider the role of pedagogy in other areas of life than has been done so far.

Already it is apparent from these few introductory remarks that a clarification of the nature of philosophy of education is needed.

In my attempt to clarify the term, I intend to present an educational-philosophical interpretation by means of an analysis which has its point of departure in the history of ideas. Unlike the more harmonious interpretations, this interpretation entails a *reflective handling of educational antinomies,* in the province of philosophy of education.

The sense of antinomies can be limited as well as wide. In a limited sense, antinomies (anti-law) illustrate contrasts in the principles of explanations. One of the most famous examples, which is also characterised as an example of a paradox, was articulated by the Cretan, Epimenides, who claimed that all Cretans lie.

In a wider sense, antinomies can be seen as the contrasts that are part of the fundamental structure of life and which, once discovered and rendered visible, are not neutralised. Rather they become an everlasting challenge. It is not a question of semantic or logical antinomies, but of the contrasts that are part of life.

Pedagogy and educational processes are filled with such indissoluble antinomies, which are more or less obvious. Usually, they are the implicit conditions of our educational actions and recognition. They only become explicit when things turn out differently than we expected them

---

[2] KEMP P., "Tro & Filosofi: Den hvileløse tænkning, feature" *in Information* 5. Dec. 2001. See also KEMP P., "Udfordringer mellem pædagogisk filosofi og pædagogiske videnskaber" (Challenges Between Educational Philosophy and Educational Sciences) in L. G. HAMMERSHØJ, H. D. JENSEN and C. STENBAK LARSEN (eds), *Mellemværende. Festskrift til Lars-Henrik Schmidt*, Danmarks Pædagogiske Universitets Forlag, København 2003.

to; when things are not as we think they ought to be. We only become aware of the educational antinomies the moment our educational actions and reasoning fail. This happens in theory as well as in practice.

Thus, sooner or later, all parents will find themselves in a situation in which they have to ask themselves what right they have to force their opinions and values on the child. As adults we naturally feel that we do the right thing, since we do not raise our children in accordance with our personal opinions and attitudes as much as according to what is commonly recognised as "good", "valuable" and "just". Nonetheless, we are left with the insoluble problem which consists in our anticipating the future of the child without having any knowledge of it. We cannot know whether our standards and values will turn out to be a problem for the future life of the child. On the other hand, we must anticipate the child's future life. Abstaining from educating the child with the argument that we do not know its future and therefore should wait until we know more about this future, would result in a brutal and inhuman childhood. We have no choice. When bringing up a child we must act without any certainty, which aspect epitomises the antinomian structure of the education and which cannot be ignored.

However, it is not just in the actual upbringing of the child that we are confronted with educational antinomies, the knowledge of which is likewise important in our roles as professional teachers or educators. What kind of task is it really that one has as a professional? On the one hand, you must represent what is general meaning whatever society dictates in terms of laws, rules or a cultural canon. We appreciate the contents of these and find them worth preserving and worth passing on to the next generation. On the other hand, the educator and the teacher are also responsible for the individuality of the child, who cannot be educated on the basis of universal rules without losing its individuality. What then should the professional do in order to neither deprive the child of its individuality nor overrule the more general educational regulations of society? Teachers and educators must consider both aspects, and thus find themselves in what you might call an antinomian challenge. Consequently, when all is said and done, it is understandable that their job is problematic, overwhelming and ambiguous. There is no escaping this antinomy, irrespective of your professional level, and irrespective of the number of school canons we formulate, be they artistically, literarily or democratically motivated – they will not neutralise the contrast consisting of the idea of the universal and that of the individuality of the child respectively.

We are challenged by educational antinomies in our actual experience as well as in our professional performance. The challenge does not only consist of the contrast itself, but also in the fact that antinomies have a substantial content. They bring into play a matter that concerns and therefore calls for a deliberate attitude and responsible conduct.

However, to be able to commit yourself on an educational level, a certain amount of knowledge of pedagogy is imperative. If you have no idea what is educational about pedagogy, or what constitutes an educational recognition and action, you could insist that anything is educationally relevant with the result that you would no longer be able to commit yourself educationally.

Thus the way is paved for the philosophy of education, whose job is to delimit pedagogy. There are no simple and linear solutions to this delimitation, which, as mentioned above, will not lead to harmonious and idealistic explanations but rather to disharmonies, paradoxes and above all educational antinomies. By taking an antinomian point of departure we underline the fact that our immediate, educational experiences are, to a certain extent, contrasting and doubtful.

This opens the prospect of educational-philosophical *reflection*, whose aim is not to neutralise the contrasts but to look for answers which do not simply allow for several solutions but likewise pinpoint and retain the fundamental educational ambiguities.

Such an approach moreover emphasises the aspect that the relations between pedagogy and philosophy will dissolve if pedagogy does not take into account its antinomies. In this respect, there is no such thing as an issue of an educational nature which is not of a philosophical nature, too – otherwise they cannot be considered educational issues.

PHILOSOPHY OF EDUCATION IS NOT A THEORY OF SCIENCE

If we consider the current development of the relations between pedagogy and philosophy, and in particular the question concerning the specific educational traits of pedagogy, we will find that there are two different ways of going about it, however neither of them is likely to lead to a notion of pedagogy.

One of the methods, you might say, is based on the idea that the "educational aspect" is of minor importance and is split up into a number of subgroups that have either a function or a specialisation as their point of departure. Thus they refer to either special or social pedagogy, or to the pedagogy that occupies itself with babies and youths. In the same way you can organise pedagogy in groups according to various subjects such as educational psychology, educational sociology, educational anthropology and philosophy of education, too. Even if this grouping can be convenient for organisational as well as educational reasons – it does not result in a proper understanding of pedagogy, but rather in a number of occupational pedagogies lacking coherence.

The other one of the common methods does not differ much from the first one when it comes to elucidating the nature of pedagogy. Rather than organising pedagogy in groups according to subjects or disciplines, this method arranges it in classes according to various theories of science. In this way an attempt is made, either to infer educational knowledge from theories of cognition, or, on the basis of scientific criterion, to find out whether pedagogy is scientific altogether.

Thus there are theories of humanistic pedagogy, behaviouristic pedagogy, the pedagogy of the arts, hermeneutic pedagogy, critical pedagogy and constructivist pedagogy. These theoretical groupings do explain various scientific attitudes which also have an educational significance; nevertheless, they do not result in an independent notion of pedagogy.

Neither does a scientific-theoretical examination of the scholarly character of pedagogy. Such an examination usually contents itself with indicating that pedagogy is not scientific, seeing that it lacks a specific object and research method, the absence of which they try to compensate for by applying the theory of science – and lately also philosophy – so that pedagogy will be treated on the same footing as the other sciences. That pedagogy is not even a theory of science – since, in practice, it is a behavioural theory, which is of an earlier date than the theory of science – paradoxically, cannot be considered in a scientific-theoretical examination.

To really comprehend philosophy of education and to delimit pedagogy you should neither organise the educational aspect in provinces and functions, nor should you exclusively focus on the theory of science, but rather try to discover interfaces between philosophy and pedagogy. In other words, what you need is to illustrate *the educational aspect* of philosophy and *the philosophical aspect* of pedagogy.

A double perspective like this is found among conventional educators, who articulated pedagogy in the break between pre-modern and modern times. When re-examining this break it will be clear that pedagogy is a way of action – a practice – that assumes an antinomian character in its movement from pre-modern to modern times. This movement radically changes the character of philosophy of education in the sense that the educational aspect distinguishes itself from the philosophic province, and thus we will be left with two distinct yet interconnected reflection instances. Paradoxical as it may sound, pedagogy disengages itself from the province of philosophy in order to be able to ally itself with it. Or put differently, we cannot define philosophy of education properly until both pedagogy and philosophy have entered into an independent and reflexive relationship.

THREE ANTINOMIAN CHALLENGES TO THE PHILOSOPHY OF EDUCATION

As mentioned earlier, the essential thing to do is to return to the conventional – and forgotten – educational tradition, which originates in Antiquity, and which differentiates between *educational philosophy, cultural philosophy and educational philosophy.*

Unlike the common belief, the history of concepts does not infer the Greek concept of pedagogy from the *paidagogos* concept (the slave who took the child to school), but from the *paideia* concept, which was the science of the *human education and upbringing.* A fundamental educational-philosophical concern, which, until the 18th century, entailed that theoretical pedagogy lay within the province of practical philosophy, all the while the institutional, educational practice was the concern of the church and the state. Only in the course of the 18th and 19th centuries did this division change, and pedagogy systematically began differentiate itself from philosophy.

Three antinomian aspects in particular present themselves as modern, educational challenges: the first of these is the question concerning the correct, educational behaviour or upbringing (I). The second one is the question of the educational process without educational ideals (II), and lastly, there is the question concerning the issue of pedagogy in theory and in practice (III). Let us dwell on these separately for a moment.

I. As regards the antinomian question when it comes to the correct upbringing, J.-J. Rousseau's novel *Émile ou De l'éducation* (1762) is considered paradigmatic. In this work as well as in his political treatise *Du contract social* (1762), Rousseau makes the antinomian challenge of upbringing in contrast to the idea of the free individual and the political individual. On the one hand, the freedom of the individual to live his or her life in accordance with his or her personal values and political attitudes, on the other, the demand of the community for political participation. Not only will the upbringing to freedom be a paradoxical challenge, but at the same time, it will be additionally radicalised in the light of the political upbringing. It seems impossible to combine the two of them although they are interdependent. The upbringing to freedom presupposes free and democratic terms, which, however, can only be established by free people.

In the preface of the novel, Rousseau calls attention to the educational paradox by articulating that *we have no knowledge of childhood*. This was the beginning of the modern conception of childhood, which recognises that the purpose of education can no longer be to introduce the child to a particular social, cultural, occupational and political set of rules. Education must be considered an educational support to the free and rational sovereignty of the child to create its own future. Instead of basing the upbringing on a given attitude, Rousseau bases the upbringing according to the *indefinite learning nature* of the child. The child is awarded a liberty of action that does only firm up in the educational process. Rousseau's answer to the modern, educational antinomies is thus a trinity consisting of the open learning nature of the child (nature), its relations to the world (the objects) and the educational encouragement of the adult (man). In this trinity, the educational behaviour must be *negative* according to Rousseau in the sense that the adult recognises the nature of the child and encourages the child to self-activity.

II. Whereas Rousseau formulates the principles that underlie the modern educational theory, Wilhelm von Humboldt (1767-1835) makes the categories of a new paradigm of education his theme[3]. Whereas, in pre-modern times, you lived according to an educational ideal without problematising its complex of problems, modern times are characterised by people living according, not just to one, but to several educational ideals, and therefore must problematise the significance of education.

When Humboldt in the opening of his thesis *Theorie der menschlichen Bildung* (around 1790) points out that it would be a great achievement if someone could formulate an inclusive theory of the education of human kind, it is due to his conviction that such a theory does not exist.

Instead of drawing up some harmonious canon of education, Humboldt calls attention to the interplay of *man* and *the world*. Our thoughts and our actions are always an attempt to grasp our own humanity. However, this endeavour can only be realised in an interplay and in connection with something that is not ourselves. Humboldt characterises this "something" as "the world", and educational processes as free and vital connective processes. Man is open to the world, and in this openness he

---

[3] OETTINGEN, A. von, "Dannelsesfilosofi i lyset af det moderne" (The Philosophy of Education in the Light of the Modern World), in A.-M. EGGERT OLSEN (ed.), *Pædagogikkens filosofi,* Roskilde Universitets Forlag, 2004.

grasps himself as well as the world without sacrificing one for the other. Man does not invent the world, and neither is man merely a product of the world. The antinomian aspect of this interpretation of education consists of the notion that, in some curious fashion, man must be able to distance himself from the world in order to understand himself and the world.

When Humboldt points to these two categories it is as a response to two fundamental questions that emerge with the birth of the modern way of thinking. Firstly, the question of how a human being/person in modern times can learn to *become* a human being, and secondly how this human being can continue to live a human life in a world which is differentiated. From a modern perspective, man is constantly exposed to an involuntary alienation from the control mechanisms coming from financial, political, normative, social, scientific and technical conditions.

Humboldt contrasted these factors of alienation with a *public education (öffentliche Bildung)* that discusses the relations between man and the world, so that man in modern times can leave the discussion permanently open to educational challenges and tasks. A fundamental, educational, theoretical principle, which is not affirmative and ideal when accounting for education, but rather reflexive and antinomian.

III. Reformulating upbringing and education inevitably entails an updated justification and legitimisation of theoretical pedagogy. From a historical point of view, J. F. Herbart was the first to emphasise the importance of pedagogy to focus on its own issues and to develop an independent "research province[4]". Herbart's intention with this division was not to clear pedagogy of philosophy. On the contrary, the relation between the two should endure but, unlike before, the relation should be consciously contemplated. With no independent educational reflection and with the introduction of the new theories on upbringing and education, there was a considerable risk that they would insist that everything which was absent at that time and which they wished for in future was essential from an educational point of view. This, in other words, resulted in a complexity of educational opinions and attitudes with no criterion for determining which of the various formations of theories could be claimed to be *educationally* valid.

Yet as a consequence of the demand for an independent educational science, the issue concerning the relation between theory and practice

---

[4] OETTINGEN, A. von, *Det pædagogiske paradoks* (The Educational Paradox), Klim, Aarhus 2001.

immediately arises. Should you then abide by a paradigm of natural science or choose an empirical perspective? Herbart considered both options untenable. The limitation of the former of the options consists of the fact that pedagogy is not dealing with a natural object that you can explore theoretically and experimentally, and to which you can subsequently apply the results. The limitation of the latter consists in the fact that experience only lets us know how "something" was or is, but not how it could and ought to be.

Herbart thus subordinated the issue concerning theory and practice within the field of pedagogy to the notion of *educational tact*. This tact recognises that educational practice can only become valid through theory. However, an educational theory can exclusively communicate a common perspective through practice. Individual decisions, issues and choices cannot be captured by theory. Consequently, theory cannot replace educational experience either, seeing that pedagogy always deals with the actual child and not a hypothetical one. Therefore, the other element that educational tact call attention to is the fact that you can only learn about educational conduct in practice – however, only if you have been scientifically schooled first; meaning after having taken into theoretical consideration what *possible* problems and choices he might be met with, and what *possible* pitfalls he might be exposed to. With this ambiguous but also paradoxical description of the relation between theory and practice, Herbart recognises that pedagogy as a science does not simply seek out its object of investigation like other sciences, but always finds it in the form of a *specific task*. This means that going directly from theory to practice turns out to be just as problematic as going directly from practice to theory. Pedagogy is a science that emanates *from* practice and aims *at* practice – and this ambiguous aspect in itself demonstrates an antinomian structure.

To summarise the above, you may say that the classical notion of pedagogy in modern times is differentiated into three parts. Firstly, there is the reflection on the *educational conduct* the purpose of which is to point out principles that should function as guidelines for an educationally valid conduct. Secondly, there is the reflection on what is educationally normative which discusses the central principles of a modern reflection of education in the relation between man and the world. Thirdly, there is a self-reflection on pedagogy in the form of an educational-philosophical reflection on the issue of theory and practice.

All three parts emerge as a result of antinomian issues, and each one of them entails an educational-philosophical reflection. Consequently, we do not only need philosophy of education in order to discuss the scientific or normative character of pedagogy, but also in order to point out principles of educational technologies. The latter of the three, in particular, has been neglected by philosophy of education, since, at a very early stage, it convinced itself that it has nothing to contribute to the actual educational conduct[5].

Despite this disregard for educational technology, the three antinomian fields show the necessity for an educational-philosophical reflection that preserves the contrasts. It is not a question of formulating a philosophy of education which removes the paradoxical aspect of the educational conduct, replaces the openness of education by applying affirmative ideals of education or reduces educational professionalism to naïve benevolence. On the contrary, the object is to insist on an educational-philosophical understanding which includes the controversial and disharmonious aspects. Only in this differential and non-harmonious understanding do the three antinomian questions in principle remain our own – although, in the light of new challenges and social descriptions, they call for a new attitude.

THE STUDY OF THE EDUCATIONAL WORLD OF PHENOMENA AND ISSUES

Even though, as mentioned, it would be wrong to claim that we in Denmark have a pronounced educational-philosophical tradition, this is not true for Knud Grue-Sørensen's philosophical and educational works. As the very first professor teaching pedagogy, Grue-Sørensen made an attempt to made use of philosophy to organise and throw light on the educational terms and language. Not because he thought that pedagogy could become a harmonious unity, but because his point of departure was likewise antinomian.

Grue-Sørensen's works locate themselves somewhere between *the philosophy of upbringing* and *philosophical pedagogy*. On the one hand, he insisted that the central concern of pedagogy was the notion of upbringing in a wider sense, dealing with all questions concerning the indi-

---

[5] OETTINGEN, A. von, "Pædagogiske handlingsteorier i differencen mellem teori og praksis" (Educational Theories of Conduct in the Difference Between Theory and Practice), in A. von OETTINGEN and Finn WIEDEMANN (eds), *Mellem teori og praksis – aktuelle udfordringer for pædagogiske professioner og professionsuddannelser* (Between Theory and Practice – Topical Challenges for Educational Professions and Occupational Educations), Syddansk Universitetsforlag, Odense 2007.

vidual's developing into a human being. Today, you might call this philosophy of education.

On the other hand, he used philosophy to shed light on the basic concepts of pedagogy and criticise the contemporary educational euphoria, especially if it became too harmonious. In his philosophical and educational publications alike, Grue-Sørensen's overall interest was whatever was *specifically human*. That which, referring to I. Kant, comes down to the question of "what man as a freely acting creature makes of himself, and what he can and must make of himself[6]."

In this broad sense, it is made clear that humanity is not just something that all human beings obtain automatically; it is also always a task that is given them. In this sense, man does not merely live his own life, seeing that at the same time he will always represent part of *human life*. A human being is something you are as well as something you become, in that you must answer for your humanity throughout life. In this respect, pedagogy signifies the adults' responsible way of helping the child understand humanity as a lasting task. It is with this understanding in mind that Grue-Sørensen problematises pedagogy as he, in all his works, persists within the antinomian and paradoxical aspects of pedagogy.

However, his ethical and philosophical studies are inspired by the same educational issue. From an ethical point of view, it is a matter of maintaining *the inalienable*, the will – or you might say the liberty – to preserve an ethically binding responsibility. Referring to philosopher, Leonard Nelson, Grue-Sørensen spoke in favour of *objective ethics* whose arguments were rational rather than scientific and which argued that man loses his humanity – his reason – when he loses himself in value relativism[7].

Just as human liberty can be lost ethically, this can also happen on a cognitive philosophical level.

In Grue-Sørensen's major philosophical work – his dissertation – he studies *reflexiveness*. A phenomenon that, according to Grue-Sørensen, conveys what is specifically human – that which distinguishes man from the animals and which epitomises human liberty. Thus there are phenomena which are characterised, odd as it may seem, by being cause and effect alike in the same process. For instance, we can *discuss* language *using* language, and in this way we never escape language. In

---

[6] GRUE-SØRENSEN K., "Pædagogik og antropologi" (Pedagogy and Anthropology), p. 12, in *Pædagogik*, Vol. 1, n° 3, 1971.
[7] GRUE-SØRENSEN K., *Vor Tids Moralskepticisme* (The Moral Scepticism of our Times), Hagerup, København 1937.

the same way, we can *be* conscious of *being* conscious and being capable of recognising something, all the while we recognise that we *are capable* of recognising. Language as well as consciousness and recognition are true reflexive phenomena, seeing that they can consider themselves, be applied to themselves and relate to themselves[8].

This brief description already clearly indicates that Grue-Sørensen in his dissertation anticipates a number of topical discussions within the fields of philosophy, sociology, psychology and pedagogy respectively.

Sociologist, Ulrich Beck, among others, refers to the "reflexive modernisation" thus signalling that modern consequences reflexively feed back into modernity itself[9]. As you will know, Niklas Luhmann, referring to biologist, Humberto Maturana, introduced the notion of *autopoiesis*, which inter alia implies that autopoietic systems do not replicate their structures from the surroundings, but that they construct them themselves "through their own operations[10]".

If you have a look at a more educational linguistically philosophical approach, you likewise come across the argument of reflexiveness. For instance, making Bateson's philosophy his point of departure, N. Buur Hansen emphasises the child's "reflexive process of learning", and M. Hermansen emphasises "learning level four", which means that you "contemplate your reflection as contemplating your process of learning[11]". Lastly, you might turn your attention to child psychology, which claims that an infant, within the first couple of months, develops a "dawning self", which among other things implies that it can think about thoughts in a reflexive fashion[12]. These references alone should make it evident that the notion of reflexiveness is used in many connexions. In this respect, Grue-Sørensen has contributed an essential study; yet the study in question has been disregarded in the greater part of the recent, educational absorption in the phenomenon. Unfortunately, Grue-Sørensen himself has not explicitly made the reflexiveness category the theme of

---

[8] GRUE-SØRENSEN K., *Studier over Refleksivitet* (Studies on Reflexivity), J. H. Schultz Forlag, København 1950.

[9] See among others U. BECK, A. GIDDENS, S. LASH, *Refleksive Modernisierung. Eine Kontroverse*, Suhrkamp, Frankfurt a. M. 1996.

[10] LUHMANN N., *Einführung in die Systemtheorie,* Carl-Auer-System Verlag, Heidelberg 2004.

[11] BUUR HANSEN N., *Pædagogikkens treklang* (The Three Facets of Pedagogy), Carpe Gyldendal, København 1999 and M. HERMANSEN, *Læringens univers* (The Universe of Learning), Klim, Århus 1997.

[12] STERN D., *Barnets interpersonelle univers* (The Interpersonal Universe of the Child), Hans Reitzels Forlag, København 1995.

an educational discourse. Meanwhile, it is beyond doubt that this was an implicit part of his understanding of pedagogy and his understanding of the phenomenon of "learning" in particular.

To Grue-Sørensen the fact that man possesses a *reflexive ability to learn* is a manifestation of what is specifically human. He repeatedly underlines that the ability to learn is not learned, but that pedagogy must presuppose this ability in order to avoid coming up against massive initial difficulties. Consequently, when it comes to man's obtaining an understanding of and an insight, we enter into a reflexive, not to mention paradoxical, situation. True insight, meaning a person's agreeing or disagreeing with something in accordance with his or her own conviction, can neither be predetermined nor determined, rather it depends entirely on man's own free process of recognition and learning. According to Grue-Sørensen, the only solution is to couch "the truth in a version that stimulates the insight of the other when you teach. This can be done more or less effectually, but the most important and crucial prerequisite of success lies with the pupil[13]".

In this assumption lies the conception of an edu*cational a priori*, which manifests itself in man's reflexiveness, and which legitimises, sets bounds on and makes the educational action possible. As Grue-Sørensen puts it: "There are prerequisites concerning human nature that underlie the educational theory, especially the so-called *a priori* prerequisite, the idea that there is something innate in human nature, something that cannot be implanted by someone else[14]". An *a priori* which remains latent even when the learning is accomplished, with the result that the learner is unable to focus on the learning process itself.

To avoid any misunderstandings, the following should be noted: Grue-Sørensen's understanding of the reflexive structure of learning does not refer to a "self-referential" system which, so to speak, emerges spontaneously and autopoietically. A human being's learning in principle presupposes *the other*. Just as recognition presupposes that there is "something" that can be recognised, and that "the self" can only be conscious of its own existence because it has something other than itself.

Here we can only point out by implication and with a broad outline how Grue-Sørensen makes the connection between philosophy and pedagogy. For him it was all about using philosophy to get a better idea of the

---

[13] GRUE-SØRENSEN K., *En analyse af lærerbegrebet* (An Analysis of the Term: Learner), in *Pædagogik*, volume 2, n° 2, 1972.
[14] GRUE-SØRENSEN K., *Veje og afveje i pædagogisk teori* (Right and Wrong Tracks in Educational Theory), p. 22, *Pædagogik,* volume 6, n° 1, 1976.

educational world of phenomena and issues. In this way, he adhered to the idea that pedagogy is not just a technique or an instrument, but a human way of practice that, like other methods of practice, can only be described in simple and linear sentences and solutions to a limited extent. Thus, criticising his contemporaries, who demanded that educational methods be based on science, Grue-Sørensen emphasised that "you cannot just equate pedagogy with educational technology. I would much rather approach the matter from a different angle, from above, you might say, and say: *pedagogy is the study of the educational world of phenomena and the educational world of issues.* That is about as general as it gets. And then again, it is not desirable that it should get any more general[15]." Philosophy of education, or perhaps you should say philosophical pedagogy, is a study that examines a specific practice.

When Grue-Sørensen thus critically and philosophically considers his educational contemporaries, he does not distance himself from other scientific methods or the educational practice in general – on the contrary. Without philosophy the educational theory and practice lose the broad perspective. Others have phrased it more radically by claiming that any attempt to point out or delimit an educational issue immediately and inevitably refers to philosophy[16]. There is no such thing as an educational issue which is not also philosophical. Even when we immediately consider questions such as "learning" and "teaching" along with other similar phenomena to be empirical matters, they always imply an interpretation of *liberty*. When the child learns, is taught or undergoes an educational process, it does not pass through an evolutionary phase which we can account for empirically. It is a question of a *meaningful action* which makes pedagogy a philosophical issue.

What is particularly valuable in relation to Grue-Sørensen's educational works is probably not as much the theoretical consequences he articulated as the fact that he insisted on the importance of philosophy of education, at a time when everybody else was looking for empirical methods. This clarification of philosophy of education is obvious in Grue-Sørensen's address from 1969 on the occasion of the foundation of the Department of Theoretical Pedagogy at the University of Copenhagen. In this connection, he expressed his scepticism towards the strong specialisation within the province of philosophy. "Specialists who have

---

[15] GRUE-SØRENSEN K., *Om den mulige nytte af teoretisk pædagogik* (About the Possible Benefits of Theoretical Pedagogy), p. 1186, in *Gymnasieskolen,* volume 49, n° 21, 1996.
[16] PETZELT A., *Pädagogik und Philosophie,* in *Einführungen in die pädagogische Fragestellung,* published by W. Fischer, Lambertus-Verlag, Freiburg im Breisgau 1967.

no knowledge of the coherent whole within which they engage in their speciality are likely to end up on barren paths. They may very well know how to approach and solve the various questions, but to determine whether the solution of a given question is of any educational significance in this regard, a broader perspective within the entire field of pedagogy is needed. Often, the secret is not to master some technique that allows us to solve this or that question, but to be able to pose good and essential problems, to be able to ask in the right way[17]."

Whether or not pedagogy can confine itself to asking questions, we shall leave unexamined at this point. Time has in many respects shown us that Grue-Sørensen had a good point when he called attention to the idea that pedagogy risks becoming addicted to methods when it loses its general view. Time and time again, he warned against pedagogy spreading beyond its natural province and assuming *absolute, educational power*[18].

THE NOTION OF PEDAGOGY AND EDUCATIONAL VALIDITY

With this understanding of the relationship between pedagogy and philosophy, Grue-Sørensen embraced a particular Neo-Kantian philosophy of education, which unfortunately was not to play an important part in the educational development.

Although Neo-Kantianism represents a large number of movements and tendencies within the educational province, these do however share the understanding of philosophy of education as a theory of reflection whose job it is to delimit pedagogy in relation to other sciences as well as to its own principles. Their point of departure is not the educational practice but the question concerning what can fundamentally be said about pedagogy. The Neo-Kantians tried to formulate principles of the pedagogy as pedagogy. For example, it is not difficult for us to consider pedagogy from an ethical or a political point of view. Thus they formulate ethical principles that pedagogy must conform to, to avoid committing an act of ethical injustice. Or they point out political and democratic categories according to which pedagogy should be regulated in order not to end up being unpolitical and undemocratic respectively. And likewise we

---

[17] GRUE-SØRENSEN K., *En indvielse* (An Inauguration), p. 101, in *Årbog for Dansk Skolehistorie,* 1969.
[18] See among others K. GRUE-SØRENSEN, *Om begrebet værdi, dels generelt dels i relation til opdragelse* (About the Concept of Value, Partly in General, Partly in Relation to Education), in *Pædagogik,* n° 3, 1975; and *Veje og afveje i pædagogisk teori* (Right and Wrong Tracks in Educational Theory), in *Pædagogik,* n° 1, 1976.

may ask ourselves what educational principles pedagogy must conform to, to be educational at all?

This question is not first and foremost aimed at any particular educational practice, but at the concept of pedagogy – its self-description. That this reflective process does not disengage itself from the practical aspect of pedagogy is clear in that the purpose of the reflection is partly to protect the practice, partly to develop it. In other words, behind the Neo-Kantian reflection on the pedagogy of pedagogy is a recognition of the educational practice, and not – as you often read – a disqualification. It is a recognition which stems from the assumption that you cannot act in an educationally responsible way until you know what constitutes and legitimises an educational conduct and recognition as being, in fact, educational.

It comes as no surprise that wishing to reflect on the boundaries of pedagogy as pedagogy is one of the fundamental ideas in Kant's critical philosophy and in his lectures on pedagogy.

Especially when lecturing, Kant made clear that man is responsible for his own development, seeing that no such thing takes place instinctively and spontaneously. This fact necessitates certain educational skills, which either evolve mechanically – meaning without being planned and according to the given circumstances – or "judiziös" – meaning according to *rational principles*. Since the former of these can end up producing defects and shortcomings, Kant concluded that pedagogy should build upon reason. Without an "idea of reason" – which according to Kant signifies a "notion" of pedagogy – there is a risk that the educational responsibility from one generation to the next will be instrumentalised and random. This does not mean that the idea or the notion is non debateable, as Kant himself pointed out, but merely that the older generation cannot undertake the educational task in a defensible manner, without a conceptual clarification.

It is exactly this subject of *educational validity* that, to some degree, constitutes the common motivation in the Neo-Kantian philosophy of education. We can find it in the works of, for example, Leonard Nelson, Paul Natorp, Theodor Litt, Theodor Ballauff, and today, among others, in Jørg Ruhloff and Wolfgang Fischer, but also in Dietrich Benner's general pedagogy. Even though Benner would not characterise himself as a Neo-Kantian, he nonetheless takes inspiration from their educational-philosophical ideas in particular[19].

---

[19] BENNER D., *Allgemeine Pädagogik,* Juventa, Weinheim und München 2005.

He is particularly influenced by philosopher and Neo-Kantian, Richard Hönigswald (1875-1947), who opens his study of the foundation of pedagogy with a somewhat odd formulation; namely that pedagogy's problem is that, at the end of the day, it can only be understood educationally, seeing that behaving educationally is always a communicative activity – a form of conduct and not a reflection as such. To Hönigswald, pedagogy is always "an action and not a reflection[20]".

This should be considered in a purely fundamental sense, since the question of what constitutes the foundation of pedagogy does not arise until the educational conduct becomes problematic in practice, the motive for reflecting is to communicate a more deliberate notion of pedagogy. We only begin to wonder about the true nature of pedagogy when our daily educational actions fail, when pedagogy loses its familiarity. Thus the intention of self-description again becomes educational in that the reflection on pedagogy – whether it is scientific, theoretical or philosophical – will itself appear *educational*. As Hönigswald writes, its aim is not a reflection in the actual sense of the word, but an *improved conduct* in practice, no matter if this reflection takes place within or outside of the scientific sphere. The motivation that underlies the reflection is to *communicate* a better notion of pedagogy, and it is this motivation for communication that is the very core of pedagogy.

The crux of Hönigswald's analysis is the notion of "communication", which, once again, can only be understood on the basis of the demand for "validity". The idea of pedagogy – that which constitutes pedagogy – is the fact that man lives in a cultural transmission. This signifies that we could not have a conception of pedagogy and educational practice if we did not live in a intergenerational and cultural community of communication[21]. If we did not believe that "something" was worth passing on, and that this "something" could actually be passed on from "somebody" to "somebody else", the notion of "pedagogy" would not be possible at all. Thus educational conduct presupposes a *subject matter*, a *time* and an *interpersonal community*.

Immediately it would appear that Hönigswald's ideas are in accordance with Schleiermacher's claim that pedagogy is the transmission from one generation to the next. On closer inspection, however, it is

---

[20] HÖNIGSWALD R., *Über die Grundlagen der Pädagogik,* p. 11, Verlag von Ernst Reinhardt, München 1927.
[21] HÖNIGSWALD R., *Pädagogik und Philosophie, Pädagogik und Geltungsgedanke,* p. 28, in *Pädagogische Grundprobleme,* published by M. Heitger, Verlag Julius Klinkhardt, Bad Heilbrunn 1969.

striking that he, to a greater extent than Schleiermacher, emphasises the methodical and the volitional aspects, and within the cultural sphere he distinguishes between scientific and non-scientific transmission of culture. Every single cultural product or expression – be it scientific or non-scientific – obtains its meaning by virtue of its relation to a value. The criterion of values – that which substantiates the value, and which cannot be substantiated further – is that they "count" and consequently are valid. This, too, should be understood in its fundamental sense in that "validity" as a notion is the condition for something to be of value and therefore can be passed on. In this way, a given reflection on the notion of pedagogy is closely connected to a reflection on the idea of *the cultural transmission*. It is not culture as such that constitutes the crux; it is rather its potential for being transmitted. According to Hönigswald man is committed to a truth requirement – or you may call a transmission of reason – and this is exactly what constitutes pedagogy and philosophy, too, in that Hönigswald characterises the latter as the overall reflection on "the system of validity[22]". Consequently, the notion of validity is not educationally indifferent. On the contrary, it determines the educational conduct. The concept that something "counts" – that something has a truth and validity value – is in principle independent of the recognition of its "validity". It is not the recognition or the lack of it that is the criterion of the validity value. On the contrary, it is the validity value that *demands* recognition. Truth "is" not because we recognise it as "truth", but because it "is" true, we must recognise it. The idea that validity *must be recognised* as well as the aspect that it *can be recognised* are the fundamental principles of educational practice and consequently also of philosophy of education. The object of the educational practice is the methodical and intentional transmission itself, all the while philosophy of education is the reflection on the conditions of realising this transmission.

This educational-philosophical perspective likewise has consequences that concern school and learning. Seeing that validity is not dependent on a subject, but at the same time demands recognition, the subject as an instance has already been established. Without the idea that the subject can affirm the demand, the demand makes no sense. In connection, subjectivity signifies the opportunity to *actively* determine and with that recognise validity as valid, truth as true and objectivity as objective.

In this way, a communicative community has likewise been taken into consideration in that the possibility of recognition of validity in-

---

[22] *Ibid.*, p. 31.

cludes any conceivable subject. In principle, no one can be excluded when defining validity. According to Hönigswald, this becomes a fundamental principle for the modern school and its presentation of a valid content. The school first and foremost represents an ethical and cognitive principle, whereas its function as a national institution, among other functions, is of secondary importance. In principle, anyone in the educational process – teacher and pupil – should be considered free, not just in his or her process of recognition, but also in his or her will to obtain truthfulness. To Hönigswald, as was the case with Grue-Sørensen, *learning and teaching* are an ethical concretisation of the human possibility of recognition. That is to say that processes of learning and teaching are ways of wanting to illustrate validity within time. Since "truth" as a concept demands recognition, *wanting* to learn becomes an ethical obligation towards truth. Learning – and this goes for teachers as well as pupils – means wanting to learn about truth for the sake of truth. And we may add: due to the existence of "truth", we can learn as well as teach.

This perspective implies a specific understanding of freedom, which, according to Hönigswald, is not just any freedom, but rather the will to one's own *freedom of recognition*. That is to say a freedom that is closely connected to the case, or rather to objectivity. You could say that man is free on account of his ability to learn to act and think truth.

With the concept of freedom of recognition the mistaken belief that it is the task of the schools to transmit a *specific* educational canon, which the next generation should merely learn to confirm, is obviated. It is validity itself or, to be more precise, the very objectivity in relation to the case, which legitimises school activities.

Concluding Remarks

Grue-Sørensen's and Hönigswald's studies alike show that philosophy of education is more than a distant art of abstraction and that it can also contribute to actual educational phenomena and issues.

You can always discuss whether the Neo-Kantian position, in particular, holds the educational antinomies open, or whether, at the end of the day, its main preoccupation is to find an overall principle of reason? It is a discussion which we need not touch on seeing that my main purpose here was to pinpoint the relationship between pedagogy and philosophy.

In this attempt, my point of departure was the assumption that pedagogy – due to its inherent antinomies – needs an educational-philosophical approach. However, not any approach will do; what we are dealing with is a *reflective* handling, which systematically tries to describe educational antinomies and which, in the reflective process, endeavours to search for and advance alternative ways of conduct, which address both the actual educational practice, educational professionalism and research.

Thus, philosophy of education is neither anti-empirical nor normatively neutral and least of all unscientific. In relation to empirical research, its role is to clarify and describe in detail the various *educational* concepts and understandings, which to research are tacit conditions in the evaluation of the educational reality. In relation to normative ideas and ideals, the educational-philosophical contribution could be a discussion of what constitutes educational normativity. In this way, philosophy of education can likewise contribute to the public discourse by analysing, interpreting and problematising educational ideas and tasks. In this respect, the philosophy of education is assigned a task whose purpose is to *search for and describe meaning*. This, however, does not mean that it should set itself up as a judge of what is valuable in the educational practice and what is not. Its task is rather to pinpoint and throw light on the challenges and antinomies with which the educational practice is confronted.

You may criticise such a philosophy of education as being too reducing or for cherishing a scepticism which more than anything else ends in a paralysis of action. In other words, there should be a limit to how paradoxical and how antinomian the description of the educational province is.

It can be difficult to dismiss such an accusation since it is true that it may be the consequence of focusing too much on the contrasts. On the other hand, you should not disregard the antinomian aspect on the grounds that you cannot endure the challenge.

In spite of this discussion, you must remember that philosophy of education only comes into being when an educational practice fails. The point of departure is always a broken practice, which triggers off the educational-philosophical reflection. This break connects pedagogy and philosophy, and a pedagogy that fails to appreciate its relationship with philosophy therefore always ends up underplaying its own qualifications. It will abstract from the fact that its fundamental problems cannot be clarified without an educational-philosophical reflection.

Yet, this does not signify that pedagogy is subordinate to philosophy, and that philosophy can merely confine itself to reflecting *on* pedagogy. If philosophy regards pedagogy as some kind of more or less interesting appendage, which does not really have anything to do with philosophy, philosophy likewise fails to appreciate its own foundation. If, on the other hand, it takes its relationship with pedagogy seriously, it also takes itself seriously. Thus you can regard the relationship between pedagogy and philosophy as an open, discursive, problematising and challenging relationship beyond ideal and harmonious definitions, and you can define *philosophy of education as a reflective handling of educational antinomies.*

THE CONCEPT OF FREEDOM BETWEEN RELIGIOUS INTERPRETATION AND POLITICAL APPLICATION

Henrik VASE FRANDSEN
(School of Education, Aarhus University,
Campus: Copenhagen, Denmark)

1. THE AMBIVALENCE IN THE EXPERIENCE OF FREEDOM

Freedom is an ambiguous concept, and, similarly, the experience of freedom is something that can never be contained in unequivocal terms[1]. On the one hand, we experience freedom as the capacity to take action. We experience ourselves as free in the fact that on the basis of ourselves we are able to make something new. We are capable of beginning something that wasn't there before, something that was not present prior to our decision of carrying it through. Our freedom shows itself in the fact that we have the ability to begin or change something; something that was not present before or was not present in the same manner as after our intervention. We have the experience of ourselves as beings that are capable of beginning; which also mean that we have the experience of ourselves as beings that are capable of interrupting some course or a process.

On the other hand, we also have the experience of ourselves as beings that have not begun ourselves. Moreover, it is innate in our experience of how we are that we *could not* have begun ourselves. In this way the experience of freedom points towards an essential limit; i.e. towards the fact that we have to be present in order to be able to experience ourselves as free beings. Before I was there, before my very existence, I was not free. Or to put it otherwise: We all come into being by virtue of other peoples and other things – which of course is obvious in the case of birth, but is also true when we think of education as well as

---

[1] In the following, I profit among others from I. U. DALFERTH, *Freiheit und Liebe. Selbstwerdung nach Levinas und Rosenzweig*. Unpublished manuscript.

of other human and social relations, friendships, school attendance, and further of the experience of my own body and of ourselves as material. We grow and age without any decision, we are familiar with ourselves in illness, when we have reserves of strength, and when we lack strength; we also discover ourselves in sport, eroticism and sensuality in a broad sense and in many other kinds of *impressions* that affect us and change us and, as it is sometime said, "makes me into who I am". In short, the phenomenon of birth, which is not only the birth of the body, precedes and exceeds every experience of freedom, because the phenomenon of birth escapes my experience. Since I was not there before my birth, neither could I be free prior to my birth. Therefore, prior to my freedom, prior to the experience of my *capacity to begin*, there is another beginning which I have not initiated, but which by contrast has initiated me. Consequently, our experience of freedom moves in two directions, namely that we *can* begin, but also that we *cannot* begin our selves. Prior to our freedom there is another beginning; another beginning that is not mine. But I am here by virtue of this other beginning. Before freedom there is something that is not freedom, but there wouldn't be freedom without it – and this experience is innate in the experience of freedom.

In this way, an old and classical problem is raised, namely: How can freedom arise from something that is not freedom? Or to put it another way: How can my freedom be the result of some other freedom foreign to me?

The question is classical, it belongs to the genre one might call "the unsolvable questions" and it occupies a central role in modern philosophy whatever the cadre might be – philosophy of education, political philosophy or philosophy of religion. When freedom is not an unequivocal concept it stems from the fact that freedom seems to be describable only in an aporetic manner. One might dispute freedom, one might even restrict freedom, and in fact this is done every day; but if freedom is restricted this is precisely something that demands justification, and again: such justification will have its recourse to the idea of freedom.

2. HANNA ARENDT'S CRITIQUE OF THE CONCEPT OF SOVEREIGNTY

In an essay entitled "What is Freedom?" Hanna Arendt outlines the fundamental form of the difficulty that we encounter in the concept of freedom. The issue is about a contradiction between, on the one hand our conscience and consciousness and, on the other our daily experience of the world which we comprehend according to the principles of causality.

In all *practical* matters – ethical, political, religious, educational – we take human freedom as an evident, rightful and "true" value. Freedom has the birthright so to speak, and it is upon this assumption that we give laws to society, that we make decisions, that we build up institutions like schools and the judicial system, that judgements are given in court, that we make contracts and agreements and so on and so forth. Without individual freedom, the institutions of society would only be binding in the sense of constraint, oppression and fear of reprisals. But at the same time we proceed according to another assumption which seems to be no less obvious, namely that to anything that is, there must be a cause; from nothing comes nothing, and therefore no existence does not have a cause. The doctrine *nihil sine causa* underlies how we most often understand the physical world; to understand some occurrence or some sequence or development means to identify what causes this occurrence or this development. And what is more, this way of understanding things does not restrict itself to the exterior and physical world, but is applicable into the most secret recesses of the individual itself, since we are also the results of alien and foreign causes, whether they would be biological, psychological or social. The free man too is subordinated to the machinery of causality. Man is, like every other thing in the world, a derived effect, a result of irrational and anonymous causes. – Which is a consideration that can also be given the formulation that *a free man never appears in the world*; since everything in the world has a cause, and since what has a cause cannot be regarded as freedom but only as consequence and derived effect.

However, if freedom is never manifest in the world, is it then a genuine freedom? This is the critical question Hanna Arendt raises in her essay. To her, the freedom that is never manifest in the world is the freedom of the will, and so she attacks a dominant conception in Western culture. Freedom of will, which we know for instance in Kant, is a freedom that is not simply free as the wind; the will obtains its qualified freedom through imposing laws on itself, that is by preserving its own interior causality. But precisely this freedom of the will does not manifest itself in the phenomenal world. The *liberum arbitrium* does *not* appear, it cannot be seen, and this is why it has no meaning to Arendt in a political sense. Freedom in a *political* sense cannot be anything but *freedom of action*, not a freedom of will. Seen politically man is only free in action and solely as long as he acts. A freedom separated from action is not political freedom: "Freedom as related to politics is not a phenomenon of the will[2]". And even more, the freedom of the will would be entirely without political significance if it did not open towards a positively dangerous political conception: Freedom of the will puts the emphasis on the will, on the "I-will", and the only form of regime that originates directly in the "I-will" is tyranny[3].

According to Arendt, freedom of the will is an idea that emerges in Western culture from the Christian religious tradition. In her historical interpretation the issue is first about St. Augustine – and before him St. Paul – and their influence on western thought. Freedom understood as some kind of sovereignty that unfolds in the "interior man" presupposes the very discovery of this "interior man". This discovery is closely connected to early Christianity, and it is formulated for the first time by St. Paul in the religious experience of "what I do is not what I want to do, but what I detest" (*Romans* 7,15). Since the essence of the will is to command and be obeyed, it is a quite monstrous experience that St. Paul refers to here. It is the bizarre experience that the two elements of "I will" and "I do" do not coincide. The will is here in some kind of conflict with itself; and the discovery of the "interior man" is precisely the discovery of this interior conflict, a conflict that in Augustine can be formulated as the simultaneous presence of "I-will" and "I-will-not". This conflict does not take place between reason and passion, it is not a conflict between *intelligibilis* and *sensibilis*; on the contrary it is a conflict and a duality *within the will itself* – and it is from this experience of "the dark 'chamber of the heart[4]'", from the experience of this inner duality that the idea of the free will grows, i.e. the idea of a reconciliation between what I will and what I ought – between will and duty. Or to put it in another way: In continuation of this discovery of a conflict in the "interior man", the possibility opens of an ideality of the will that would not be divided in two; and this ideal of the undivided will is entitled the will's *sovereignty*. Sovereignty, independence, undividedness – those are to Hanna Arendt the ideals in the dominant Western tradition of "inner freedom". It is a possibility that arises first with St. Paul and early Christianity and then makes its entry in Western philosophy with St. Augustine.

To Arendt however, this is a derivative conception of freedom, and she makes it the object of her critique. Behind the movement where free-

---

[2] Hanna ARENDT, "What is Freedom?", in *Between Past and Future. Eight Exercises in Political Thought*, Penguin Books, New York 1993 (1st ed. Viking Press, New York 1968), p. 151.
[3] Cf. *Ibid.*, p. 163.
[4] *Ibid.*, p. 158 (cit. AUGUSTINE, *Conf.* L. 8 ch. 8).

dom is separated from the political efficacy she sees an attempt to "arrive at a formulation through which one may be a slave in the world and still be free[5]". To her, the idea of an interior freedom and sovereignty has a derivative character in the sense that "the experiences of inner freedom ... always presuppose a retreat from the world where freedom was denied, into an inwardness to which no other has access[6]". It is against this background that Arendt launches an alternative conception of freedom, designed as an exclusively political conception under the title *virtuosity*. In opposition to the apparent quasi-Christian and much too religious coloured sovereignty and "inner" freedom, she poses the idea of a "freedom in action" and virtuosity; concepts that are supposed to clarify the independence of political experience, its *sui generis* status. Behind this concept of virtuosity lies of course Machiavelli; but more fundamentally the issue is about the almost banal experience of spontaneity, i.e. that the experience of being free and the experience of being able to begin something new is one and the same[7]. Here there would be no division, no conflict and no duality but, if one can put it so, "pure action". Somewhat surprisingly it is once more in St. Augustine Arendt finds support, but this time in *De civitate Dei*, Augustine's only "political" work. Here Augustine no longer speaks of freedom as an internal human disposition but as something that characterizes human existence in the world: Man is a free being since man is as such a beginning. Man is a beginning in the sense that the individual is born into a world that was already created and will also continue to be after the individual's death. Man is, so to speak, a beginning inside a world that has already been put into operation. "Because he *is* a beginning, man can begin; to be human and to be free are one and the same. God created man in order to introduce into the world the faculty of beginning: freedom[8]" – she comments. The guiding thought here has to do with the relation between what is already there – knowledge, history, predictability in quasi-automatic processes – and the new, the unexpected, the *event* which is both interruption and beginning.

In continuation of Hanna Arendt's essay I would like to propose two comments:

First: It is quite obvious that Arendt in no way wishes to promote religion or some kind of "religious metaphysics". Towards the end of her

---

[5] *Ibid.*, p. 147.
[6] *Ibid.*, p. 146.
[7] *Ibid.*, p. 166.
[8] *Ibid.*, p. 167.

essay she speaks about the "miracle", and she gives here the following salute: "... we know the author of the 'miracles' [in quotation marks, *Sic!*]. It is men who perform them – men who because they have received the twofold gift of freedom and action can establish a reality of their own[9]". Consequently, Arendt definitely denies a theological perspective and places herself without any ambiguity in an immanent anthropological-historical perspective. It is from this perspective that she criticizes the concept of sovereignty by accusing it of being a figure of only an "interior" freedom; "interior" and thus, ultimately, an illusionary freedom! But in fact, in doing this her criticism of the "freedom of will" more or less follows a traditional thesis about religion's nature; namely that it is some kind of ideological-mental construction, an intellectual and cultural product whose *function* (always the "function") is to justify some deprivations or to give a compensation for the needs of identity, material deficiency, political shortage or whatever. Seen in this way, religion expresses a sort of fetish in hypostasis, but in sum its *raison d'être* originates in nothing but pure human needs[10]. The "inner" freedom has, according to Arendt, this precise function: to explain how one can be a slave in the world and yet still be free. Without any doubt religion can serve such a function, but the more radical question is whether we understand what "religion" means, if we obstinately hold on to such a model. It is probably because Arendt persists with this model and this perspective that, even if she seeks the religious roots to the notion of freedom, she avoids the narratives of liberation and the visions of freedom that are manifest in the Judaeo-Christian tradition (*par excellence*: the Exodus narrative in the Jewish tradition, the empty grave in the Christian tradition). These narratives are struck out as illegitimate by the simple suspicion that they express some ideological counter-images of the historical and societal situation in which they are formulated. But – to be honest – there is no thought, no idea, no imagination that are able to avoid such criticism. Neither political utopias nor religious narratives nor educational ideas can avoid, shall we say, the "suspicion of causality"; and this goes as well for the criticism of those ideas – the critique itself is also subject to the "suspicion of causality". Here we are dealing with a general historical condition as to how we can approach human culture, which

---

[9] *Ibid.*, p. 171.
[10] A quite refreshing discussion on religion, as well as on the very theoretical concept of "religion", is in Luc FERRY & Marcel GAUCHET, *Le religieux après la religion*, Grasset, Paris 2004, pp. 28 ff.

might suggest that religion, politics and education has much more in common than would normally be recognised.

Secondly, the notion of *virtuosity* as a concept for a genuine political freedom seems to me strangely empty in its capacity of being a practical category (and both "education" as well as "politics" and "religion" belongs to the practical world). Of course it is clear that in all this "event" and "spontaneity", as well as the celebration of "the new" and "the unexpected", operates a kind of translation of the religious idea of transcendence into historical and anthropological categories. It is the event *in* history that *goes beyond* history. Here one might sense the influence of Heideggerian paganism. But strikingly, Arendt leaves in silence the question of what normativity (that is: what genuine practical pertinence) one might attribute to the "new", except that it is new and unforeseen. It seems that events are neither autonomy nor heteronomy to her; events are a-normativity pure and simple; an a-normativity that she interprets in an almost naturalistic direction, which seems clear in her exegesis of the religious discourse on the miracle. Everything considered, events in Arendt seem to mean nothing but the interruption of a context. And obviously, every time something *begins* there is also necessarily the sense of rupture. But contrary to what Arendt seems to think, I find it doubtful that every rupture will have the sense of beginning and therefore of freedom. What excludes the possibility of the rupture's sense being the final end, the terminal event (the "big bang" in an inverse perspective, the "final bang")?

3. THE APPEAL AND THE OBLIGATORY VISION OF THE WORLD

In continuation of Hanna Arendt I would like to encircle another idea of freedom, an idea that might be understood as the common source both of the political utopia and of the religious relation to the world. This other idea of freedom is linked to the appeal. The point of departure in this meditation is to be found in Emmanuel Levinas' concept of "testimony" (especially in *Autrement qu'être*) and in Jean-Luc Marion's thesis on the "saturated phenomenon" (formulated in particular in *Étant donné*). However, I shall confine myself to tracing two traits that seem particularly characteristic to me. Firstly, the appeal is always pronounced in the name of somebody else, and pretends to be sincere in this reference to the other. Secondly, in the final analysis, the appeal can only be heard in the response that I make to it; only from the very moment when I make a response to the appeal can I have an experience of the appeal.

1. *The appeal addresses itself to me in the name of another.* The appeal does not consist primarily of some new information about the world; first and foremost it is an impression and a demand. But the source of this demand withdraws itself; the "first cause" of the appeal does not reveal itself to me. This trait is confirmed both when some organisation – like the Red Cross or *Médecins sans frontières* – launches an appeal for the benefit of somebody (for instance the victims of a cataclysm or a war), and when some public person pronounces an appeal (Dalai Lama, Ghandi, the Pope, the President, the "intellectuals" (if they still exist), etc.). The appeal addresses itself to me *in the name of somebody else*; the appeal is in service of somebody other than the individual or the organisation that actually pronounces it. So, there is reference to the other in the appeal, and with this reference there is also the pretension of "frank speaking". Without this "sincerity in the application" the appeal will not be heard at all. Or perhaps better: If I do not hear the sincerity in the appeal when it claims to be at the service "of the other", I will not hear the appeal at all but something else, perhaps an attempt to manipulate. Now, moving on to the encounter with a concrete individual in distress that appeals to me to intervene: it would not be less wrong to say here, that this individual forms the source of the appeal. It is of course possible, and likely, that this other person in need addresses himself directly to me, but even here this demand does not take place solely in his name but also in the name of others, like for instance in the name of justice, in the name of God, in the name of life, in the name of humanity, etc. In this way every appeal carries with it a kind of implicit reference to another name; a name that in the end remains unknown but yet forms the appeal's genuine source – which means that the appeal preserves its anonymity along with its approach towards me. What is more, one has to maintain by contrast that if the source is known, if we know "who is making a demand" or the appeal's "ultimate name", then we fall outside the position of being the appeal's target. If the appeal is to be heard, one must "give ear" to it, meaning that one gives in to the appeal, that one submits oneself to the appeal's sincerity in its reference to the "other name" – without any knowledge of the other name, which does not appear before consciousness.

2. To this we can add the second trait, namely that *the appeal will only be heard in the response I make to it*. The recipient is necessary in order for the appeal to manifest itself; and the recipient only enters into his role as recipient from the very moment he responds. Here we have to take notice of the fact that the appeal is not an object-phenomenon; it

does not manifest itself "in the world" like an object that offers itself to our knowledge. On the contrary, the appeal is a kind of intentionality, a will, which affects me and influences me in that I only know the appeal in the influence it exercises over me. Therefore, to know the appeal's signification or its "will" coincides with the movement where the subject takes it upon himself to pronounce the appeal. The only one who knows the appeal's signification is the one who subjects himself to the appeal by pronouncing it. The appeal cannot be pointed out as a phenomenon alongside several other phenomena, but the one who responds *testifies* to it. The issue here is about the dimension of the elevated and the "very high", that to which I do not have access by research or by examination, since the appeal withdraws itself from any direct knowledge. There is only access to the appeal in subjecting oneself to its pre-eminence. In the appeal we are dealing with alterity and heteronomy; a will strange to me, but a will that becomes my own from the moment I speak and so *pronounce* the appeal myself and in this way respond to it. Without this dimension of the elevated, the appeal would transform into something else: a seduction or a political manipulation or simply a vulgar advertising for yet another and still more vulgar product. In the appeal the encounter with the transcendent occurs, the encounter with what goes ahead. The appeal is not a phenomenon in a trivial and common understanding since it does not manifest itself; but – as an essential point – it gives a new vision of the world. It gives an obligatory vision of this world that we usually call the practical world; this world wherein certain actions are necessary and sometimes even urgent. The appeal does not give itself to my sight, but it orientates my sight of the world; the appeal does not itself appear, but rather makes the world appear to my eyes, the world wherein there is not only true and false but also good and evil, and therefore urgent obligations which cause that from time to time there are absolutely indispensable actions.

Returning now to Hanna Arendt's critique of the concept of sovereignty, it seems to me that what she misses in her study is sensitivity towards the fact that "the new" does not simply "happen" in the manner of a mere coincidence; rather one has to say that the new only arrives by struggling with the old. No genuine utopia – religious *or* political, presupposing that it makes sense to make such distinction at this level – no utopia or vision can be cut down to the character of a mere occasional coincidence; rather it imposes itself with the character of *necessity*. It is because of this necessity that the experience of a utopia is never the experience of something that "I have chosen"; it is not a "choice" in the banal sense that I could have chosen otherwise if my mood had been different this morning. – This danger of the arbitrary is precisely what threatens if one promotes virtuosity as the sole category of political freedom. Of course it is a matter for each person to choose the utopia and its obligation, but this does not change anything about the fact that the obligation *arrives*; that it *presents itself* to me and therefore maintains the character of something that transcends. In this way any utopia of a different world retains the trait of something *given*; there is something which demands me and imposes itself, something which calls upon me.

The issue here is the way in which the practical sight of the world has the character of an appeal. In the appeal I find it possible to make a common formulation about the way in which the obligating or binding is experienced in both politics and religion. Something appeals, but regardless of what causes this appeal (to be exact: we do not know the cause), it belongs to the appeal that it introduces me to a new way of seeing the practical world. Thus the division of the will into a simultaneous "I-will" and "I-will-not" can be interpreted as a form of subjectivity's hesitation in face of the appeal; we might say that it is like a conflict between "my will" and "the appeal's will". Naturally it is heteronomy and transcendence that is at play in the urgency and the pressing character of the appeal; but it is freedom as well, since *the appeal gives me the possibility of engagement and beginning*. Precisely by imposing itself on me it demands my action, it urges me to begin; and so it forces me to assert my freedom. This is the sense of the rupture. The new and the surprising – what Arendt calls "the event" – is not about what happens in the world in the mere capacity of unpredicted interruptions; this would be freedom reduced into tourism and the exotic ("oh!...how very interesting!"). On the contrary: What is in play here is that the world may appear in a new way, namely that, unexpected and surprised by it, I understand that the world is a place where action is necessary. The surprise, the unforeseen, the new, the unpredicted, all these are characters of the appeal. Or, to be more precise: surprise is a character in the *signification* that the world might take on according to the appeal, at least if it is heard and answered[11].

In this sense, freedom begins as given freedom; and any genuine free act (Arendt's *virtuosity*) begins against the background of such an

---

[11] For a more detailed study on the appeal (and with extensive references to E. Levinas and J.-L. Marion), see H. V. FRANDSEN, "Transcendence of the Appeal – Sovereignty of the Subject"; forthcoming at Mohr Siebeck, Tübingen, in A. GRØN, S. OVERGAARD and I. DAMGAARD (eds), *Subjectivity and Transcendence*.

initial passivity. And finally: Even if it is not Arendt's intention to proceed in such a direction, I would nevertheless like to conclude by quoting once again her last sentences: "... we know the author of the 'miracles'. It is men who perform them – men who because they have *received the twofold gift of freedom and action* can establish a reality of their own" (my emphasis). Is it simply a "slip of the pen" when she writes by implication about freedom and political action as something *given*? – suggesting that political action refers back to a kind of passivity and perhaps even to a form of transcendence lying before the ordinary distinction between active and passive, before the distinction of spontaneity and automatism, before we separate the cause from the effect? Against Arendt's condemnation it is necessary to maintain that even if the "freedom of the will" does not appear in the phenomenal world, this does not imply its political indifference; by contrast it is in interior conflict that decisions about the practical world's face are made; and consequently about which actions are necessary. In short: Without the idea of sovereignty, neither philosophy of education nor political philosophy nor philosophy of religion has anything to gain if they want to continue to be regarded as normative and practical philosophies.

I would like to express my gratitude to Shane Mackinlay *for his talented and indispensable editing of my English text.*

EDUCATION AND PLEASURE IN PLATO'S *LAWS*

Irene SVITZOU
(Academy of Athens, Greece)

> ... τὴν δὲ πρὸς ἀρετὴν ἐκ παίδων παιδείαν, ποιοῦσαν ἐπιθυμητὴν τε καὶ ἐραστὴν τοῦ πολίτην γενέσθαι τέλεον, ἄρχειν τε καὶ ἄρχεσθαι ἐπιστάμενον μετὰ δίκης. Ταύτην τὴν τροφὴν ἀφορισάμενος ὁ λόγος οὗτος, ὡς ἐμοὶ φαίνεται, νῦν βούλοιτ᾽ ἂν μόνην παιδείαν προσαγορεύειν... οἱ δὲ ὀρθῶς πεπαιδευμένοι σχεδὸν ἀγαθοὶ γίγνονται, καὶ δεῖ δὴ τὴν παιδείαν μηδαμοῦ ἀτιμάζειν, ὡς πρῶτον τῶν καλλίστων τοῖς ἀρίστοις ἀνδράσιν παραγιγνόμενον.
>
> (Plato, *Laws*, 643e4-644b2).

THE IMPORTANCE OF EDUCATION

The whole idea of Plato's second best city as described in the *Laws*, is based on an institution to which he attributed a major part of his work, from his primary dialogues to this latest one: Education. In the *Laws* Plato explicitly shows how education should be organized and systematized in order of course to sustain and preserve the whole city status. Yet, in this ideal State of Magnesia education differs from what we may see in the *Republic*. Here, Plato puts on the table some really innovative ideas concerning the practical application of the theoretical plans and brings to light an important issue related to the aim of education itself: the happiness of men. The preservation of the city is achieved by the maintenance of the laws and this reassures peoples' eudaemonia. But the only factor that may in a way guarantee this situation is education and this is partly why in the *Laws* Plato is primarily concerned with the public character of his educational system as well as with its anthropological aspect[1].

---

[1] Cf. John J. CLEARY, "Paideia in Plato's *Laws*", in S. SCOLNICOV & L. BRISSON (eds), *Plato's* Laws: *From Theory into Practice*, Proceedings of the VI Symposium Platonicum, Academia Verlag, Sankt Augustin 2003, p.165; Yvon BRÈS, *La psychologie de Platon*, P.U.F., Paris 1973², pp.327-328; Charles HUMMEL, "Plato", *Prospects: The Quarterly Review of Education*, Unesco, I.B.E., vol. 24, no 1/2, Paris 1994, pp. 335-336;

Education in *Laws* becomes the crucial tool for many tasks. It will acquaint the citizens to "divine necessities[2]" and will provide them prosperity in every day's life[3].

It will be their guide to truth and teach them how to choose real pleasure over pain[4] by helping them to achieve their goal of discovering it and thus live happy, namely virtuous, lives.

It is never too early to be engaged in education, according to Plato. We must start even before a child is born[5]. We may think that since we are puppets in the hands of God we may do as we please and not take things seriously since one way or another our destiny will be fulfilled; but even so, we must act in *sophrosyne* and think of education as one of the most important issues in our lives[6].

Furthermore, the Nocturnal Council, through a higher type of education will be able to understand the aim of social life that is the development of virtue and the establishment of pleasure. Education will provide its members with the ability to distinguish the one among the many, that is to say to conceive the unity of virtues[7] and will take them closer to wisdom. Besides, education will bring internal harmony to people and unity to their souls. It will make them capable of distinguishing right from wrong and it is the only way that will make them realize that the caring of the soul is prior to the caring of the body since there are no other means for them to develop genuine virtues.

So great is the importance Plato attributes to education in the *Laws* that it has been supported that the *Laws* was written as "a paradigmatic text in prose literature that is being offered for the education of the ordinary citizens of Magnesia, but especially for the Law Warden who is to supervise the education of the children[8]...". And though at a first rough glance it may seem that the *Laws* is in a way limitedly devoted to the educational program of the citizens in comparison to the program for the guardians of the *Republic*, this disparity may lose ground at a second, more serious look, where it becomes obvious that the importance and the

---

Christopher BOBONICH, *Plato's Utopia Recast. His Later Ethics and Politics*, Clarendon Press, Oxford 2002, pp. 92-93, 107-108.
[2] PLATO, *Laws*, 818b3-8.
[3] *Ibid.*, 756e4-5.
[4] *Ibid.*, 726b-734e.
[5] *Ibid.*, 789d.
[6] *Ibid.*, 803d5-7.
[7] *Ibid.*, 965c-e.
[8] Cf. J. J. CLEARY, *art. cit.*, p. 166.

emphasis given in the former dialogue to the educational role, purpose, function and aiming reduces, if not eliminates that difference[9].

Before we begin to examine other aspects of education and their details we must make one remark, that is also essential for the importance of education in the *Laws*: Unlike *Republic*, education here is equally important to all the citizens (although it may vary in some quality details) because the citizens of the *Laws* are equal; they all share in their souls the divine element of *logismos* and thus the potentiality of becoming carriers of the divine law through a correct performance of education. Soul may offer Man the possibility of avoiding the bad, recognize the good and decide to follow it for the rest of his life[10]. A wise man must show mercy for other people's faults and imperfections because as we already know "πᾶς ὁ ἄδικος οὐχ ἑκὼν ἄδικος[11]" but becomes so out of lack of proper education.

THE *LAWS* AND THE LAWS ON EDUCATION

In Book VII of his founding the second best city, Plato exhibits us in full details his program of education[12]. The length only of his thorough examination shows the great importance the educational factor has for this platonic city as well as the various aspects of it that have to be taken seriously into consideration before we end up in a functional, appropriate for the citizens program, that will both be human and possible and of course effective.

He begins with an important observation[13]: We must form our remarks as suggestions rather than strict, specific laws since in family and personal life there exists a number of details (sorrows, pleasure, desires) that no one but the person himself is able to know. Still, they have the power to make people different from each other and thus they may result in disobedience toward the law if the latter fails to meet their personal needs. Another parameter that we must also consider is given in Book VI where it is clearly stated[14] that the title of Supervisor of Education (like

---

[9] *Ibid.*, p. 173.
[10] PLATO, *Laws*, 728c10-728d3.
[11] *Ibid.*, 731b3-c6.
[12] *Ibid.*, 788a-822d.
[13] *Ibid.*, 788a4-788b5.
[14] *Ibid.*, 765e1-3. In the same paragraph as well as in the one that follows (765e3-766b2) we are given the explanation of the important role of the Supervisor of Education (Παιδείας Ἐπιμελητής) that is directly related to the nature of Man and especially to children's nature and to the way Man has the ability to become the most divine creature in the universe. See also, J. LAURENT, "L'éducation et l'enfance dans les *Lois*", P.U.F.,

Minister of Education) is far the most important of all the offices in the State. Taking into consideration that children in the *Laws* belong mainly to the city and secondly to their parents (804d), we may understand the obligatory aspect of education and its importance for the city. Besides, the most carefully chosen Supervisor undoubtedly shows that unlike what had been happening till then, Plato strongly believed in the public character of Education with the last being a political activity rather than a private matter in the hands of the parents. Before we proceed in examining the specific laws on education we must note that Plato stands for another novelty of his times: Boys and girls will receive the same education since the same laws will be applied later to both men and women.

From the age of three we may begin to get the children used to discipline. It is at the same age that games will begin and it is for the children's best interest to leave them alone to discover their own games until the age of six. After that we must take them to the temples daily and let them play there under the surveillance of women especially chosen for this purpose. It is at that age exactly that the first lessons will begin divided into two main categories: those for the exercise of the body and those for the exercise of the mind and soul[15]. The first apply to the general title of "gymnastics" and the second of "music".

All lessons will take place in buildings especially made for such purposes, appropriately equipped and surrounded by other auxiliary buildings and game fields. Teachers must be paid for their jobs and all children should follow their lessons regularly. This systematic and well-organized idea of a "primary school" is of course Plato's astonishing novelty of the time[16]..

With these three main lessons (dancing, singing and poetry) we will deal later on in the passage that refers to the relativity between education and pleasure. Along with the dancing lessons, gymnastics also include other activities in various sorts of sports such as horse riding, hunting and training in weapons (sling-bow-javelin) both for boys and girls (although more emphasis is naturally given to the training of the boys since it is in their hands that the safety of the city lies). Moreover, the lessons of gymnastics also include wrestling from the two categories of which the free one *(ὄρθια πάλη)* is preferable and dancing in armor because they pro-

---

Revue Philosophique, 125e année, Paris 2000, pp. 46-47 ; A. E. TAYLOR, *Plato. The Man and his Work*, University Paperback, 1960[1], pp. 475-479; E. VOEGELIN, *Plato*, Univ. of Missouri Press, Columbia/London 2000, pp. 259-263.
[15] PLATO, *Laws*, 796a ff.
[16] *Ibid.*, 804e-805b.

vide useful information to the boys about battle and prepare them for the case of a war.

Let us now examine the other branches of education that is the arithmetic, the geometry and the astronomy. Plato feels embarrassed speculating about the little knowledge that his contemporary Greeks have on these issues, so he tries in his Magnesia to prevent the citizens from making the same mistake[17]. Astronomy has a distinct place among these lessons because of its close relevance to God and to the essence of the universe[18]. In this lesson it is really important to correct a number of wrong ideas and misunderstandings about the planets and their movements. Astronomy, apart from its use in every day's life, is, according to Plato in the *Laws*, an attempt to put theology on a scientific and explicable basis; it is in a way what we could call a kind of proof of God's existence. So of course, not only cannot it be missed in such a detailed and carefully planned program of education but as we see in book XII members of the Nocturnal Council may only become those citizens who are well educated, apart from others, in astronomy and mathematics (of a higher level of course) and have clearly and completely understood the theology of book X and the priority and causality of soul in the universe.

To return to the education of children and of the rest of the citizens, although a lot of people are not so attracted to mathematics and geometry and do not show great abilities in them, they all must be taught these lessons and reach a minimum point of necessary knowledge on the subject in order for them to avoid inherit their ignorance to the next generations.

And with these lessons the educational program of the *Laws* is completed. If all aspects of this program are followed carefully and accurately in their details we just may succeed in our goals and achieve a life of internal harmony and pleasure, a life of virtue and happiness for all, according to the laws of Gods and to the laws of the State. By the proper guidance young citizens will grow up to be well controlled and well educated adults, totally balanced, brave, true citizens of an ideal, yet practically possible, second best city. The goal of the educational program of Plato will then have been fulfilled.

---

[17] *Ibid.*, 819d5-820e7.

[18] For further information on the importance of astronomy in the *Laws*, see books X and XII and suggestively the following: L. BRISSON, *Lectures de Platon*, Vrin, Histoire de la Philosophie, Paris 2000, pp. 259-262; L. STRAUSS, *The Argument and the Action of Plato's Laws*, The Univ. of Chicago Press, Chicago/London 1977, pp. 184-185 a.e.; P. KUCHARSKI, *La spéculation platonicienne*, tome 1, Publications de la Sorbonne, Paris 1971, pp. 73-75, 79, 87; A. E. TAYLOR, *op.cit.*, pp. 447, 452, 498-500.

EDUCATION AND PLEASURE

In a philosophical level

In the *Laws* from 634b and in the lines that follow we are informed that manliness consists in confronting the appeals of *hedony* and that the only way of learning how to do that is to come close to it, face it and finally, beat it. One can do that by training (i.e. education) and by exposing himself little by little to those pleasures, which he wants to learn how to deal with. In order to do that Man has to be convinced of the superiority of justice and law by appeal to pleasure or pain since virtue becomes now the agreement of reason and pleasure, brought about through education[19]. Law receives here an anthropological sense. Education turns out to be the path and the way that will guide men (especially children) towards the correct type of *Logos*, the one that will be revealed by Law. It will become the agent that will instate Law both in the souls and in the minds of Men assuring thus their only way to be truly happy[20].

In *Philebus* as well as in the *Laws* pleasure (and consequently pain) is rather "isolated" and studied almost *per se* concerning human life. It quite becomes an ultimate purpose, what all mankind is looking for throughout their lives and education is a matter of correctly seeking and formulating the feelings of pleasure and pain. Yet, because of a possible deterioration or even diminishing of its results throughout life[21] Gods have given us the Muses along with Apollo and Dionysus. Both young citizens (mainly children) and older ones must learn to be pleased by God's gift, the odes[22].

A child's first experience of life is his acquaintance with pleasure and pain. The aim of education is to teach him to feel so for the correct things[23]. There is no better way to conquer such an education than through singing and dancing (i.e. through teaching the children how to transform their godly given gifts of sensing music and movement into a real ὄρχησις and μελωδία, using of course another gift of Gods to mankind, *Logos* (reason) and *Nous* (mind).

---

[19] S. SCOLNICOV, "Pleasure and responsibility", in S. SCOLNICOV & L. BRISSON (eds), Plato's Laws: *From Theory into Practise*, Proceedings of the VI Symposium Platonicum, Academia Verlag, Sankt Augustin 2003, pp. 125-126.
[20] Yvon BRÈS, *op.cit.*, pp. 125-126.
[21] PLATO, *Laws*, 635c7-d6.
[22] *Ibid.*, 659d-e.
[23] *Ibid.*, 653a.

Thus, pleasure becomes an essential part of human education and the tool in the hands of the teacher and the legislator, giving them the possibility of correctly guiding the citizens towards virtue, namely towards *eudaemonia*. This is the reason why the legislator must not grant total freedom to poets and musicians in order for them to practice novelties, because they might be catastrophic to citizen's *ethos*. Living a just life in which education keeps the man safe and away from wrongdoing through the correct use of music, poetry and group dancing is the best possible way of living and therefore the most pleasant one. Music brings harmony into Men's souls, dancing gives control and spiritual pleasure, and through the participation into this mystical event a wonderful task is achieved: the seeking of the ultimate good. And for the elderly who may not have the mood to participate like they used to when they were younger, a little wine will give them enough spirit to act like they were young again.

Anyway, the legislator must not forget that the people he wants to "attract" to the just (and most pleasant life according to Plato) are humans and not Gods. This is why he must *persuade* them that this kind of life will indeed be the happiest (since Man will from nature choose something pleasant for him and of course not painful). What Plato intends to show now[24] is that even to a man in desire of a life full of pleasure the ethical way of living according to the law is much more pleasant as long as the rules are correctly and carefully formed and executed. These rules generally say that men long for the presence of pleasure in their lives and for the absence of pain while a neutral situation is not desirable but still is much more preferred than pain.

It is not in the aims of this paper to analyze the platonic theory of calculating pleasure and pain in the *Laws*[25] but to detect the place of pleasure and its importance in Plato's educational purposes. Still generally, we may say that taking a serious turn towards human psychology and theory of human motivation[26] Plato acknowledges that pleasure and pain determine our way of acting and make us decide or not to follow

---

[24] *Ibid.*, 732e-734e3.

[25] For further information on this subject in the *Laws* and in other later dialogues see F. C. WHITE, "Plato's Last Words on Pleasure", *Classical Quarterly*, 51.2, 2001, pp. 469 ff.; D. LAMBRELLIS, "Plato's Philosophy of Education", *Philosophical Inquiry*, Aristotle Univ. of Thessaloniki, Vol. XXV, Summer-Fall 2003, n° 3-4, pp. 127-133.

[26] A. LAKS, "The Laws", in Chr. ROWE & M. SCHOFIELD (eds), *Greek and Roman Political Thought*, Cambridge University Press, The Cambridge History of Philosophy, 2000, Chapter 12, pp. 275-278; D. FREDE, "Plato's Ethics: An overview", on line in *Stanford Encyclopaedia of Philosophy*, © 2004, ch. 5 "The Late Dialogues", pp. 10-11.

certain rules. It is rather a kind of a motivational hedonism[27] in which we all prefer pleasures to pains considering their sizes (frequency, intensity, magnitude and their opposites). If anyone chooses anything different than this predominance of pleasures over pains, he speaks so out of ignorance and in need[28] of experience.

This is when education is once more seriously involved in human's seeking for a pleasant life. The word *ignorance* shows that the lack of appropriate education may cause severe mistakes in a man's choice for a lifetime and therefore cost him his happiness and a life deprived if not of any pleasure, at least of the right pleasures for him and thus, a life in a predomination of pain. Hence, in order for a man to choose wisely, education is indispensable in the course of leading a happy life (i.e. a life according to justice and to the rules of the City).

Let us not then pay so much attention to those who protest against a just legislator who has the right to control "private cases[29]" because a civilized life is only possible under the correct uses of the three most intensive appetites of men: hunger, thirst and sexual desire. In this case the education of the Judge is crucial for letting him understand people's needs and then so is the education of people for making them follow the just rules and live correctly and therefore happy, in a just city, the laws of which will provide them security and well-being.

In a practical level

The three applied aspects of pleasure according to what is mentioned in the *Laws*, as we have already seen are dancing, music and literature. Plato speaks for a different approach in teaching dances for boys and girls and this is strange because it seems to be the only difference he acknowledges in his educational program for both sexes. Perhaps it is a matter of different capabilities in body movements or another serious anthropological look into the psychology of children and into the special needs of their souls that differ between boys and girls (although he himself does not give any explanation about this. Or even, as J. J. Cleary puts it "perhaps we should not attach any importance to this anomaly, since the Athenian Stranger is mainly interested in excluding from the education of the young citizens the dubious kind of dancing associated with comedy[30]".

---

[27] See A. MOORE, "Hedonism", on line in *Stanford Encyclopaedia of Philosophy*, © 2004 A. Moore, pp. 1-3.
[28] PLATO, *Laws*, 733d.
[29] *Ibid.*, 780d-781d.
[30] J. J. CLEARY, *art. cit.*, p. 168.

The whole program of education must start as soon as the child shows the first signs of sensitivity for rhythm and melody. All citizens of the community must participate to this worshipping of the Muses and the older ones are allowed to use some wine in order to find that sparkling mood existing in the younger and to participate into the whole event with the appropriate joy. Besides, it is them who are meant to choose the "official anthology" of music and songs for the young and Plato thinks that this way, whoever is charged with such a task has a lot more probabilities on one hand to make the correct choices and on the other hand of course to make the most pleasant choices for the young ones that would both fit and satisfy them.

Because soul is prior to body, the second indispensable aspect of pleasure in education, music, is more important than dance that mainly cultivates the body. Since music is an expression of universal harmony accompanied by certain features of mimesis and taking into consideration that man is subjected to the same laws with the universe[31], it makes quite a big difference which model (the good or the bad) is going to be imitated by the children. Hence, music that follows certain rules that apply to the amelioration of soul is superior to others[32], better in fulfilling many educational purposes and thus, finally, more pleasant. Furthermore, the correct choice and performance of dancing, of musical plays and of games excludes the danger of insulting Gods, as it is possible to happen most of times with tragic poetry, and gains their protection[33]. Besides, it is the appropriate way of spending our leisure time. Given the fact that the work of the slaves will supply the citizens with the basic goods, the main task of the latter should be living virtuously, in discipline and according to the rules of the city, leading lives of a leisure that will be dedicated to moral perfection through virtuous activities[34].

Concerning literature[35], the third and last aspect of education immediately connected to pleasure, the main aim of the legislator should be the composition of a proper poetic anthology suitable for the purposes of education. Those whose work is the making of such an anthology must at

---

[31] See I. SVITZOU, "Necessity in Plato's *Republic* X and *Laws* X", in *Hasard et Nécessité dans la philosophie grecque*, Centre de Recherche sur la Philosophie grecque, Académie d'Athènes, Athènes 2005, pp. 72-74.

[32] E. MOUTSOPOULOS, *La musique dans l'œuvre de Platon*, P.U.F., Paris 1959, pp. 347 ff.

[33] PLATO, *Laws*, 644e-654b.

[34] It is interesting to see the example that Plato gives us in favour of this measure: the Egyptians once again become a model for the correct way of educating (819b1-d3).

[35] C. DESPOTOPOULOS, *The Philosophy of Plato* (in Greek), Academy of Athens, Athens 1997, pp. 246-253.

least be at the age of 50 and well appreciated for their good taste in order for us to be sure that they will choose the best for the young citizens. All children must at least learn how to read and how to tune up their lyres but if the teachers understand that a child is not so talented they must not press him very hard for fear that he will no longer feel pleasure in learning but hatred or fear. This is another worth noticing remark of the depth of platonic psychology and experience revealed in the *Laws* and conquered by Plato through maturity of age. He tries to fulfill his citizen's long for pleasure and happiness knowing that in the opposite situation they might just not become what he would expect for the sake of his city.

CONCLUSION

There is no doubt from what we have so far seen that education is a major issue for Plato in the *Laws*; perhaps the most important one. Aim of the education is to make people decide what to keep and what to avoid from what they love or detest. It is the only approved way of understanding their own feelings, of distinguishing between pleasure and pain and learning how to control them and how to be brave in facing them. Education in the *Laws* is the explicit program of lessons and trainings, totally systemized and organized to its last details in its practical applications, the path that will guide men to a pleasant, eudaemonic life. For Plato, education is the way to show a deeper understanding of the human nature, it is his second and best look into the possibility of people living in harmony with the universe, near Gods, according to the Law, in virtue and because (despite?) of all that in happiness. Pleasure is its means and its aim.

EDUCATION – A LASTING VALUE

Evanghélos MOUTSOPOULOS
(Academy of Athens, Greece)

1. THE CONCEPT OF VALUE

Before embarking on the main part of my subject, education as a value, let me first probe my title a little. The adjective 'lasting' that I have attached to the noun 'value' calls for some explanation and justification. The notion here is essentially one that implies, at least in normal usage, some centre of interest attracting the consciousness and in the process showing itself to have certain advantages, for consciousness if not per se. This is also a centre in motion, to the extent that it radiates in the direction of consciousness. It would be true to say of value – value in general and in particular – that it has been much discussed. Does a value owe its existence to the consciousness that has created it? Or does it exist independently of that consciousness, in other words as an absolute? Various forms of subjectivism have from time immemorial clashed with various forms of objectivism instituted in this case. The controversy remains a live one, and I shall not enter into it now, since I have dealt with it at length elsewhere[1]. Instead, I shall opt right away for a 'moderate' solution. I shall claim only, that a value has its birth in consciousness, from an intensely felt need (prior to being projected on to a background of objectivity) to ultimately find its justification in its universalization at some level of intersubjectivity.

Here everything takes place in motion. On the one hand, there is a value's rising motion up to the point where it is self-sufficient, rounded off by its falling motion in the form of radiance. On the other, there is the extrusive motion of consciousness, rounded off by its motion in search of its own product. Lastly, there is the lateral motion of consciousness that

---

[1] Cf. E. MOUTSOPOULOS, *Phenomenology of Values* (in Greek), 2nd éd., Univ. of Athens Press, Athens 1981; *Idem*, *The Itinerary of Mind* (in Greek), vol. 3: *Values*, Hermes, Athens 1977.

seeks to legitimate its product relatively to the similar products of every other consciousness, the latter also being in exactly the same state of motion. The intersubjective nature of these contrary and reciprocal motions is itself proof of the quasi universality of those needs (and hence those desires and aspirations) whose objectivized result values are. This result finds its confirmation, at least in part, in the process of intersubjectivization. This means that any value in itself acquires the status of reality, simply because it expresses a group of realities that have been experienced by a collective number of individual consciousnesses.

Nor is this all. The dynamic of the relationships set up between consciousness and values declares itself through a genuine form of kinetics. Here I may mention the process known to acoustics and optics as the Doppler-Fizeau Law (or 'Doppler effect'). This states that the pitch and loudness of a sound emitted by a moving sound source will vary, in relation to a static observer, as a function of distance and the source's velocity. The same effect is true of a moving observer in relation to a static source, and also of a moving source in relation to a moving observer. The closer they come to each other, the higher and louder is the sound as perceived. The further away they get from each other, the lower and softer the sound proves to be.

The same phenomenon can be found, *mutatis mutandis*, in the respective behaviour of consciousnesses and values. It is all as if the value were coming closer and reaching the consciousness from its angle of radiation; and then as if consciousness itself were carried towards the value by virtue of the importance the latter has for it, seeing that what the value stands for is a primal experience with enhanced power derived from objectivization and maintained by a fundamental gravitational field of intersubjectivity. Thus above and beyond its supremacy of origin, a value acts as if it in effect enjoyed its own autonomy, allowing it to impose itself on consciousness and giving it chances of success that depend on the degree to which it corresponds to the inherent needs and desires of consciousness, needs and desires that will henceforth be experienced as sovereign aspirations. This behavioural model is undoubtedly the one operating in any normal consciousness. Other 'resistant' types of consciousness seek to favour negative values whose tenor is best expressed by the Greek term *apaxiai* – 'devalued' values.

In this connection we must accept that value has the status of transcendental reality inasmuch as it is at the same time a paradigm and a norm. In the fashion of Plato's Ideas, value, so far as the ensemble of its functions is concerned, finally makes its appearance, quite independently of its early history, as an *ontôs* on – a being in itself. Not long ago I published an article insisting on Plato's ontological realism[2]. My grounds for this view are that Plato's *Theory of Ideas* rests on recognizing they have a double nature. They are both beings and values. To take an instance: justice can only be conceived of if we take into consideration its normative nature and its need to be always applicable at the human level. The same goes for the other Ideas. Let me repeat: origins apart, the values as previously defined behave identically. Raised to the rank of entities *par excellence*, they call for respect and moreover they find every consciousness ready to act on them promptly. In terms of status, they have been promoted from desires and aspirations to models that cry out to be applied. For good and all, they show that they are naturally capable of being experienced intersubjectively, and thus quasi universally.

However, not each value, to be sure, can always be felt equally intensely. The dialectic is one that corresponds to a value's axiological kinetics. Some values show themselves at the very start, in primitive man, some come later. Others again go into temporary eclipse, like the subjects of a symphonic movement, only to reappear later in an enhanced form. Lastly, there are those that, though slow to enter the consciousness, establish themselves for good and all once they become part of its repertory. Such is the case with education. It can be thought of in various complementary lights, and these will be studied in more depth below.

2. Education as a Value

Education – just like Being in Aristotle – is used in various senses, both when it refers to a value and when it refers to a practical activity; and it can also appear in various guises. Apart from formal teaching, with its stage set of teacher and taught, 'schooling' being the name for the most official of its layouts, there is instruction, where the aim is taken to be a specific form of apprenticeship, to be distinguished from training, thought of as an advanced level of specialization, and culture, the path to a general enhancement of knowledge, a path more often than not depending on the voluntary enthusiasm of a free agent. Once more the Aristotelian categories of Being come to mind, for what we are dealing with here is designations that are on each occasion only approximately countable and that are difficult to list exhaustively, because their sense is masked in their practical application. Nevertheless, the aspects of educa-

---

[2] Cf. *Idem, Platon, idéaliste ou réaliste?, New Images of Plato. Dialogues on the Idea of the Good*, Akademia Verlag, Sankt Augustin 2002, pp. 318-330.

tion that have been singled out here display features that notoriously cannot be regarded as representing specific behaviours with peculiarities fixed by current usage, despite the confusion they are prone to lend themselves to elsewhere.

From that point on, one arrives at imputing what is recognized about value in general to the value of education in particular. Of course this procedure can hardly be likened to a rigorous geometrical theorem: that is due precisely to the possible confusions we have just mentioned. Having said this, education as a whole seems to show all the features of a value – as much by the grounds that make it an object to aspire to, as by its reflection upon individual consciousnesses, first manifested as respect, and then as acceptance, even before it establishes itself as an efficiently organized institution. It is from these successive stages, typically, that there emerges down the ages the stance of consciousness towards education in whatever form it has evolved into; though this is not to underplay something that has never varied throughout education's long history, namely the universal respect for the educated person. Here it is important to distinguish between the various forms of education, according to what state each describes. As a generalization, these are structures ordered so as to highlight what is normally flawless continuity. Interruptions are in this respect conceivable, to a greater or a lesser extent, but they will create difficulties that cannot in principle be overcome. How many painful repetitions are needed, how laboriously one has to strive, if one is to catch up with missed opportunities! That is why education should ideally be able to go on its way without let or hindrance, following a reasonably well established programme, if it is to prove itself beneficial, let alone salutary.

Let us examine the interior of education's global layout a little more closely. It will be recalled that this includes schooling, instruction, and culture. The first of these is of the nature of a constraint. The second implies full technical competence. The third is free enriching of consciousness by acquiring new value dimensions. This being so, education is surely a uniquely desirable value to acquire and to hold on to, come what may. Its purpose is not simply to accumulate knowledge; on the contrary, it aims to make good use of knowledge acquired, and above all, it may well be, to let all human beings profit thereby. Here we are in fact talking about continuous creation of values in the service of humankind, for its well-being and for the advancement of human dignity. This formal aspect of a concrete value system apart, safeguarding the positive aspects of genuine equivalence in creating values is something we cannot do without. It should be kept in mind that education is a value constantly in progress. There are two main reasons for this. Firstly, the field covered by education is an ever-widening one. Secondly, education develops in depth, becoming to a greater and greater extent not just a medium but a real guarantee that consciousnesses are in touch with one another. It is the best expression of a triumphant value system.

This means that we can imagine a grading of the aspects inherent to the value 'education'. This grading has to do with levels of schooling, instruction, and training, crowned by culture. These various levels are in constant rapport with each other. Together they define a value domain in which consciousness sets up relationships between epistemological, aesthetic, or moral values (as the case may be) and in which the boundaries of a value category are not always clearly defined, because their applicability is so fluid. As well as being axiological, however, education is also methodological. It assumes an organized approach to its subject, one that shows it to be an orderly process whose aim is the achievement of a journey with special advantages, an enriching of the spirit. By this token the methodological nature of the process is seemingly inseparable from, and indeed adds weight to, its axiological nature. Here methodology and value system become the two main portals making up education's structure. Without them, education would not be able to go forward in search of its goals. Emphasis should be laid on the fact that in the sector in question, the above two factors are all of a piece: putting them into relationship with one another corresponds to a reality that is beyond question. This key aspect of the problem is one that overshadows the whole of the educational value system.

Within the system, as a result, purely axiological issues are inextricably bound up with fundamentally epistemological issues. This happens to such a degree that these two orders of thought manage to strip off their original nature and melt into a well-balanced whole, where the prevalent conception is one whose dominant note is that it wholly centres on the postulate of well-being. Such a mixture is *prima facie* strange; but on mature reflection it proves to be quite reasonable. Indeed, the epistemological aspect of the question harmonizes perfectly with its value aspect. At this level, then, what is involved is a conception that felicitously combines the aspects of both types of activity that consciousness engages in.

3. EDUCATION: VALUE AND VALUES

The need to investigate the qualitative weight of education in general, even before starting qualitative research on its various aspects, is thus evident. It was Descartes who said, and rightly, that human reason can arrive at the truth by itself[3]. Admittedly in most cases reason is only too happy to accept the support of the educational process, which enables it to kick off in its quest for a truth that it will afterwards have to discover by its own means. The support may of course sometimes put reason on the wrong track from the very start. But even this will eventually be of benefit, insofar as any intelligence is capable of correcting itself once it is free of the grip of a defective, not to say vicious, education. For all that, no educational process is inevitably disastrous. For many centuries, astronomy was dominated by the erroneous teachings of the Ptolemaic system, which had ousted Aristarchus' heliocentric system. Yet, despite this dominance, many pertinent questions were raised that needed only to be incorporated in the Copernican system for them to be correctly conceptualized. By and large, truth, as rightness, is not attained without a sustained effort of the consciousness; and it is slow to make itself clear, after much trial and error[4]. Only rarely does the light dawn on the spirit in a single burst. When Archimedes shouted eureka! in his bath, his discovery looked at first sight like a brainwave but was in fact the result of a concatenation of circumstances resonating to the very precise requirements of a given piece of reasoning. Likewise, there are many instances where teaching has made a contribution that was later seen to be defective, on the way to a theory that was finally agreed to be correct. It is good enough simply to have all the possible variants of a hypothesis in view first, before opting for the best one, by definitive reasoning flowing from sufficient preparation of the consciousness through adequate education.

Moreover, as I have tried to show elsewhere[5], error is not so very obviously the same thing as falseness, and the erroneous as the false. To borrow a metaphor from the army, error is more like a sighting shot. As a 'pre-truth state', it is part of the domain of truth, with the same credentials as rightness, and all that it is opposite to is the falsifying nature of the mendacious that stems from a desire to alter, contrapuntally, what is correct. Education when well organized and, this above all, properly administered, shows itself to be salutary, even if it has some deficiencies. It gives one the authority to take one's bearings on virtually everything that reason acquires and successfully to apprehend most fields of knowledge, enabling one also to overturn such errors as may crop up. In this sense,

---

[3] Cf. R. DESCARTES, *Discours de la méthode*, 1.
[4] Cf. E. MOUTSOPOULOS, *Thought and Error* (in Greek), Athens 1961, pp. 120-122.
[5] Cf. *Ibid.*, pp. 37-52.

education can be seen as reason's route to independent action, starting from a certain formative point. For, as we have already said, reason has no reason to disdain preliminary assistance when starting up its engine – and even better is assistance when the engine is actually running. Within this process, education reveals itself as spurring reason on to emancipate itself, in the short or long term, from its guardian. Education offers consciousness many levels of profit, the most important of these being an apprenticeship that starts in repetition. Of course this is not a matter of 'flogging a dead horse'; on the contrary, it implies acquiring a set of habits that actually liberate reason from a number of constraints quite foreign to any need and obstructive to the exercise of the rational faculty. Emancipated itself from its *ad hoc* connections, yet thriving on their substantial assistance, reason uses its own means to seek the true in the form of the correct.

In parallel with a controlled education, planned, regulated, and prescribed, we can conceive of another education governed by the preferences and specific orientation of consciousness, which make it independent of any imposed prescriptive rules. We refer here to culture. This is an autonomous education that does not scorn to give pride of place to certain rules of method used with profit in carrying it out. While claiming to be the process of acquiring complementary aptitudes, what it really and truly turns out to be is that element which marks the distinction between a cultivated person and any other person. The same can be said of a group of people all of whom have received a similar or identical education. Culture itself is a different matter: it makes itself specific to a particular person, thus individualizing itself. Wherever there is culture in the real sense, it is acutely personal, and even unique for each case. There is of course such a thing as 'group culture', where a set of values are experienced communally, but from this axiological groundwork rises a whole system of values acquired by a strongly personal axiology in which all consciousnesses are to all intents and purposes called upon to play an active part. Consciousness never tires of this kind of culture. It imbibes at this spiritual Fount of Youth without ever quite slaking its thirst, for such is its nature. Ceaselessly it acquires new forces that enable it to ingest, and always to its advantage. The more plentifully it acquires, the readier it is for new acquisitions. If education's destiny is to ensure a basic minimum of knowledge, of culture it can be said that it is never complete. The solider culture is, the more riches the spirit gets from it, and the more eagerly. 'Cultivating one's garden' means, in this context, 'enriching one's spirit' – not simply by piling up knowledge there, but (and above all else) by accustoming the spirit to make a hierarchy of kinds of knowledge from a value standpoint, once one has submitted them to minute critical examination. The eighteenth-century general theory of 'differentiation of taste' and the conditions that produced it come to mind. The theory was based on an Aristotelian model[6]. A region's climate, it claimed, influences the character of its inhabitants. This theory rubbed shoulders with Montesquieu's[7] concept of the effect of environment on the spirit of laws; and with Kant[8], and, at a later date, Hippolyte Taine[9], both of whom saw environment as having an effect on art.

That Aristotle's ideas were taken up again in the Century of Light should not surprise us, even though conditions then were not at all the same as for Aristotle when he produced them. The problem was one which he encountered when formulating his theory of measure and moderation, whereas the representatives of modern thought took over the concept in order to underline the relative nature of mentality. And so this new reading of the term 'culture' came to join its classical form of *paideia*, the term so admirably elucidated three quarters of a century ago by Werner Jaeger. Granted that a given society's culture is formed on the basis of a shared mentality, nevertheless personal culture can only fashion itself by going in search of individually investigated cultural values. This is what makes the richness of a spirit henceforward claiming to be a value in itself so important. And this is what makes that spirit different from every other spirit. The Greek term *paideia* will not exactly translate the term 'culture' across its whole range, for it fuses and confuses the meanings of education and culture. There is no such problem with the Greek term *didaskalia*. This designates education lavished according to some system. Once one looks into the etymology of all these concepts, the general sense of the term 'education' then becomes all the clearer. In actual fact, whereas culture means 'voluntary and continuous enriching of the spirit', teaching (with due regard for the etymology of the corresponding Greek *term didaskalia*[10]) ought to denote the act of 'putting back', or 'putting in trust', one's know-how for any who can profit by it. Following the same train of thought, education ought to be the act of 'leading' the spirit along the furrow of an apprenticeship that is also pre-

---

[6] Cf. ARISTOTLE, *Politics*, H7, 1327 b 23-33.
[7] Cf. Ch.-L. DE SECONDAT, b. DE MONTESQUIEU, *L'esprit des Lois*, 1748.
[8] Cf. I. KANT, *Beobachtungen über das Gefühl des Schönen und Erhalenen*, Kanter, Königsberg 1764.
[9] Cf. H. TAINE, *La philosophie de l'art*, Paris 1865, chapter II.
[10] This term also denoted the representation of a theater play.

arranged and predisposes to personal culture, something to be pursued *ad infinitum*.

However rigidly structured it may be, the human spirit unquestionably has the quality of being pliable enough to let itself be led to the starting-point and then to be able to build up, in the long run, a whole armoury of knowledge and essential principles to act as its bearings and prevent it wandering all over the place once it is emancipated. In this sense, a young person is invited to buckle down to acquiring all the know-how that the wisdom of the ages judges indispensable for the preparatory stage of training, even if this means breaking free once one possesses the mental tools that guarantee both that one can pursue the acquiring of original knowledge *ad infinitum* and also, and perhaps even more importantly, that one can enrich one's spirit with values as yet ignored, though incidentally experienced during one's discoveries. Something should also be said about the particular case of the quantitative accumulation of new values that gradually ends up in a qualitative enrichment. This allows one to break the accepted limits without Hegel's 'crucial' passage, from a given state to another state, any longer being necessary.

Here we are on familiar ground – the concept of kairicity[11]. The concept emerges from the background of Hegel's philosophy[12], but I shall not make use of it in my reflections on education, or at least not as presented here. This is a case of kairicity, but purely in the sense of a choice made within a process whereby consciousness favours one value over another as the value that will govern its action. Thus the axiological pivot in this case is not a passage from one quantity to another, but rather the cardinal importance of a given value for setting up a personal value hierarchy that determines what priority it has. In spite of appearances, the operant concept of kairicity rests not on a mechanistic idea but on an exclusively dynamic idea. As I have dealt with the question of kairicity at length elsewhere, let me at once pass on to examine an issue that is becoming, it seems to me, more and more topical.

4. THE RIGHT TO EDUCATION AND THE RIGHTS OF EDUCATION

It is undeniable as a proposition that every human being should and can make good use of advanced education and culture, and under the most

---

[11] Cf. E. MOUTSOPOULOS, *A Philosophy of Kairicity* (in Greek), Cardamizza, Athens 1984.
[12] Cf. *Idem*, *Histoire et temporalité chez Hegel*, Hegel-Jahrbuch, Jouvence, Roma 1981-1982, pp. 39-51. Cf. G. W. F. HEGEL, *Science of Logic*, ed. Lasson, I, pp. 383-384.

advantageous conditions, to boot. This is a topic which I have dealt with elsewhere, laying stress on the quality of culture to be looked for, and in particular on the relationship that needs to be established between quality and value of acquired culture. I shall now turn to the prospects for enlarging the domain that relates to the cultural value system, one of the favoured aspects of education, within the educational value system as a whole. There is general agreement that in the far past education was a matter for the individual. The status of the teacher, like that of the pupil, was dealt with under civil law. Only with Plato, and secondarily with Aristotle, was there any question of education becoming institutionalized, something that in any case did not happen in the lifetime of either. The nucleus of an educational institution for teaching and research had to wait for the creation of the Bibliotheca Alexandrina. Destined to go through various ups and downs before it was finally destroyed completely, the Alexandrian Library long provided the model for many a medieval institution – these being placed, at least in the West, under the guardianship of Holy Church – before coming to serve as a model for universities and schools at all levels of education. This being so, it was recognized that all, without exception, had a right to an education, with the Church guaranteeing access to instruction for anybody able to benefit from it. Here was a democratic development, and responsibility for education would subsequently pass to the State. Education as a value was acknowledged to be a good for sharing amongst all, with ignorance now seen as an evil that rebounds on society itself.

This was an idea that had first been put forward by Socrates. For him, however, it only applied to individuals. Not until modern times was it put into practice by the State. So it came about that the right to education acquired the sense of the usufruct of a value that was universal and, as I have argued throughout, lasting. It flows from this that one should try to ensure access to education, by every means possible, making it compulsory. The goal is to protect all citizens: those with a long pedigree as well as those recently integrated into society. On this subject, today it is highly desirable that the fruits of education should also be enjoyed by refugees (whether political or economic) from Third World countries. Indeed, they should, I think, be given priority, so as to avoid the dangers encountered in societies where such groups have difficulty in adapting and acculturation. It all depends on how well one can organize the broadening of institutions and the deployment of the particular means required. Education – still in the sense of a value – also deserves to attract the attention of the authorities as regards the goal of steadily improving its quality. To this end, there can be no restrictions, financial or other, and every sacrifice is an imperative necessity. The right to education entails as its corollary the idea of respect for the rights of education. These rights presuppose that the access roads are kept open and that the services provided are increased, without losing sight of the fact that what goes for 'developed' societies does not necessarily go for the whole world. Education can moreover be equally effectively experienced as a value in search of particular values. This is true of research, of the maximization of young people's talents and individual potential, and also of 'problem' subjects (autistic and dyslexic children, 'difficult students', and so on), where one has to insert a certain amount of personalized 'special education' side by side with 'integrated education'.

Next, there is no dodging the issues raised by present trends in education. I mean its dogged attempts to respond to the changes in mentality that have taken place in our day and age, at the expense of its true condition. Clearly these changes are mainly due to the growing importance of technology in our lives. Technology demands that we reinforce the teaching of certain subjects to the detriment of others that were traditionally popular, and rightly so. Notably, we can see a continuous falling off of interest in the humanities to the advantage of 'hi-tech' sciences, the immediate result being ruthless cuts in curricula and staff in what was once a favoured area. And yet we know how crucially important the humanities were, not so very long ago, in moulding the character of young people and giving them a grip on reality. On the same tack, how disappointing it is to see the prominence given to physical education in the curriculum! It is not that there is anything wrong about physical education in itself; but it does nevertheless have a negative effect insofar as it encourages hopes of quick and easy success, with considerable cash rewards from systematic levies taking a disproportionate chunk of the income of the sports-loving public. Less obvious are the damaging effects of encouraging the young to make a career of doubtful taste as an 'artist'. It will give them precarious fame and astronomical fees, thanks to their accomplice the public, which fills the cinemas or buys their recordings. This reduces the number of souls interested in high art to a minimum, which is to the detriment of the general cultural quality of a society.

Is there any way to reverse what is at first sight an irreversible situation? In the first instance this is the responsibility of the State and its authorities. Their role must be to see to the restructuring of curricula and a more logical and equitable distribution of teaching matter. They must not try to re-establish a seriously disturbed order of things wholesale, but to improve the guarantee of an education – so far as this can be done – by, even if only in part, putting right a deplorable situation at the heart of which can be observed what the always topical Nietzsche called a 'transvaluation of values'. Yet this is a task that falls equally on the citizens themselves. They in their turn must stop choosing the easy way out that ultimately leads to ruin. The values traditionally conveyed by the teaching of the humanities are worth putting back in place. Any civilization that wants to call itself democratic ought imperatively to preserve these values and promote them. The humanities are worth reintroducing liberally into curricula, and worth giving a dominant place, not so much because they are an apprenticeship pure and simple but because they are a tool for moulding character and a guarantee of a controlled humanist attitude worthy of human genius and fit for any culture, no matter how prestigious. As conquests, science and technology are certainly no less prestigious. But they can never detract from the human achievements that have been their own proof from ancient times onward and that are so cardinally important that they enjoy the same esteem as science and technology, and in the same degree. Now it is thanks to the humanities on the curricula that education as a value deserves to be described as 'lasting', and for this reason alone it may continue to deserve the description.

Education, that pre-eminent value, cannot deny its past without destroying itself. One need only recall the prestige once upon a time enjoyed by students who were 'strong at composition' and who had a keenness of mind equal to that of the best mathematicians. Nor should we forget that, in our own day, the boss of the biggest multinational producer of computers had to get his employees to learn Greek, this being the language best suited to the machines. You cannot destroy what has been firmly established with impunity. Sorcerers' apprentices, please note.

5. Education and Philosophical Teaching

It is above all through philosophical teaching that education establishes that it is a universal value. At the Twentieth World Congress of Philosophy in Boston, there was a round table discussion, organized by the Association of French Language Societies of Philosophy, about the structure of philosophy teaching in France and in partly French-speaking countries. The discussion took stock of the present state of philosophy teaching in Belgium, Quebec, Tunisia, and of course within France itself. There were no details of the situation in Switzerland, or in other countries where French is one of the main languages. There were four panel speakers, and in the discussion which followed, it became clear that only in France could philosophical teaching be said to have unambiguous, and therefore satisfactory, status. In actual fact France is the only one of these countries that offers philosophical teaching and not just teaching of philosophy. This implies a separate attitude and, already, a whole philosophy at official level. This noteworthy difference makes not simply for a transmitting of knowledge but for the birth of a mentality that encourages the questioning spirit among young people. Was that not what the teaching of Socrates himself was all about?

Wherever the French teaching model was in use, one could still, even a few years ago, observe more or less the same situation; and it was entirely due to the clear thinking in curriculum development strategy. Manifestly the diversifying of teaching so as to prise it free from the 'hold' of French 'supervision' ended in an undeniable loss of credibility and in the depreciation, for good and all, of the teaching itself. This was followed by a loss of orientation, because there were no clear guidelines to attach teaching to. The same want of transparency in intentions and goals pursued can be witnessed in French-speaking or partly French-speaking countries outside France. In Quebec, for example, the main shortcoming is lack of will on the part of the State to see all its citizens, without exception, acquire at least the rudiments of philosophical culture and to use them to good purpose. The real reason for this attitude is, we may be sure, that there is a certain well-concealed mistrust of the philosophical spirit and the values it conveys. In all these countries it is only too easy to see the calamitous results of this hesitancy and scepticism: the gap widens between the philosophical elite of university professors and the man and woman in the street, who have been deprived at the very outset of a quality philosophical education.

A unified conception of philosophy teaching would be no bar to philosophical activity on many fronts. Far from it: such activity would be a matrix for acceptable operative shades of intention and actualisation without limit, and these would help sustain the richness and vitality of a centuries-old philosophical tradition open to all trends and all aspirations. Philosophy, when understood as a genuine groundwork for questioning and not as a form of sophistry, becomes a weighty weapon for anyone who can wield it with integrity and courage, so long as he or she can ignore vulgar prejudice. Philosophy is evidently not quite the same thing as rhetoric. But if we look into it, philosophy has been doughtily defended in France by outstanding philosophers who were also enlightened politicians – Victor Cousin, to name but one. It was they who helped chisel French philosophical teaching into shape and give it that profile that juts out among all the other great national traditions of philosophy. The emergence of a dialectic is discernible, between the French model of philosophy as taught in secondary schools in France, and the corresponding teaching model in Italy. In the case of France it is a matter of looking at philosophy thematically; in Italy, philosophy is looked at from the historical point of view, and the apprenticeship is spread over three years, one each for classical, medieval, and modern philosophy, reminding us of Kant's distinction between philosophy itself and the philosopher. So it all depends on what dosage we use to test out the methodical mixture of each of these dominant trends. In France, philosophy is practised in an appealing way that is heightened by the transparency, a legacy from Descartes, with which, in most cases, its various topics are treated. Even Bergson, who was certainly no Cartesian rationalist, was happy to benefit by this clarity. In short, there is now a sort of common language in which to broadcast a whole host of theories and styles of thought and discourse connected with philosophical activity. Thus the teaching of philosophy comes to crown the work of education. This is exactly what Socrates meant. A young person initiated into philosophy becomes skilled at applying this apprenticeship in all domains and at all levels of thought and action. At the same time, he or she is actualising education as lasting value. And this in its turn ensures the conscious permanence of human dignity.

VALUE-BASED LEADERSHIP IN EDUCATION

Guttorm FLØISTAD
(University of Oslo, Norway)

THE PROBLEM SITUATION

The system of education in advanced countries finds itself in a curious situation. Students of all ages are subject to a variety of forces, often pulling them in conflicting directions: Society requires the highest level of knowledge in order to master competition in a market-driven economy – at the same time as the dominant trends of the market by way of entertainment and consumption impact upon the conditions for success. The market is a continuous threat to our most vital interest, our ability to focus, to study in depth. This is a necessary requirement for turning knowledge into experiential knowledge.

Experiential knowledge is knowledge that means something to you, it is personal knowledge. This, I take it, is a necessary requirement for someone being creative and innovative.

Teaching of values is even more difficult. You may certainly teach values, but you cannot teach the essential part of it, that is, commitment. Commitment is even more personal than knowledge ever can be. To make students of all ages committed to values, that is, to their community, is a far harder task.

I shall briefly comment on some of these difficulties in the modern society, and point to ways of survival.

THE CHALLENGE

The ideal requirements for anyone entering working life are well established. In addition to a high and sufficient level of professional knowledge, you should also have learned to cooperate with colleagues. Cooperation involves training people face to face, listening to them and taking them seriously. Cooperation involves an awareness of being part of a group and co-responsible for its social and professional success. The training in the group may be a valuable contribution for one's encounter with those who use your products and services. The idea of customers being part of the company is well known, as well as the idea of a company's co-responsibility for the local community.

It goes without saying that no system of education is in a position to fulfill all of these requirements. In most cases experience from working life will be necessary.

Education systems differ, of course, from continent to continent, also among advanced countries. In Japan, for instance, group training from primary schools onward is an integrated part of individual growth. Cooperation is built into the individual training (White 1987, p. 27). This, I take it, is how Japan has combined the Western notion of individuality with the Japanese traditional religion (Shinto) and the customs and traditions related to it.

In the Philippines, school children are from the beginning trained in thinking in terms of Philippine cultural identity. Authorities have worked out four volumes for different levels, all dealing with value transmission within their cultural identity. The volumes are, no doubt, among the best strategies for counteracting the culturally destructive impact of globalization. Cultural identity is necessarily local and national if it is to be something to which one may be personally attached.

In the United States, the Mormon family training of children and youngsters supplements their school education. Monday evening is a family evening, organized by some of the children. The program consists of reading, story telling, dancing and playing. The family evening is training in cooperation, in religious attachment and leadership from childhood onward. The Mormon missionary training provides the youth with language training, covering all continents. The service to American diplomacy and business is unique.

Examples from other cultures such as these fulfill to a large extent the requirements of practical life.

I have myself written a book on value transmission in schools, including in the Philippines and among the Mormons. Most examples are from Norwegian schools. Many teachers and school leaders know how to motivate children and youngsters for the hard process of learning (Fløistad 1996). But certainly not all. The situation in many families and in modern societies in general makes it perfectly understandable. The following is a brief description of how it is experienced, and the consequences for the human mind.

THE TROUBLESOME REALITY

Newspapers sometimes provide information as to the mental health situation in an entire population. Frank Furedi, professor of sociology at the University of Kent, Canterbury, analyzed British newspapers in the period 1980-2003 to find out about their use of some key psychological terms like 'self-esteem', 'trauma', 'stress' and 'syndrome'. It turned out that the journalists' use of these terms showed a "phenomenal increase" during those years, especially in the 1990s. These and other findings are interpreted as emotional vulnerability subject to therapeutic counseling. Furedi's book *Therapy Culture* (2004), with the telling subtitle *Cultivating Vulnerability in an Uncertain Age* offers a diagnosis of the modern (postmodern) culture. Lower self-esteem, higher stress and more traumas turn our culture into a therapy culture. The effects on families, school children, students and teachers are rather sad: Children as young as nine and ten talk about feeling "stressed out". Stress clinics are available in many areas. Children in Liverpool have access to aroma therapy, foot and hand massage as well as "lavender-soaked tissues to help reduce stress and aggression" (Furedi, p. 1).

University students in the UK are no better off. 53% suffer from anxiety at "a pathological level" (according to a survey). One in ten students seeking help is suicidal. It is maintained by some researchers that the schools themselves, contrary to every intention, serve as "the groundwork for depression" (Furedi, p. 8).

The situation appears to be much the same in other countries. Stress, anxiety, depression, escalating violence and the use of drugs are now common features. Violence among school children is perhaps best known from the United States. 50 million Americans each year are developing mental health disorders. 80 million have already experienced therapeutic treatment (Furedi, p. 9). Clinics for mental health problems in babies are popping up (25,000 babies in the USA enter the world and abandoned). In addition, quite a few children living with their parents (mostly the mother only) are unwanted. According to Peter Struck, 53% of the mothers in the Sachsen region of Germany would prefer more personal freedom instead of the child (Struck 1996, p. 59). In Germany, as many as 1.4 million children are hit by parents every year, 300,000 so heavy that they suffer for a long time afterward. In Australia, according to Dr. Catherine Scott, the education system is gripped with fear caused by the behavior of their students (Furedi, p. 8).

The list of articles and books in psychology and psychiatry dealing with increased "vulnerability" are nearly pouring out – as is the therapeutic professionals. In the years between 1970 and 1995 the number of mental health professions quadrupled in US and Britain (Furedi, p. 10). No one should be left alone with their emotional troubles.

What is the upshot of all this? Now, the conclusion drawn by Christopher Lasch (1984) that "Education is at an end" appears somewhat hasty, although the mental and socio-cultural disintegrating forces in the US and European countries are frightening. The market-driven economy doesn't think that way. And still, there are sufficient people around who manage to acquire sufficient competence for the job market. However, that is not all there is to say. Even in a small country like Norway with a workforce under 2 million, as many as about 700,000 are out of work on national insurance due to physical and mental exhaustion and suffering.

What is, perhaps, even more serious is what the profound unrest in modern societies says about the historical development and the school curriculum: They have both failed. I take the school curriculum to embody the great prospect of the European Enlightenment, the modernity. Every one of us should become self-governing individuals finally freed from authoritarian forces, acting only from our own free will. The basic principle of the free will is the (Kantian) moral law: Acting morally is to act on behalf of the humanity in ourselves. Self-realization involves both a concern for ourselves and for others. In other words: An individual's socialization is part of his self-realization. Self-realization without regard for others promotes selfishness. "Regard for" means learning by cooperation and mutual respect.

Every one knows the outcome of recent historical developments: Increasing selfishness in learning, entertainment, consumption, marriage and competition in working life. The idea of the self-governing and socially responsible individual is bound to lose the battle between himself and outside forces. Some of us may soon be gripped by a strong feeling that we are moving toward a new type of slavery, victims of impersonal economic powers. The main lesson from humanity should not, however, be forgotten, that we become individuals only in so far as each "stretches out to others" (Kaplan 1970).

POSTMODERNISM

The Empty Raincoat. Making Sense of the Future written by Charles Handy (1994) appears to be a precise description of postmodernism, the age after modernity. Having lost sight of ideals of modernity, we don't know where to go. We have lost the direction. It makes little sense to hold on to the idea of self-realization in the desert, where "anything and everything goes" (Usher and Edwards 1994, p. 26).

The substance that should fill the coat is lacking, despite all our equipment, commodities and money. Or, to be more precise, every individual is left with the task of creating his or her own meaning, without help of transcendent powers.

Song texts in Pop music are, in fact, sometimes more revealing than books in philosophy and sociology. In Roger Waters' *Amused to Death*, a text reads:

> Doctor, doctor,
> What is wrong with me
> This supermarket life is getting long
> What is the heart life of a color TV
> ----
> The little ones sit by their TV screens
> No thoughts to think
> No tears to cry
> All sucked dry
> Down to the very last breath
> Bartender what is wrong with me
> Why am I so out of breath
> This species has amused itself
> Amused itself to death, to death
> We watched the tragedy unfold
> We did as we were told
> We bought and sold
> It was the greatest show on earth
> But then it was over.

French philosophers have given a more positive evaluation of postmodernism. Lacan, Derrida, Foucault and Lyotard are the most important names. No unified definition appears to be possible. No such definition would, anyway, be in accord with the idea of postmodernism itself: No comprehensive or totalizing definition or system of ideas is any longer within our range. This seems to be just a consequence of the postmodernist denial of the universality of reason. According to Derrida, it is impossible to arrive at *one* truth, because there is always interpretation. Instead, what one finds is a multiplicity of truths, depending on how a text is being understood (Derrida 1986; Usher and Edwards 1994, p. 120).

Lyotard offers a different explanation of the individualizing trend in postmodern thought. For him the technological culture of Western societies has created computers and other instruments as well as art objects that leave it to every one to make sense of for himself. Anything like total mastery is out of question (Aronowitz and Giroux 1991, p. 60).

That reason is local and not universal is acknowledged long before the emergence of postmodernism. Reason, in the sense of scientific reason and method, is not applicable in the humanities, let alone to the ethno-philosophical traditions in other continents. This is an insight in Ranke in German historicism, and later on in Rickert, Dilthey and, with even greater emphasis, in Gadamer's philosophical hermeneutics. Production and interpretation of literary works are both culturally determined. Gadamer is certainly not a postmodernist. He belongs squarely within the modernist tradition. His idea of the coherent and perfect interpretation is not an individual enterprise; it aims at contributing to *sensus communis*, of vital importance to any humanistic culture. Postmodernism appears to dissolve relationships and mutual commitment between people. Everyone should be sentenced to freedom, as Sartre presumably would say.

Postmodernism's effect on education is hardly discussed by the main authors, except in Lyotard. There is, however, a lot of articles and books written on the subject. The theme is complicated, since the school curriculum is modeled after the ideology of European Enlightenment and the demand of the market economy. There are, however, clear signs that education policy within the OECD countries has recognized that individuals are different and that the standard curriculum should be adapted differently. As Lyotard says, everyone should pick from the curriculum what he or she prefers according to his or her abilities (Lyotard 1984; Aronowitz and Giroux 1991, p. 60). However, given the circumstances, postmodernism cannot simply be a rejection of modernity. Instead, postmodernism has to use those aspects of modernity that can help, for instance in turning the individual into a participatory subject instead of remaining an object dominated by others. This is a condition for creating "a radical democracy" (*ibid.*, p. 59).

However, this and other postmodernist ideas are up against much the same disintegrating forces as is modernity. Disintegration is by no means identical with individualization. Postmodernism needs attentive, self-conscious and powerful people. The modern mass culture, as it appears, tends to eradicate individuals as individuals, turning them into passive, intoxicated recipients. Most classes in schools all over Europe and the US are likely to have some of these students among them, sometimes almost the entire class. They all need a rescue operation.

IT IS NEVER TOO LATE

The following example is taken from a school in Norway with just under 300 students, boys and girls aged between 14 and 16.

The situation is well known from schools all over the Western world: Unrest, inattentiveness or mental absenteeism, depression, powerlessness, violence, suffering from conflicts at home, lack of intimate friends, use of drugs and slow learning progress. Many, or most of the students in the class, usually function satisfactorily. In the school I have in mind nearly half of the students had become drug addicts. The teachers discussed whether to stay or apply for positions elsewhere. What interests me is the steps taken by some teachers to restore a vision of the ideal school in the classes.

Ordinary teaching according to the curriculum did not function. The students had to be challenged emotionally and activated in entirely different ways. A music teacher and some of his colleagues put up a strategy in four points.

• Every student should be member of a rock group.

• All students should perform sequences of great Norwegian and English dramas for their parents and the local community (Ibsen, Shakespeare).

• Everyone should create a piece of art or handicraft with a view to exhibiting it in the local community.

• Together the students should run a café for elderly people in the community.

The school had a section of rock music. The school got some money from the local and regional authorities (they knew what was going on) to buy and rent instruments. Two teachers attended a course in rock music at a high school to be able to organize the students in groups and guide their choice of instruments. Two professional rock musicians were hired from the town and the school kept open day and night.

The students came, even those who hadn't been at school for some days and weeks. They picked an instrument and began their training. In the course of six months altogether thirty groups were established, involving all the students. They agreed to prepare two CDs, where the students themselves should write the texts and compose the music. They should write about their lives, about their loneliness, depression, desperation, sadness, experience of meaningless, about suicide. Both CDs were called *Future*. Few of the students had ever had any future. They were under way to get one.

To compose songs, it pays to know some mathematics. The argument may not go home to professionals. To the students it worked. The additional purpose was to motivate students to pick topics from the ordinary curriculum. Aesthetic experience is our primary motivational background. To bring out their musical talents the students needed a soloist. Among the students was a girl aged 14, who several times, privately and in public, had demonstrated her qualities. However, as she was heavily addicted to drugs, she hadn't shown up for weeks. The music teacher searched for her, found her among her companions, picked her up and engaged a professional singer for her training. In the course of two years the project was successfully completed.

The rock project motivated the students, in between also to study Norwegian and English language and literature: They should perform sequences of Ibsen's *Brand* and *Peer Gynt* as well as Shakespeare's *Hamlet* and *King Lear*. A professional instructor picked the students for the various roles and helped them to give fully acceptable performances for the local public. Nearly all the students were involved.

To prepare the exhibition, the students were asked to paint scenes from their own life. The exhibition turned out to be a moving and powerful reminder of what young people encounter and suffer in the new world. Their use of colors told us about their emotions.

To organize and run a café, providing coffee, tea, sandwiches and cakes, all homemade, is an achievement in itself. To encounter elderly people by serving them is a new and most valuable experience for young people. The elderly people were storytellers, acquainting the students with the history of the community.

At the end of the two years the students said: We love going to school, we love learning. After the three years of the middle level curriculum, the students had to pass on to a different school elsewhere. They wouldn't leave. The music teacher and his colleagues were entitled to say: We have realized our vision: *None of the students should leave the school without suffering privation.* The students had a feeling that they had been "rescued". Their own power and optimism had been released through an attachment to a school community with new ways of learning.

I know of many school communities in Norway and abroad in need of a similar cultural renewal. However, I know of even more that could do with much simpler steps.

An example shows how a restless and inattentive student may be brought back to himself and to the class community without medication.

The use of Ritalin to calm down restless and inattentive young people has nearly exploded in recent years in most Western countries. Some of the causes are mention above. In a community in Southern Norway with just a few thousand children, about 500 of them were in the course of a few months reported to the school authority. The teacher couldn't handle them any more. In a school in the United States most students pile up at the health office in the morning to get their dose of Ritalin (Boston Globe 2000). The case is referred to by a Norwegian psychologist Joar Tranøy, who is highly critical of the evidence for using Ritalin against ADHD at all. The evidence is not significant. He refers to several physicians and psychiatrists. The title of their books are telling: *The Hyperactivity Hoax* by Dr. Sidney Walker and *No more ADHD* by Dr. Mary Ann Block. Others call ADHD just an invention.

> Having spent seven years in primary school, repeatedly reported to several health authorities, of no use, a boy aged 12 entered the secondary level. The school director, together with her social worker, carefully planned his reception. Almost immediately upon his arrival he was invited to the Director. That was nothing new to him. It happened every year. This time, however, he was received very friendly and served soft drinks and cakes. Skeptical as he was, he just waited for the usual hard words. Instead he was appointed assistant to the school keeper. Eight hours were planned so far for £4 an hour, paid to him in advance. He was, of course, taken by surprise. He brought the money to the social worker, asking him to follow him back home. Because, he said, if I show my parents that much money, they immediately will accuse me of theft. So he did. The social worker told the parents what a fine son they had. Contracts were written and signed, lasting one month, one for his behavior at home, including homework, one for his behavior at school.
>
> The school director and her social worker waited anxiously to see what happened. A month later the boy came to the social worker and handed him £16, saying: I have worked four hours and earned £16. The remaining £16 I want you to take care of. A month later, his task accomplished, he turned up asking for the rest of the money. The contracts were renewed. They both asked themselves, was it that easy to cure destructive behavior? All went well in nearly three months. Suddenly the boy's orderly behavior changed. He stiffened, letting nobody touch him physically or orally. The director and the social worker tried desperately to reach him. Continuing throughout three hours without succeeding, she gave in, the social worker did not. He grabbed the boy, dragged him into his car and drove deep into the surrounding forest. They started walking, in silence. After two hours the boy, totally exhausted, stopped and said, presumably giving the explanation of his entire unruly

behavior: "I just wanted to know whether you too would betray me, leaving me alone[1]."

What is needed in all schools is emotional and conceptual incitement. The subtitle of a book by two American psychologists should be studied by all teachers: *Raising Cain. Protecting the emotional life of boys* (Kindlon and Thompson 1998). The same applies to girls. No study of curriculum can do without motivation. Our motivational powers are rooted in our emotions and our knowledge.

A proposal: Every day in school should begin as follows:
• *With a song*. Singing creates community. Let the students choose the songs themselves. They may perfectly well choose songs from their favorite CD. But songs of a more national and local kind should be part of the repertoire. The songs should of course all be known by heart. Singing may moreover contribute to the students' way of speaking. Rhythm is part of both proper singing and speaking. There are schools which, with great success, turn hundreds of children and young people into huge choirs guided by professionals. Quality is required for public performances[2].
• *Telling stories and fairytales* are necessary in order to take care of conceptual language. The pictorial culture is threatening our conceptual capacity. And learning and communication require a highly developed conceptual language. I know that the postmodernists hold that the great narratives have come to an end. Some of us don't think so. Great narratives originate in history. And it belongs to philosophical hermeneutics to have shown, most systematically, that knowledge of history is necessary to enrich our present and future lives. Postmodernism holds that history is out.

It is certainly not easy to catch the attention of young people. A young teacher, who was fond of reading from books, discovered that no one listened. Especially the boys were bothered by the "senseless" stories. He continued reading 15 minutes every day. He tried, however, to find books that he thought would interest them. Finally, after a couple of months some of the students woke up and

---

[1] The case is given to me by the social worker involved, Svein Olav Nordlien. He is widely known in Norway for his eminent ability to amend destructive behaviour and relationships in children and their families. He is a genuine "field worker".

[2] That music is used to create a community experience is known all over the world. Music bridges the gap between people and creates a feeling of belonging. If I were to recommend a book on music relating to the recipient, my best proposal is Jon-Roar Bjørkvold, *Det musiske menneske*, translated into English and several other languages.

asked for the books. After about four months a major part of the class came up to him on a Friday afternoon and asked if he were willing to meet with them and read to them on Saturday as well. There is sometimes someone who knows better than others.

• *By reciting a poem* chosen and prepared by the students or by the teacher. Reading and listening to poems may be a profound both emotional and cognitive experience. In view of the richness of the world's poetry, listening to poems could give you a first acquaintance with other cultures. In view of the school's multicultural students, knowing each other's poetry would help create personal relationships.

• *By talking together*. Topics for discussions are many. They could start on the objective level, about problems and challenges in the local culture, how children and elderly people are taken care of, loneliness in the community, drug abuse, crime and its causes, marriages and how they succeed or fail, and consequences for the children. Slowly the class would be able to approach a more personal level, to reflect upon, following the model of Socrates, what the students think of themselves and how they behave toward others and how they think how they should behave. What can I do to promote the climate in the classroom and in the school yard? How do I behave towards the other sex?

As everyone knows, there is usually among us, young and old, a frightening lack of self-reflection. We just act or we don't do anything, waiting for something to happen. Socrates never got tired of having people confront themselves. He lost his life for it. He thought it was worth it.

Although the curriculum in most schools, I take it, contains topics for strengthening the class community, most often this part is neglected to the advantage of the professional topics and language. The common language, the language of social and cultural relationships, is impoverished. The tendency is further promoted both by the pictorial culture and the market-driven economy with its steady demand for professional knowledge. A fellow of the London School of Economics (Martin Jaques) has stated that development tied to the "selfish, market-driven economy is eroding our humanity" (*The Guardian* Oct. 1, 2004). To start every morning at school by singing, reading, listening and discussing could save it.

The students' attachment to institutions and subjects of study is vitally important for the learning process. The opposite of attachment is alienation. Alienation blocks motivation and attentiveness. There is much to be said for the view that the overwhelming culture of media and consumption divert attention from the learning process.

Attachment or the lack of it has always a history. It goes back to the family, more precisely, to the behavior of the mother. In the first year the mother is the center of the child's attention (Ayers 2003, p. 61). After birth, maybe just a few seconds, according to Ayers, the child directs its eyes toward the mother. This appears to be the decisive moment in the child's life. This moment decides to a great extent whether the child will succeed in developing self-esteem and self-confidence in relationship to other people and to the world. As Winnicott says (Ayers 2003, p. 63) "the mother and her face play a vital mirroring role from the moment of birth. The child needs to be received and recognized by an emotionally engaged mother, reflected in the baby's eyes. This is, or should be, the maternal care: The nature of maternal care determines the quality of the baby's development."

She facilitates the infant's realization of inherited potentials through her emphatic reflection of her infant (Ayers, p. 63). It is through a visual eye-to-eye contact that the "playful communication" may arise. This is how development of attachment initially proceeds.

If the mother's eyes show sign of anxiousness, loneliness, despair, hesitation and even rejection, the foundation is being laid for the child's insecurity. Lack of self-confidence makes it difficult to establish social relationships. An example from *Wednesday's Child* dealing with 800 women in London (*The London Sisters*), all of whom suffer from depression, shows what can happen. A group of social psychologists asked the women whether they remembered what possibly could have caused their suffering. The book reports of series of physical and psychological neglect, antipathy, role-reversal, violence and sexual abuse. In my reading the reports raise the question as to whether parents and families with such destructive behavior have the right to privacy and be respected for it. I am not in doubt about the answer. It is certainly in most cases not a police matter. But it should be a case for teachers in schools and kindergartens.

What is the upshot of this for the teachers and the school community? A school community may be called a mother at a higher level. With a few exceptions the same that is required of a mother is required of the school community, of the school directors and the teachers. The children and the pupils have to be seen and be acknowledged. Direct eye-to-eye contact is vitally important. Eye contact is the beginning of personal relationships; it is the beginning of attachment.

Schools, classes and students of all ages do of course differ. In most classes, there are some students who need special attention and help. The need for help may be reduced by contributing to the students' higher self-esteem and self-confidence. Cooperation in small groups, discussing subjects from the curriculum and various other types of social training, guided by a teacher, are necessary. The best way of bringing restless, inattentive and lonely students back to the community is, in my view, long-term personal relationships.

GENDER IDENTITY

The school is not only an extended mother. It should also be a masculine role model. Clear role models for both sexes are necessary for the development of gender identity. In this respect the family, though not always, may function as a sufficient social unit. A main reason, as the Italian psychiatrist Luigi Zoja points out, is that the 20th century is the story of the missing father (Zoja 2001).

Developing gender identity is a notoriously difficult task. Freud once said that it is the most difficult topic there is. What is reasonable is to say that, since men and women have both a similar and a different physiology, they have both a similar and a different way of thinking – I cannot imagine that a person's mental life is isolated from the rest. This is also shown, for instance, in research into men's and women's mental health and illness (cf. f. inst. Dora Kohen 2000). Simone de Beauvoir maintains, at the conclusion of her book *Le Deuxième Sexe* (1949), that, in order to be respected and acknowledged, women should adopt the rationality of men.

However intelligible that may be from the point of view of her own situation and her relation to Sartre, I take it as an insult against women. In view of what man, maybe especially the European man has been doing over the centuries in terms of fighting against, and destroying, other people, de Beauvoir's conclusion is even more bizarre. This is also the view taken by most feminists in the latter part of the past century (for instance Adrienne Rich). It is not the nature of woman to destroy life, since one of her basic functions is the opposite. Adrienne Rich thinks in opposition to de Beauvoir, that being a mother is an optimal experience for a woman. It goes without saying that being a mother (or having the potential for it) and other capacities outlined above, cannot be replaced by man and his way of thinking.

However, determining the character of the woman's mental life is not an easy task. The only book I know that deals with it by itself and not in relation to man is written by a psychoanalyst in the Jungian tradition, Clarissa Pinkola Estès, in *Women who run with Wolves* (1992). Women are giving birth, are caring, receiving, organizing rituals in the family and elsewhere, and they are faithful, however only when they are respected for what they are, just as free and wild as the wolves. Fathers too have an important role in the family. Together their task is to bring their children out in the active world with a sufficient self-esteem and self-reliance.

Boys and girls need both their parents as role models to develop a balanced mental life. This is to say that children of both sexes are mentally constituted under the influence of both role models. It follows that boys and girls acquire the same set of female and masculine mental qualities, only that the emphasis differs. Girls and women are caring in the world, boys and men are active. To put it differently, women are caring and active, while men are active and caring.

Both role models are needed to turn children into distinct and balanced personalities. At the outset they are both mostly tied to their mother. In her liberation from the mother a girl has a more difficult task. She is to develop into a woman on her own and needs a father who all along acknowledges her as a distinct person. If he is not available, the liberation process from the mother will suffer. The ties to the mother are likely to continue in one way or another (the Norwegian psychiatrist Jarl Jørstad).

Boys may be more successful in liberating themselves from the mother, due to gender difference. However, boys need a father to succeed, and to guide them into the world.

This is theory. The praxis in our age is different. Zoja is undoubtedly right in characterizing the 20th century as a history of the absent father. In the US more than 3.1 million children are living with the mother only, the father has never been seen. In Germany 75% grow up in a one-parent family, mostly with the mother. In addition, they have no sister or brother (Struck 1996, p. 130).

In the course of their development the children are sometimes turning to the mother and sometimes to the father, according to their needs. Children without a father develop an excessive longing for him. They are not easily attached to the school community. Luigi Zoja asks: Does the history of the missing fathers explain the current crisis? (Zoja 2001, p. 82.) It would certainly be a great help for these children if the school had distinct male role models. Their process of socialization is anyway difficult enough.

As compensation these children automatically search for models elsewhere: Often boys find it in action movies. That these "heroes" hardly ever are the best models, needs no argument, in addition to the fact that the visual media to a large extent have destroyed family relationships (see f. inst. Struck 1996, p. 204, and 2004).

Learning by computer, however efficient, can hardly be said to comfort these children. A computer can never replace the distinct personality of a teacher. A teacher believes in what he is saying. He or she *stands* for the content of his teaching and conveys the personal significance to the students. This is a major point in rhetoric – and, I take it, a contribution to the formation of gender identity.

School, Family and Local Community

To grow up is to grow into. It is to grow into a family culture with its family relationships, its manners, customs and rituals. In the course of the years it is to grow up into a local, national, European and global culture. The order is important if you want to support the development of a proper commitment on the various levels. As the main program for small, local schools in Norway states: If you are to become a world citizen, you have first of all to learn to be part of a family and a neighborhood. Otherwise you will not succeed in developing attitudes of respect for others. And you will not be able to recognize that cultural identity – involving the feeling and knowledge of belonging to – should be given priority over everything else. Cultural identity is moreover the base for a sound economic activity. "Sound" means: to see economic activity, not as a goal in itself, but as a means to strengthen the cultural activity with its web of personal relationships.

Everyone knows that it is no longer so – if it ever has been. Despite our riches we have not succeeded in creating the wellbeing of everyone. Our religion and humanistic attachment are weaker. We have exchanged our geographical stability *(stabilitas loci)* with a space flow *(mobilitas loci)*. Man is regarded as a resource for productivity instead of as a value in himself.

If you still are living in the same place, you are mentally still on the move, due to the invasion of stimuli from media and consumption. In both cases personal relationships suffer, due to lack of care. We are hardly present to anyone – let alone to ourselves. To grow up is to grow away. As a leading European architect, Rem Koolhas says: Modern capitalism which organized the reduction of all social life to a spectacle, is incapable of presenting any spectacle other than that of our own alienation. A well-known Norwegian architect, Christian Norberg-Schulz, holds the same: The tragedy of modern man, he holds, is the loss of a stable space (Norberg-Schulz 1980). The trouble is that basic human needs have not changed. Against our needs we, or most of us, are not at home any more.

The situation makes cooperation between families, schools and local communities more cogent than ever. The chief responsibility is with the school director and the teachers. They have to agree upon a common strategy for meeting with the parents and upon a list of values and problems to be discussed with them. The point is that there should be standard procedures for all meetings and discussions in all classes. The teachers may sometimes have difficulties in agreeing upon, and be committed to certain values. That parents very often are uncertain as to which values should be conveyed to the children in this turbulent world, and sometimes between themselves, are well known. Institutions in the surrounding community are rarely used to cooperate with schools. In a fragmented society everyone functions best by himself.

Despite this, there are at least two basic values that everyone involved should be able to agree upon: *Equality* and *respect*.

Regional cooperation between school authorities in Southern Norway, the VAAR project, resulted in the following list of themes to be raised at the meetings[3]:

- Social unrest and lack of attention among the pupils and possible causes and how to deal with it.
- The teachers' methods of teaching. Are they acceptable and do they pay sufficient attention to the need of the pupils? The students' own culture determines, to some extent, what they have access to.
- The students' use of media. The school has the right to raise the question for discussion. It is well known that extensive use of media reduces the students' attentiveness and learning conditions.
- The students' use of drugs, its spread and causes, and steps to be taken. Youth culture representatives as well as the police should be involved in the discussion.
- Mobbing, violence and vandalism at school and in the local community.
- Working-out a common value base for school and home.

---

[3] The project called VAAR, designating three regions in Southern Norway, where members of the teachers' union cooperated to work out an extensive document concerning school, home and local community cooperation.

It goes without saying that none of these challenges can be solved once and for all. On the contrary, in the present-day society with the weakening or even disappearance of Christian and humanistic ethics of duty, they presumably cannot be solved at all. The challenge has to be dealt with by way of a long-term value transmission. The process requires cooperation between students, teachers and parents as well as with the local community, hoping to improve the current situation and counteracting destructive behavior.

Among the numerous topics to be raised for discussion and action, sometimes especially with the parents and sometimes with the students, may be:
- Are you a friendly person?
- Willing to cooperate?
- A nuisance to others?
- Respect for those who are different.
- Bad language.
- Are you a negative person?
- Are you audacious in your answers?
- Do you greet others in a decent way?
- Are you expressing your gratitude upon receiving a gift?
- Are you a helpful child by nature?
- Are you looking at schoolwork as natural challenges?
- Are you noisy during teaching hours?
- Are you caring for your fellows at school?
- Are you against schoolwork, against national holidays, against learning anything, against everything at school?
- Are you a joining-in fellow?

Discussions of these and other topics and questions are all parts of value-based teaching and leadership.

VALUE-BASED SCHOOL CULTURE

Values are primarily moral values. Moral values are ethical values in action. Ethics as the theoretical base of morality is a practical discipline. As a practical discipline, ethics is both easy and most difficult to convey. The reason is simply that whereas it causes no trouble to teach values, you cannot at the same time teach commitment to values. And commitment to values is just what ethics as a practical discipline is about.

For this reason ethics as a theoretical discipline, a discipline of long standing, no longer suffices. Defined as a theory of justification of value, ethics is of course a most important discipline. Rational justification does, however, not bring forth commitment. The translation from knowledge and justification to commitment requires, I take it, a long process of interpersonal exercise. Ethics therefore, in the traditional sense, needs to be supplemented by practical advice.

My proposal is as follows, in four parts:

• *Ethical Values*

A selection of the best known ethical (or moral) values should be listed. They are all relational values, indicating qualities in interpersonal relationships. The following five values will do: Respect – Equality – Forgiveness – Justice – Trust.

It is hardly necessary to teach anyone these values. We all know them by way of our enculturation process. We all know the difference between right and wrong. It is all too understandable that in a world of consumption, media, hastiness and a level of violence never seen before together with an increasing insecurity, a lot of us are left with words without commitment. Our freedom is left on its own, without direction. "We are living in an age of unreason" (Charles Handy 1996). Many, perhaps most of us, are still in many ways committed. The rest of us, I am sure, would like to join. Now and then, however, confronting the postmodern society, I take to be a sign of good health, to ask, committed to what? Are the Western societies moving in the right direction?

The overall message of the values is that ethics applies to every human being, irrespective of who we are, how educated we are, which position we have in society or what we have been doing. Everyone is at any time considerably more than any of our actions. This is not only a Christian message. It is equally valid in other religions and in Humanism.

How then, does knowledge of values translate into commitment? Several steps of mediation are needed.

• *Ethical Norms*

Norms are rules of action and behavior. In view of the variety of working places, the question immediately arises whether there is any sufficiently general rule valid for everyone everywhere. From our encultural processes we all know there is one, usually called *the golden rule*. This rule is central to all cultures and religions. It is the rule of mutuality in behavior and action. In *Christianity* it runs: Everything you want others do to you, you shall do to them (St. Matthew 7.12.) In *Islam*: No one of you is a believer until he wishes the same for his brother as he wishes for himself (Sunna).

However, knowledge of the golden rule is by itself hardly of much use. Commitment does in no way follow from knowledge of this rule either. That explains the thefts every year worth half a billion Euros in Norway from shops and stores. Everyone knows that it is wrong. "You shall not take anything from others, because you don't want them to take anything from you." Knowledge often differs from action and behavior.

At least two more steps of mediation are needed.

• *Ethical Rules*

Rules are of two types, *formal* and *informal*. Formal rules are first and foremost the ISO systems of rules, notably

ISO 9000-1-2-3 and 4, which are rules for securing the quality of products and services,

ISO 14000, prescribing a responsible use of resources, and

ISO 18000, covering rules for the preservation of health, security and environmental qualities.

These international systems of rules are, no doubt, all modeled after the golden rule of mutuality: Every business enterprise should offer products and services to the market that the companies themselves would want to buy. And all companies should be an example of responsible use of resources from the beginning to the end. The employees obviously belong to a company's resources. Human beings are our most valuable resource, the saying goes. However, human beings are primarily in no way a resource to anything. Ethics teaches that human beings first of all are valuable in themselves. If respected as they are, most people are willing to do their best. It goes without saying that the same applies to parents, to children and young people in the classroom. Thoughts such as these, I take it, should be added to ISO 18000, that is, rules for taking care of the employees' health, security and environment. If not taught and discussed in the classroom, at least in part, working life will suffer. Quite a few schools in Norway, following other European countries, have organized even children in small enterprise units. They are themselves responsible for choosing a leader, a personnel manager and an accountant, and what sort of products they should produce and sell, or what services they should offer to the local community. The unit is also responsible for the use of all the money they earn, often several thousand Euros. Sometimes they take a trip abroad or to another community at home. They practice "knowledge in action".

The overall purpose of the enterprise unit is not to earn money. The purpose is moral practice. It is application of moral values in cooperation, exercising mutual respect and acknowledgement. This is in all situations necessary steps for achieving optimal results and at the same time preventing selfishness and corruption. Earning money is a by-product of moral qualities in the group.

The most successful of the international systems of rules is no doubt the first one. To the rules securing high quality of products and services are tied strict control and reporting systems. This has, no doubt, reduced the number of accidents and dissatisfied customers. The food and clothing industry certainly follows, or tries to follow, the rules of production. However, it is not that easy to care for workers in other, low-cost countries. It is of course highly stimulating to receive food and clothing from foreign cultures. However, due to the competition in the market economy and to speculating shareholders, part of the food and clothing business produces endless series of foodstuff and clothing that no one has ever asked for and no one really needs.

Evidence is at almost every shopping center. A highlight can be observed in some of the greatest shopping centers in the world. I once visited a center in Kuala Lumpur, where Shakespeare's *Hamlet* was performed on a stage: Reciting *To be or not to be*, the actor showed a lady's handbag. Together with the voluminous entertainment and advertisement from TV channels, the Internet and the cell phones, we are virtually invaded round the clock. In the US every citizen is every day victim of 3,000 advertisements (Jean Kilbourne 1979, p. 12). Freedom of choice is certainly a value for most, or all of us. Freedom led astray is rather a heavy burden. We are, as it were, dragged out of our reliable relationships. Too much freedom creates bewilderment, no longer being in command of ourselves. Our minds are emptied. Lack of communal values causes unrest and violence. For the same reason our parliamentary system cannot work properly. Selfishness is and has always been incompatible with democracy. It violates the golden rule. A fundamental question forces itself to the fore: Is democracy as we know it from Locke, Mill and others, really compatible with the market economy as we know it today? What is certain, is that there are numerous arguments for saying, no. What is equally certain, is that politicians and others should be very cautious in holding up the Western type of democracy as an ideal for the rest of the world. Institutional democracy is certainly not enough. Culturally-based communal values are an equally important base for the political system.

The discussion of this cluster of topics and challenges begins at home and in the classroom, not only in the business units. That would, hopefully, be a contribution to reducing the level of corruption.

• *Informal Rules of Ethics*

The general ethical values have a wide range of informal applications both in private and public life. They range from rules of good manners and a variety of rules structuring our private and public rituals to rules of community building in schools, companies and administration on all levels. No one is anywhere supposed to study or to work for himself only. We are studying and working to enable us to achieve some common goal. Selfishness, although sometimes hard to avoid, is rarely a pleasant encounter.

Many companies, though not all, have a document stating their type of value-based leadership and culture building. The document usually opens with some statement about core values and continues by applying these values to their specific way of doing business, to their competence, products and services. I have myself dozens of such documents at home. A number of local and national administrations have similar documents. The same applies to a number of professions. A recent book has the title *Ethics and Values in Psychotherapy* (Tjeltveit 1999). The conflict is between scientific and value-based therapeutic approach. Tjeltveit goes for the moral approach. To help people, to care for them is certainly a moral issue. Farming has long had an ethical guidebook. Animals have a right to be cared for.

In my work with schools in Norway I discovered new ways of motivating children and pupils together with building a class culture based on general values. The pedagogical strategies to achieve this vary immensely. It depends on the teacher's personality, his pedagogical and social creativity, his knowledge of the local history, its manners and customs, old buildings and ancient roads, its songs and celebrations and of working life. There is usually more to a local community than standard textbooks of history reveal. There is much in the history that excites the interest of children. And engagement in one subject often easily translates into other areas. Some examples are given above (cf. Fløistad 1996; chap. 27).

THE FOUNDATION OF COMMITMENT

To develop a necessary relation between knowledge of values and personal commitment to values is obviously no option. The personal dimension involved in commitment is individual and subjective. The golden rule and formal and informal rules for value-based leadership and behavior are certainly important steps to secure commitment. A fourth and final step may be added, especially to strengthen the interpersonal relationships. Traditionally a strong social web is to a great extent self-correcting. The following three points are in my view relevant.

• *Personal Relationships*

Children need care, in families, in kindergartens and schools. Care gives them a feeling of belonging to someone, in the beginning to the mother and father, later on to wider social networks. The feeling of being cared for, and belonging to, gives self-respect and self-confidence. I take it as a matter of fact that quite a few children in the postmodern society are not sufficiently cared for – far too many, I would say, in view of the examples above.

The situation challenges the teacher. Professional knowledge is necessary, but not sufficient. In most, if not to say in all classes, there are children whose behavior asks for more. They ask to be cared for, due to earlier failings. To relate personally to the children is only the beginning. A teacher should be able to go behind the surface of unrest and inattentiveness and ask for the causes. Some knowledge of the family history is a minimum, as well as some training in conversation about sensitive matters. Some socio-pedagogical knowledge and training together with some preliminary knowledge of how unruly behavior should be diagnosed, appear to be a necessity. The point is that children and pupils shouldn't, in case of some learning disability, be removed from the classroom and referred to professionals other than the teacher. In view of a number of books on the subject, I am convinced that a great many children and young people suffering from unrest, inattentiveness and lack of self-confidence can be helped by establishing (or restoring) lasting personal relationships both with the teacher and friends. To compensate for loss of caring relationships take time. A teacher should therefore teach the class several hours a day. Otherwise the child would hardly develop attachment to him (cf. Struck 1994, p. 174; 1996, p. 225).

Caring is an active relationship. It may express itself in many ways. Acknowledgement is one of them. To be acknowledged is to be made visible within a class or a working community. It is to be declared a valuable member. It is rarely a question of great effort. Often it is simply a matter of being seen and shown signs of confidence. For instance: A well-known teacher approached his retirement age. The weakest student in the class, hardly competent in any subject, was asked to hand over a bunch of flowers with a few words of thanks. The rest of the class expressed loudly their disbelief in the teacher's judgment. The student, however, did it so well that he was admired by the entire class. The admiration motivated him to study hard again, as he had been doing in earlier classes.

Caring may also involve creating order and beauty in the classroom. Already Plato taught us about the close relationship between aesthetics and ethics, between an experience of beauty and commitment. It enhances the effect if the students themselves are responsible.

Personal growth is a necessity if relationships are to thrive. The greatest source of proper self-development is certainly not new technology, new books, new clothes for teenagers or new incomes in whatever field. We all have some fore-knowledge of it already. What is really new is what most of us have forgotten, our history. It is a remarkable fact that interpersonal relationships are almost infinitely richer than all our doings, information technology included, ever can be. And it is richer due to our historical background with everything that it involves: Its political history and conflicts, its philosophy and its literature, poetry and art, its religious rituals and its beliefs, its folklore, its social classes, its poverty, suffering and death. Cultures have never been isolated from each other. Even in the history of local communities (*in casu* Norway), the presence of other cultures is evident: The fairytales are often transmitted from the Middle East and from India. Almost everyone has some knowledge of *1001 Nights*. A variety of superstitions have been imported from "abroad".

The lesser you know of your world-wide background, the poorer your relationships tend to be. And conversely, the more you know of your fascinating and frightening background, the more you may inspire yourself and your fellowmen. Education and schooling are supposed to provide you with a cultural foundation for further growth.

• *Rituals*

Personal, caring relationships need dialogical care. The standard prescription in all religions and cultures are rituals. Rituals are regular social training areas. They are an exercise in being present to others, much needed in a hasty living. A cultural foundation is what binds us together. In our education from primary school to university, even sometimes in families, the ritual training is poor, if not non-existing. This raises the question of whether we later on are sufficiently prepared to be and to work together with others.

It is the teacher's responsibility to ritualize the class community and to assist families in restoring lost traditions.

• *Leadership*

Society is changing. Families change, often to the effect that parents fall apart and the development of children's self-reliance and gender identity suffer. School curriculum does not change, at least not in a way that changes in society require. The curriculum itself should design steps to rescue children from unrest and other learning disabilities. If not, it rests entirely on the teacher and the school director.

The discrepancy between changes in society and the training of teachers has long since been accounted for.

> The speed of change has been unprecedented. The schools have not kept up to a level even approaching that necessary to fulfil their proper function. Nor, it must be said, have the institutions traditionally relied upon to train teachers, their lag has been as great as that of the schools (Blackington and Patterson 1968, p. 174).

Although written nearly forty years ago, in the USA, it still deserves to be read. Recent reports make the same point.

The training of teachers still focuses on professional education. Although necessary, it is in no way sufficient. Reasons are given above. Teachers have the hard task of compensating for the loss of self-reliance and duty in many children, and even excellent professional teaching may fail. What is sometimes required, is given in the stories above. Standard descriptions can hardly be given.

In the past school directors have (in Norway) usually been appointed on the basis of a long-standing teaching career. Recently additional criteria have sometimes been applied (f. inst. motivational power). As far as I can judge, the education authorities have a long way to go before something like a value-based leadership in educational institutions can be established. Some of the difficulties stem from the position itself: The sheer amount of work related to the position of a director, often turns him or her into a bureaucrat, often against their will.

To some extent the same applies to teachers. Unrest in the classroom, inattentive children and low results, especially in mathematics, call for frequent evaluation and reporting – so the authorities think. Maybe a different strategy in the long run would pay off better: To ask the teachers to intensify their personal caring relationship to "lost" children may create conditions for learning. Attachment to someone usually motivates self-development.

There are of course certain problems involved in this strategy. Children suffering from deprivation of some kind continue to suffer after working hours. If there is a well-functioning family or caring friends around, it may be OK. If not, there should be someone at school, preferably the teacher together with the social worker. Then the question arises as to compensation. Some teachers of the idealist camp won't ask for extra money. To care for the children is an integral part of their privileged position. I know of many. Others, in some areas perhaps the majority, stick to their working time and are not willing to extend their time at school. They are probably confining their role to being a professional teacher only. To partake in the education of the children is an alien thought. If they are to do anything extra at school, f. inst. counselling or chairing a commission or even a professional discussion, they demand additional payment. Teachers such as these have, it seems, fallen victims to the postmodern culture of money and self-endorsement.

The logic of their restricted self-definition as a teacher will hardly work. To quote Peter Struck: *Neue Lehrer braucht das Land* (Struck 1994). They seem to have forgotten that in order to succeed in conveying knowledge to children they first of all have to secure their attention and interest – usually a quite different task than instructing them about the laws of nature.

In addition, a minimalistic teacher has taken on an extra burden, to keep an eye on the minutes and hours and extra positions that exceed their ordinary working time. It goes without saying that this attitude further impoverishes the quality of the personal caring relationship to children and parents of the day.

It remains to be added that the schools are society's last chance to provide young people with values. Armed with values, we may even hold on to the fact that "life is our last chance[4]".

BIBLIOGRAPHY

ARONOWITZ Stanley and GIROUX Henry A., *Postmodern Education. Politics, Culture & Social Criticism*, University of Minnesota Press, Oxford/Minneapolis 1991.
AYERS Mary, *Mother-Infant Attachment and Psychoanalysis. The Eyes of Shame*, Brunner-Routledge, 2003.
BIFULCO Antonia and MORAN Patricia, *Wednesday's Child. Research into Woman's Experience of Neglect and Abuse in Childhood, and Adult Depression*, Routledge, London/New York 1998.

---

[4] The title of a book by the German Professor of Educational Science, Marianne Gronemayer, *Das Leben as letzte Gelegenheit*, Wissenschaftliche Buchgesellschaft, Darmstadt 1993.

BJØRKVOLD Jon-Roar, *The Music Within: Creativity and Communication. Song and Play from Childhood to Maturity*, Translated from Norwegian: *Det musiske menneske* (1989) by William H. Halvorsen, Harper Collins, New York 1992.

BLACKINGTON III Frank H. and PATTERSON Robert S., *School, Society, and the Professional Educator*, Holt, Rinehart and Winston, INC, New York/Montreal/London 1968.

BREEN Dana (ed.), *The Gender Conundrum. Contemporary Psychoanalytic Perspectives on Femininity and Masculinity*, Brunner-Routledge, The New Library of Psychoanalysis 18, New York 1993.

FLØISTAD Guttorm, *Om å kunne mer enn man kan. Verdiformidling i dagens skole og samfunn*, Høyskoleforlaget, Kristiansand 1996.

FUREDI Frank, *Therapy Culture Cultivating Vulnerability in an Uncertain Age*, Routledge, London 2004.

GADAMER Hans-Georg, *Wahrheit und Methode*, J. C. B. Mohr/Paul Siebeck, Tübingen 1960. Translated into English 1984 by Garret Burden and John Cumming.

JAQUES Martin, "The selfish market driven economy is eroding our humanity", *Guardian*, Oct. 18, 2004.

HANDY Charles, *The Age of Unreason*, Business Books,London 1989.

HOLMES Jeremy, *The Search for the Secure Base. Attachment Theory and Psychotherapy*, Brunner-Routledge, New York 2001.

KAPLAN Abraham, "Individuality and the New Society", in *The Sanctity of Life*, Vol. 2, Seattle 1970.

KILBOURNE Jean, *Deadly Persuasion. Why Women and Girls Must Fight the Addictive Power of Advertising*, Foreword by Mary Pipher, The Free Press/Simon & Schuster, New York 1999.

KINDLON Dan and THOMPSON Michael, *Raising Cain. Protecting the Emotional Life of Boys*, Ballantine Books, New York 1998.

KOHEN Dora (ed.), *Women and Mental Health*, Brunner-Routledge, London 2000.

LYOTARD J., *The Postmodern Condition*, University of Minnesota Press, Minneapolis 1984.

NORBERG-SCHULZ Christian, *Genius Loci. Towards a Phenomenology of Architecture*, Milano 1980.

PERELMAN Lewis, *School's out*, New York 1993.

STRUCK Peter, *Neue Lehrer braucht das Land. Ein Plädoyer für eine zeitgemässe Schule*, Wissenschaftliche Buchgesellschaft Darmstadt, 1994.

STRUCK Peter, *Zuschlagen, Zerstören, Selbst-zerztören. Wege aus der Spirale der Gewalt*, Wissenschaftliche Buchgesellschaft Darmstadt, 1995.

STRUCK Peter, *Die Kunst der Erziehung. Ein Plädoyer für ein zeitgemässes Zusammenleben mit Kindern und Jugendlichen*, Wissenschaftliche Buchgesellschaft Darmstadt, 1996.

STRUCK Peter, *Die Schule der Zukunft. Von der Belehrungsanstalt zur Lernwerkstatt*, Wissenschaftliche Buchgesellschaft Darmstadt, 1996.

STRUCK Peter, *Die 15 Gebote des Lernens Schule nach Pisa*, Wissenschaftliche Buchgesellschaft Darmstadt, 2004.

TROWELL Judith and ETCHEGOYEN Alicia, *The Importance of Fathers. A Psychoanalytic Re-evaluation*, Brunner-Routledge, London 2002.

USHER Robin and EDWARDS Richard, *Postmodernism and Education*, Routledge, London/New York 1994.

WHITE Merry, *The Japanese Educational Challenge. A commitment to children*, The Free Press/Macmillan, New York/London 1987.
ZOJA Luigi, *Father. Historical, Psychological and Cultural Perspectives*, 2001 (First published in Italy 2000).

ACHIEVEMENT MOTIVATION AND ENTHUSIASM
AUTHENTIC COMMITMENT AND ENTHUSING PARTICIPATION IN SPORT AND EDUCATION

Hans LENK
(Karlsruhe University, Germany)

I. AN OLYMPIC CLIMAX OF ACHIEVEMENT ENTHUSIASM

"Encore quatre minutes!" The loudspeaker sounds across Lake Albano, echoing back with a hollow grumble reflected from the crater walls. The Olympic final in the eights is just about to start. The shells are arranged at the take-off marks. Dull feelings in the stomach. Pull yourself together – now or never! *"Partez!"* The signal cuts the silence, releasing a hustling, bustling noise of coxswains' piercing cries, of cracking sliding seats and hasty water splashes. The great, the last race is under way. Looking back: for four years, we had lived only for this goal. For four years, there was hardly time for anything else except daily workouts, travelling to regattas, races, times, diet and exercise, trimming boats, variations in condition and shape, tactics, strategy and so on. Rowing seemed to be "the most important thing in the world". The sporting "myth" caught the imagination and built up motivation. To participate, to be in the swing of things, totally involved in this fascinating endeavour, all that seemed to be the greatest adventure of an active life. It has been a cooperative endeavour, consummated by the crew and its coach (Karl Adam), highlighting and fulfilling a "mythical" dream. *"The eights – it is the team per se"*, wrote the German poet Hagelstange about our Olympic race as of 1960 on Lake Albano in the mountainous vicinity of the Olympic City, the eternal Rome.

"One thousand metres, half way. Stay tough!" Ten hard strokes against Canada's intermediate spurt. Three quarters of a length. And still five hundred metres to go, the last quarter of the last race. Muscles and tendons strain with pain, pushing, treadling against growing resistance. Air! Breathing and coughing.

Arms, legs but clumsy obstacles. A glance out of the boat shows that Vancouver is falling back: one length. The final spurt: *"still 15!"* The boat jumps on again, accelerates once more. All the energy into this stroke – and again in that one! Darkness, buzzing ears, hoarse and coarse throat. The clumsiness seems unbearable. *"14, 15 – through"*. Falling, dropping. Breathe! Darkness, points of light – exhaustion. *"Stay moving!"* Slower paddling on, panting, gasping. Relaxation. Gradually the environment reappears. The brown shells, the coloured racing suits, the roaring grandstands.

The last, the greatest race. A dream came true, a "myth" became reality. "The structure of top-level performance is the same in any realm" (Karl Adam). Is life but a race?

Being a, or even *the*, climax of achievement and life, such an accomplishment would determine practical walks of life already a long time in advance by training, shaping mentality, personal commitment and devotion. What is the meaning of such at surface value rather useless accomplishments and achievements records rendering – at least in former times – neither bread nor pay nor rent nor sustenance nor even scholarships? Does such an Olympic success make sense in itself or just by being applauded by many?

Indeed, one does not live on bread and sustenance alone. This might – superficially speaking – already convey a partial answer. Humans seem to be the beings for whom the seemingly superfluous accrues towards a sort of necessity, amounting to or even constituting culture – at least this is Ortega y Gasset's[1] basic philosophy of civilisation, life and sport. More specifically, culture would according to him be "the daughter of sports" and of the free exuberant activities of life thus following Schiller's and Spencer's philosophy of life being creative exuberance of energy release and play of all kinds. Ortega would not – as many authors usually do – think that it is primarily not work and toil as well as self-discipline and self-overwhelming, if not self-victory, which would lead to creative achievements, but the sporting free exuberant active creativity like play and energy expenditure for fun, so to speak. Anything valuable

---

[1] Ortega would expand the concept of sports far too broadly. Any effort undertaken for itself or the exuberance of power and vital impulses would be "sport" for him. Any arts or culture – at least higher civilisation – would amount to sport: *"disportare"*, a sort of distraction is a Latin linguistic root of the concept –, would be sport *a fortiori*. Even life itself would be meta-physical effort just for itself, a sort of overflowing of energy. Ortega even talks about "the sportive, festive meaning of life" (1954). However: life is not in itself and by itself just sport and play.

for and in higher cultural endeavours would result from the surplus of this sort of joyous life, the overflowing of power and the spending of energy not necessary for sustenance. Today, we are far from such a philosophy of life which reigned for a long time in idealistic times of optimism and exuberance of this sort of really authentic and creative personal activity only despising any work and toil and self discipline. Indeed, we cannot identify anything barren, mechanical and oriented at aims and usage just with work and, by contrast, see anything vital, interesting, valuable and cultural as accruing by and originating from sport and games and play. Did not Beethoven see 5% of any creative arts as inspiration and 95% as transpiration and hard work-outs?

Sport indeed is vital life. It consists of actions, achievements, accomplishments, which humans perform. These accomplishments cannot be surreptitiously pretended or conducted by betrayal, make-shift, etc.; they in the final analysis cannot be delegated or reorganized just by orders from top. You cannot command somebody to establish a world record in the marathon or to climb Mount Everest, though you may be able to command people to march in line in military formations.

In sport, notably in athletics as well as in any sort of top-level creative accomplishments whatsoever, you have to identify with your own activities and decisions as well as plans. Training and workouts require a sort of devotion and personal authentic identification. Sport is but an exemplary realm for really conducted authentic achievements, personal proper accomplishments which I would like to call "e*igen*activities" and "*eigen*achievements[2]" (*Eigenhandlung* and *Eigenleistung*) being proper authentic self-motivated actions with which the agent would personally identify under standards of judgement and valuation as being top- or high-level, better, excellent or, on the other hand, worse or a failure. These evaluations are conducted – and judged – by the acting person her- or himself as well as from others in teams, groups and societal subgroups or even the general achieving society (McClelland).

"The structure of achievement would be the same in all areas" did our coach of the Olympic rowing team, Karl Adam, emphasize many

---

[2] Quantum physicists talk of "*eigen*vectors" and "*eigen*values" of the state matrix or observables (characterizing the projected possible experimental values of the observables "projected in Hilbert space from the quantum theoretical state function). The terminology of "*eigen*achievements" is by analogy devised after this partial translation from the German reminding us of the characteristic features of self-authored, i.e. authentic and autonomous, personal achievements proper with which the very originators really identify themselves.

times. This is certainly a bit exaggerated, but in any case, the pertinent structures are rather similar indeed so that many an experience from sport, top-level athletics in particular, might be transferred to other realms of *eigen*achievements. Nevertheless, the phenomenon of *eigen*activity and *eigen*achievement is of course much more general than just referring to the area of sport itself.

II. EXCURSUS ABOUT ACHIEVEMENT MOTIVE AND ACHIEVEMENT MOTIVATION

Achieving action and achieving are always oriented at a standard of performance or even excellence. This is true for the achievement motive (McClelland, Atkinson) as well as for achievement motivation in the narrower sense.

The *achievement motive* is a personal rather prominent need disposition or motive to generally orient oneself at high goals and to strive for these, to propel oneself foreward in order to top one's former achievements. Characteristically, the respective actions would thus refer towards a standard or even an exacting scale of performance "goodness" or effort. *Achievement motivation* can be summarized as the personal tendency and general disposition to strive for a specific goal if the achievement motive is the decisive propelling disposition. Those motives and dispositions are usually seen in context with the person's craving and striving as well as a special motive for her or his recognition by others and in one's own eyes.

In short: The achievement motive is a relatively stable personality trait, whereas according to social psychologists achievement motivation is by contradistinction the *actual(ized)* tendency or disposition – dependant on the immediate situation and therefore being rather variable – to strive and attain a distant target and succes to measure one's own performances with criteria of excellence and performance standards, once the achievement motive furnishes the impetus.

According to Atkinson and McClelland the most important axiom of the social psychology of achievement and motivation would be: The effective achievement motivation depends on the (level of the) achievement motive, but also on the (subjective and objective) probability to reach the goal by one's own activity and in addition on the special valuation and/or attractiveness of this goal: probability and attraction of this success together with the achievement motive would determine the strength of the respective actual achievement motivation.

Correlatively, according to this approach, the tendency to evade and avoid failure would grow together with the amount of the motive to avoid failure as well as with the probability of failures and the respective measure of discouragement (the second basic axiom of a simple theory of achievement motivation).

Everybody would be subject to *both* motives: the achievement motive as well as the motive of avoiding failure, indeed, however to rather different extents. The main thesis of the mentioned theory of achievement motivation would state that the overall tendency to take over and fulfil the task or achievement would originate as the difference between achievement motivation and the respective motivation to avoid failure – as well as from external motivations like, e.g., the affiliation motive and motivation.

We might hypothesize that success would be conducive or at least favourable to the expectation of further success experiences, failure would decrease this expectation; therefore failure in rather easy tasks and challenges would in the case of highly achievement motivated persons decrease the achievement motivation whereas successful performance in rather difficult and hard tasks would motivate these highly achievement-motivated subjects. By contrast, success in easy tasks would motivate rather anxious persons mostly oriented at avoiding experiences of failure, whereas failure with hard tasks would discourage them. All this seems to sound rather plausible: Easy success is not interesting for persons high in achievement motivation: The Olympic champion would not find it very attractive to compete at a local school contest.

Easy tasks however would render the rather anxious athletes more self-confident: They would take a little more risks and go on to accept slightly higher challenges.

From this theory we may derive a few simple consequences that have been multiply confirmed by many experimental tests and practical experiences:

If the probability of success and the respective attraction are the same or similar, the strength of the achievement motive would thus decide about the amount of achievement motivation. (A respective insight would hold true for the motive to avoid failure.) The (higher) the net balance between achievement and failure motivation thus decides about the overall motivation to initiate and perform an action.

The attractiveness of an highly valuated success is greater for an achievement motivated person than that one of minor successes and also stronger than for rather anxious persons. (And the other way around for subjects motivated to avoid failure.)

Satisfaction with success is usually higher on the side of highly achievement-motivated subjects – particularly within a rather uniform group of achievement-motivated persons (the social appreciation of achievement would strengthen the attractiveness).

Achievement motivated subjects would put in more effort in a situation or contest within an achievement-oriented environment than in a rather relaxed atmosphere, and they would do so more often than rather less achievement-motivated subjects. On the average, they would generally perform better in particularly achievement-oriented situations than in relaxed ones.

Being or getting accustomed to success would seem to become boring. Achievement-motivated persons would then set their standards higher (take over a higher level of aspiration – as already confirmed some seventy years ago by Hoppe and Lewin). By contrast, with ongoing failure one would tend to lower one's aspiration level.

In general, as compared to highly achievement motivated persons, the motivational dynamics would be the other way around if somebody tries above all to avoid failure. Higher achievement-motivated subjects would display a greater perseverance in staying with the efforts to solve the tasks[3].

Except a few studies – like the one in the mentioned paradoxical case of the avoidance motivated persons – the theory of achievement motivation and the overall net balance between the achievement motive and the motive to avoid failure were rather frequently confirmed and maybe seen as rather sufficiently describing many hypotheses and dynamics of achievement actions – in particular, if choices and risks according to difficulties of tasks are concerned. As a comparative theory of "more or less" highly as against lowly achievement-motivated subject this theory seems to be rather successful[4].

---

[3] Paradoxically, sometimes rather anxious persons would persevere at rather hard tasks, perhaps because other tasks and the impending transition would appear even more frightening to them. (One could perhaps distinguish two largely independent tendencies to avoid failure – namely one originating from the lack of self-confidence regarding one's own capabilities and another one as the anxiety to be confronted with negative social consequences (Schmalt)).

[4] A theory however would seem to have limits regarding extremely highly achievement-motivated persons: These would set their level of aspirations higher: They would not only choose tasks of rather medium difficulty (unsafe expectation of success), but they would rather tend to choose more difficult goals and tasks then inculcated by the median or average value as favoured by the theory. Besides, the self-interpretation of the acting subjects, their knowledge about their own motives and the feedback of success and

III. PRINCIPLES OF ACHIEVEMENT AND *EIGEN*ACHIEVEMENT

There are different principles of achievement in psychology, social-psychology and sociology: The societal and economic "achievement" has to be distinguished from the individual "achievement" of a creative and productive personal outcome of an action, which might in turn be the basis for social stratification or assessment and distribution of chances and pay, monetary and social. Achievement indeed in all these areas is dependent on evaluation and interpretation, requires as mentioned standards (or even scales) of capability, goodness, measures of difficulties, as well as certain favourable emotional individual or social conditions, e.g. an individualistic-activistic basic attitude towards life and self-responsibility as well as liberal social structures – being necessary for or at least conducive to the so-called "achieving society" (McClelland).

Achievement may be evaluated from different aspects: E.g. from the perspective of outcome, result, effort, input, competition, capability, talent, susceptibility to and/or absence of control and intervention, safety, etc. The quantitative aspects of fulfilling these standards of achievement can be interpreted as, e.g., success on the market, productivity (output-input relation), increase of output, minimization of input, fulfilment of duties and formal tasks, individual effort and workout, the topping of others or as exhaustion of personal, social or economic resources and opportunities as well as capabilities.

There is apparently no furthergoing unique measurement of the evaluation of achievement – in particular in comparison between different social realms and tasks as well as achievement structures and formats.

The so-called *"achievement principle"* (in social science) would describe material and social stratifications and rewards as well as chances of upward social mobility as well as improvement of living in return or in proportionate relationship with one's actual or potential personal

---

failure onto the subsequent self-interpretation and achievement motivation were not yet taken into account in the earlier theory by McClelland and Atkinson. — Psychologists also know the sometimes adversely affecting or hampering role of under or over-motivation. Once, a highly achievement-motivated, even over-motivated Olympic rower could only start with a pretended sedative tablet (which in fact just contained glucose as a placebo). With this placebo, he won a gold medal in the Olympics. — By contrast, there are also underachievers, who may only in very strenuous and strongly inspiring achievement situations and challenges display their optimal capability – but not yet under everyday conditions.

achievement (in particular in vocational matters). This is the achievement principle as a social attributional and/or distributive criterion).

As regards this principle, one has to distinguish the microeconomic as well as the social psychological principle of achievement, the first one relating just to economic success, the latter one describing achievement readiness or motivation in the narrower sense.

In our society, however, we have also other social principles of ascription, attribution and distribution as, for instance, principles of social support, political elections, representations, tarif conflicts, group – subgroup as well as in-group vs. out-group perspectives and ascriptions, heritage, traditions, etc.

For education and the philosophy of education, the social psychological principle of readiness for achievement and active authentic creative activity undertaken by oneself, authentic personally engaged achievement behaviour motivation and performance being self-motivated and self interested, is certainly the outstanding principle. This kind of authentic personal achievement orientation and action orientation I would, as mentioned already, specifically call "*eigen*achievement" (*Eigenleistung*, see my 1983) or more general "*eigen*activity" or "*eigen*action" (*Eigenhandlung* if no expressive increase of a scaled amount of performance or achievement is intended). There is a notable difference between self-motivated and alien determined achievement and action.

Insofar, as *eigen*achievement and *eigen*action are essential creative phenomena and moments of life itself (in particular in Western societies), these orientations and the respective principles and motivations have to be necessarily fostered and required in education. The creative social psychological principle of achievement should not thereby be misinterpreted in an economical narrower sense only. Self-motivation should as a rule be preferable to at times still necessary compulsion for achieving. Any unnecessary attempt to compel somebody to achieve should, according to an ideal outline of an achieving society by and by be tendentially reduced, should give way to the ideal creative *eigen*achievement. Our (Western) personalities would develop (only) in and by their creative *eigen*achievements. The principle of *eigen*achievement seems to me, culturally speaking as well as societally and educationally, to be indispensable.

The other large ongoing debate by social critics highlighting a hard criticism at the so-called "achievement principle" (of all three provenances) as well as the criticism of the so-called "achieving society" but the in-depth analysis of social psychological as well as educational and societal experiences and needs led up to the result that achievement orientation and the social and individual fostering of this very mentality and the respective dispositions cannot be dispensed with. Indeed, the "achievement principle" need not contravene every or any humanitarian society (see my 1976). However, it seems to be very important (which the social critics of the 60s had notoriously overlooked) to distinguish between self-motivated authentic and alien-oriented or imposed achievements and achievement expectations being notoriously of an other-directed provenance. "*Eigen*achievement" and "*eigen*activity" would prominently denote the self-motivated, self-engaged, voluntarily performed personal achievement and action. The concept also refers to symbolic achievements and such some which can be only realized or materialized and be expressed by interpretations as, e.g., in arts, sciences and many creative realms – and even in personal sports.

In an intriguing deep sense, human life is primarily "*eigen*activity", or even "*eigen*achievement", an ever-evaluable and evaluated creative personal acting or action. It is so to speak an element and vehicle of an engaging and "real" (really active) life in its original action sense. Meaning resides in acting and achieving, in self-determined, self-structured and goal-oriented "being active". Our personality – at least that one of western culture and society – mirrors itself and even constitutes itself chiefly in works and actions, in expressions and results, brought about and consummated by the individual – i.e. by actions and achievements in the wider sense. Activities of acting motor and psychical behaviour figure here as well as individual presentations: An individual might distinguish itself particularly by novel, creative, at times even unique accomplishments and achievements within the eyes of others, but also confronted to its own aspiration and expectation to go beyond her or his previous achievements, to prove oneself according to one's own judgement and to such of others. Of course, the personality does not merely mirror herself in achievement actions; it would be really at times inhuman, to judge everybody only according to her or his achievement, achievement behaviour or capability. However, achievements and accomplishments proffer a special opportunity for a distinction, self-development, self-confirmation and self-education. Within the society and cultural background tending towards levelation of everything, incurring no real menacing danger and requiring no activation of emergency reserve capacities within our usual highly civilized walks of life, action capabilities and requirements would gain a special meaning insofar as they reach beyond the day-to-day routines, motivating the human being and particular adolescents towards particular activities. In a society admitting of too little tension and challenge, to view tasks of self-probing and -confirmation the human beings create themselves some artificially designed, self-designed "tension" by make-shift challenges and risk seeking, by requiring something special from themselves. Humans would ask from themselves a characteristic personal and authentic achievement or accomplishment, maybe even in risk sports or extreme, at least some extraordinary challenges and aspiring or strenuous tasks, documenting as it were effort, self-devoting, energy release, extraordinary risk taking, endurance or, in particular, creativity. Humans are the "*eigen*achieving beings" *par excellence*. However, for a whole generation or so, facts didn't look like that. The so-called "leisure and fun society" did not seem to highlight these ideals of an active achieving being – at least at first sight. Seen from a deeper perspective, indeed, many of the respective ideas of a too lenient and pleasure oriented all to smooth and civilized small world of modern pampered and feathered youngsters seem yet to display some hidden fundamental wishes for something special in terms of reaching for the extraordinary.

Indeed, for a decade or so, for the first time again even achievement orientation and challenges of adventures, activities or at least the vicarious living of those are "in" again. This is also true for nature and risk sports in general, as well as for a considerable portion of our younger generation with respect to achievement orientation at the standards and principles of achievement. In my home country Germany, e.g., not only traditionally oriented adolescents and youngsters (at 68%) but also the "allround interested" being the most multisided and versatile ones, are (at 63%) again rather achievement-oriented (according to the *Shell Youth Study* XIII, 2000) (in the general population it is nowadays 52% as against 43% of the West-Germans and even 33% of the under 30 years old ten or two decades earlier) that considered themselves rather achievement-oriented persons. This seems to be a real turn in the obtaining trends of the last decades before climaxing in the so-called "pleasure society" and a let-it-go orientation before.

Nowadays even orientations at modernity and hedonism, as well as pleasure, seem to imply that a certain self-engagement in terms of achieving and action as well as risk taking and venturing is implied. Thus, the authors of this youth study covering the last decade in Germany state "a solid increase in achievement orientation" since 1992: "The older youngsters would more frequently profess an achievement orientation than the younger ones, the females more often than the males, the Germans more than the immigrants" (with the exception of the age section of 22-24 years old males, declaring that they would rather be achievement than pleasure-oriented). These new results amount to a remarkable turn in the traditional trend of the once fashionable defeatist mentality before.

Also sociological enquiries seem to imply that the real situation is not that negative as the well known Institute for Demoscopy at Allensbach (on Lake Constance) had announced since the end of the 70s diagnosing an enlarging cleavage between achieving activists and passivists and an overall trend not to "understand life as a task" to be tackled but just as "pleasure" to be enjoyed. For instance in metal industry in the 80s Schmidtchen conducted a rather comprehensive enquiry regarding job satisfaction, leading to some interesting results: Workers, who did assess themselves to be employed in the right way and social context would regard their work more interesting and display more job satisfaction at their working place than those who did not. Important is Schmidtchen's so-called "thesis of resources" or compensation: The more opportunities for compensation somebody has, be they psychic, physical, organisational, design-bound or other advantages besides salary, the more freedom of decisions one would have, the greater would be the satisfaction with the working place and the job, independently of one's judgement of technical progress and innovations. If anybody has many resources for compensation, this seems to be the most effective factor for job-satisfaction. According to Schmidtchen, the collaborators would then much easier shoulder special burdens, if they could avail themselves of greater resources for compensation, displaying to a higher extent a considerable job satisfaction than the others with no or less some such resources. In particular, the result showed that in conditions and situations of higher burdens on the job, personal resources like competence, value orientation, education, etc., have a more significant influence on job satisfaction than just organisational resources (whether or not one is supervisor or subordinate) and even more than pay. (79% of the collaborators confronting high job burdens would assess their task as "very good" or "good", if they had many or relatively strong *personal resources* for compensation available – as against 59% or 66% regarding just financial and organisational resources.) The *personal resources* are particularly decisive. Value orientation, personal engaging and devotion, self-motivation but also the development and the extent of a respectable margin of free dispositions and self-related responsibility would play a special role besides other personal resources like health, etc., if job satisfaction is at stake. (Similar results were found regarding new challenges in front of technological innovations (Schmidtchen 1986)).

In general – and that is really important for education and motivation for achievement and CEOs – the result is that value orientations towards activities and tasks have a significant meaning, particularly personal resources like authentic personal devotion, self-motivation, *eigen*-achievement orientation as well as enthusiastic acceptance of the respective tasks and objectives and the taking-over of responsibility and the pertinent task dispositions. Educational resources, too, have considerable influence on job satisfaction – in particular also with respect to technological innovations.

A rather simple question of education and also life in general, however, is still how to combine achievement principles with fundamental axioms of humanity. An achieving society cannot be a totally encompassing and rigorous one, just honouring only achievement in the narrower sense, but it has to be a *humane* achieving society. There is *a humanized principle of achievement* – at least ideally speaking (cf. my 1976) avoiding the extremes of achievement defeatism and total achievement fixation. This has to stay in front for education and also for the social climate within companies and firms. Certainly, engaging achievement orientation, *eigen*achievement, creative activity and notably *eigen*activity should occupy centre-stage. Self-responsibility, the extent of the margin of dispositions as well as personal engagement are necessary for education and companies as well – in particular, however, for any educational institution whatsoever. This humanisation of the achievement principle is all the more effective and conducive the more qualified, responsible and creative the respective activities are.

IV. THE STRENGTHENING OF MOTIVATION: TEAM ACHIEVEMENT AS PROTOTYPE

May one – and if so, how could one – effectively strengthen the motivation towards *eigen*achievements?

The most outstanding personal achievements are nowadays consummated by athletes – particularly those in top-level sports, where the intensity and cardio-muscular burdens of training and competitions are the highest. In particular, wherever no financial interest (like in professional sports nowadays) is at stake, it is personal will and readiness, devotion and self-overwhelming as well as self-control that would be necessary, transpiring and effective. Since most achievements are today brought about in teams, typical requirements and processes are best studied in the team sports. From the group dynamics of top-level sport teams it is possible to transfer approaches and results to other achieving groups and teams – as also, *mutatis mutandis,* even in companies and institutions of education. At least, comparisons by studying some outstanding extreme performances would as regards cases and amount of effort and energy input turn out to be quite interesting. As a member and later on coach of top-level rowing crews (*inter alia* an Olympic 8^+ gold medalist crew, 1960, an European Champion 8^+, 1959, as an athlete; moreover another World Champion eights, 1966, as coach) as well as in the fours (1958: 4^- as an athlete, and, again coaching, a 4^+ in 1965), I studied the group dynamics of crews and teams from a social psychological perspective. The respective results are discussed in my "*Team Dynamics*" (1977). Some remarkable interconnections between the internal structure of the team and external guidance as well as social environment, of competition and coaching and the development of achievement motivation are obvious. The increase of achievement motivation and the guidance of the crew or team would depend on all these factors. Conflicts and tensions within the crews as well as with the coach or leading personnel are rather common. One has to take them into account and to reckon with them: conflicts cannot fully be solved once for all, but one has to try to regulate and at times moderate, if only mitigate, them in order possibly to turn the attitudes and mentalities as well as tensions into positive achievement-increasing and conducive impulses. Not only harmonious conflict-free teams were capable of the best, even world-best achievements, as social psychologists would have notoriously claimed earlier. Leadership conflicts, group tensions and conflicts, even cliques are just normal. The World Champion eights as of 1962 was dominated by an "achievement clique" of the four allegedly strongest rowers, it was emotionally split up into these two competing cliques, each under the respective leader; the crew would nevertheless increase its overall strength[5]. Everybody had to stand out and compete against almost evenly strong spare men in the skiff and in small-boat races – in training workouts as well as in official competition. This internal competition would render the objective as well as self-assessment within the crew much more intersubjective, would by itself regulate and mitigate or even defuse some conflicts within the socio-dynamic structure. Relying on the internal

---

[5] However, there was also the second World Champion eight oar crew as of 1966, founded and coached by myself, which had only a slight competition ("leadership dual") between two rowers vying for the captain's role of the crew which turned out to being otherwise very harmonious and, nevertheless, also conducted world best achievements.

competition in small boats we had an objective standard of comparison, acknowledged by all rowers. Clique conflicts, leadership tensions could be predicted on grounds of so-called sociometric questionnaires and behavioural enquiries and could be used to manage or solve leadership tasks of the social psychological dynamics in the training camp. (For the results, which cannot be related here, see my 1977.)

However, what can be generally learned from the interconnectedness and interaction between achievement motivation and the teamwork of these crews? Internal integration and keeping together as well as external competition would vary inversely – like Homan's "laws" of microsociology, small group psychology and group dynamics would imply. In addition, however, contrary to the traditional doctrine of social psychology, clique conflicts are not necessarily detrimental, but have to be considered as normal and could be manipulated and influenced as well as used in a positive, i.e. achievement-increasing, way for the control of the group and training camp – as long as they were not that strong to really tear the respective crew apart. The success of the individual rowers is necessarily combined with the success of the crew itself: thus even internal achievement competition can be rendered positive for increasing the general achievement level of the team. Not only harmonious teams are capable of top-level, even world best achievements, but also regularly, indeed quite often, rather conflict-driven teams and crews are also. Frequently, but not always, tension- and conflict-ridden teams are more determined, more involving themselves, they seem to be more innovative, intensive and stronger: high tension of achievement orientation would express itself of course also in the social psychological relations of the crew members with one another. The rather objectifying effect of an internal competition, and – wherever this is not possible – of an open internal discussion may profitably be used to effectively regulate internal conflicts in the groups and teams. Literally as well as generally speaking, regulated internal competition would often be conducive to increasing team achievements.

The so-called "democratic" self-control of the group by using participatory decisions and the participatory style of leadership would make the regulation of internal competition more visible and more easily to handle. By this objectification many a conflict could be diffused, mitigated, regulated or even dissolved or defused. At the same time, participatory leadership would strengthen the identification with the crew and their communicative joint planning for training and races. Whoever co-operates and participates in planning would identify himself stronger with the team achievement and the cooperative planning. That very factor may – that was our hypothesis – interact with and have an impact on the thus increased personal *eigen*engagement; it might even mobilize achievement reserves, which would have been unreachable under normal motivation, say, under the traditional authoritarian style of coaching. Internal competition and, by that, extant objectifying comparisons of achievements are therefore as a rule much more effective than just preaching or admonishing or other verbal means. The principle of *eigen*achievement can therefore be conducive to strengthen the output of the group by means of in-group control and participatory leadership. Finally, also the self-motivating power of a self-gratifying activity rendering a sort of satisfaction and even "fun" in the face of top-level propelling drive and initiative plus stress may give an extra hype, because one would deeply identify with the self-chosen activity and psychic input. The urge of *eigen*-achievement within the so-called "flow" experiences (after Czikszentmihalyi 1975) would also prominently figure not only in creative, but also in rhythmical, routinely structured activities like rowing, cross country skiing and other self-gratifying activities, rendering a certain respective auto-strengthening of motivation. This also applies to team sports and teamwork in all creative realms – and notably in group education, too. In general, the characteristics of toilsome work and energy expenditure and playful activity would become fluid at the limits of the highest authentic engagement and even self-devotion for a particularly energy consuming and demanding activity.

V. THE *EIGEN*ACHIEVING BEING

What can all these experiences and social psychological results mean for the philosophy of education and for and in the anthropology of the achieving being?

Any comprehensive doctrine of the human being has nowadays to encompass many perspectives. The human being is not to be covered by just one definition or formula. Its essence cannot be characterized by just one unique trait. Any doctrine of humans, any anthropology – especially "philosophical anthropology" in practice – has to cover many perspectives, has to be pluralistic these days. The Kantian question "What is man?" can only be answered in a very complex and multifarious manner. Philosophical anthropology can today only look for unity within multiplicity and multifariousness. It has to take into account results of the human and the social sciences as well as the biological and medical disciplines. However, it cannot content itself with just descriptive summaries.

It should try to integrate in an overview and orientational guidelines some overarching central ideas of what a human being is and *should* be according to its self-knowledge and self-understanding. To work out these traits in a sort of united model would be a necessary and demanding task for philosophical anthropology today and in the future. In that respect, philosophical anthropology is partly a cognitive-descriptive discipline and in part a normative and value-oriented enterprise, too, having to somehow systematically integrate these different aspects in a methodologically viable manner.

The well-known characterization of humans as the *acting beings* (after Schütz and Gehlen) seems still to be too little specific. A rather special accent regarding human action is that potentially it is not just behaviour and action, but basically also consists of improving a goal-oriented activity according to some systematic criterion, standard or gauge, and methodical planning. In short, it is *achieving* activity in the widest sense of the word the idea and criteria of which would have to be met. *The human being is not only the self-responsible, but also the eigen-achieving being* (see my 1983). Humans, and only they, can act by ways of methodically and systematically planning, by exercising and coaching or being coached in an ever improving better way or quality, if even quantified; they can *eigen*achieve, as I say. Voluntariness and *eigen*motivation are necessary conditions of an authentic, in particular of any creative accomplishment and achievement. Achievement thus can be an expression of the personal freedom of action. *Eigen*achievement, depending on authentic personal motivation (e*igen*motivation) is an expression of the active, creative personality. The personal accomplishment is thus no pure natural product of but biological inheritance or instincts, yet simultaneously or even much more also a psychical, societal and cultural, even spiritual attainment, although certainly figuring on a biological basis. *Eigen*achievement has a very special educational significance, particularly if a symbolic achievement is at stake, rendering an economically and biologically speaking rather "superfluous" result. But, as Ortega had it, the seemingly superfluous is in some respect especially necessary – for cultural and educational development – notably for humans and humanity.

The principles of achievement and achievement comparison, of competition and equality of opportunities and chances would be almost perfectly materialized in sporting and athletic contests – in any case more objectively and fittingly than in any other realm of life. Sport seems to be the particularly apt means of expression and realm of comparison for e*i*-

*gen*achievements. Does this explain part of its fascination? Similar results are to be found for other realms of creative achievements like those in arts including performing ones as dance and play, etc., in writing and even savouring literature, in music and even in science and philosophy. These realms of creative e*igen*accomplishments are educationally speaking of the highest significance: They offer opportunities for (self-)distinction by one's own achievement within a generally conformist or concurring equalizing society emphasizing nevertheless individual values and distinction. Sports and arts symbolize ideals of high cultural achievements not required by and for day-to-day sustenance, which however renders the human being to be the creative and creatively acting, the cultural and symbolically representing being; it may thereby ascend or transcend beyond the necessity of sustenance and the securing of existence by an achievement of self-wrought and personal provenance and being highly strived for and valued. Indeed, the human being does not live on bread alone. It also lives on *properly authentic personal* achievements.

Though sport can be a characteristic paragon example of such self-stylised personal development and an expression of individual e*igen*-achievement, any other realm of *Eigen*activity, in particular in all creative fields of action – may figure in the same vein as an exemplary field for voluntarily craved-for personal accomplishments and thus become an expression of the individual creative person and autonomous personality. Any realm of e*igen*achievement is in the over-administrated, if institutionalised and over-codified and over-organized world of today an important reservation for individual achievement and active engagement. Somebody had said, that in this world of institutions it is only sport in which life still remains truly to be real authentical action. I would like to extend this towards any realms of creative e*igen*achieving, because this dynamics applies to all areas of creative and re-creative personal actions. Especially democratic societies in an administrative world are dependant on authentic motivation and readiness for achievement by member personalities and should foster these in any potential form whatsoever as effectively as possible. Self-motivated, object- and task-oriented as well as cooperative attitudes and the mentality for achievements are to be supported and honoured with a particular emphasis. Personal acting, authentic achievement are an important expression and symbol of a really personal life – at least in our action- and achievement-prone Western civilisation. Creative and productive activity in arts and sports are an attractive medium and vehicle for inculcating and leading towards the disposition for *eigen*achievements; they are especially important in a world curtailed by consumerism, and they are in particular important for adolescents, because they are at times and in appropriate forms more easily accessible than, say, scientific and really creative artistic high-level production. They might, however, at times lead to high achievement levels in turn.

The principles of achievement and objective achievement comparison by competition and equality of chances or opportunities are most easily approached in sporting training and competition. Nepotism, privileging, special relationships would count as little as property, affluence or power. It is only achievement that counts in sport – at least ideally speaking. (In professional sports as well as in any publicly impressive show-off disciplines, we have though many problems of betrayal, like doping, manipulating results, buying and pretence; this is human – all too human, indeed, but does not devaluate the ideal picture.)

Sport was understood as a societal model in which values and guiding norms as well as basic principles of the so-called "*achieving society*" (McClelland) would figure much more clearly and in a purer form than in real society. (This was for instance also stressed by the above-mentioned Olympic rowing coach, Karl Adam.) Indeed, the sporting achievement principle seems to be a purer abstraction, a rather utopian presentation of achievement behaviour and comparison, amounting to much clearer conditions, if not even greater renditions, than to be achieved in professional work, industry and economics[6]. Artistic and sporting achievement as well as any creative activity whatsoever – have indeed much in common regarding their motivational foundation. As realms of creative activities and *eigen*achievements, they are social-pedagogically speaking of highest significance: There are necessary op-

---

[6] The social philosophical critics of society some decades ago would therefore also criticize sport by reproaching that it would just mirror the achievement norms and compulsions of the working world and would thus deflect humans from their allegedly authentic "revolutionary interests". One would, moreover, imply wrongly that sport would make humans just machines or equivalents of machines, it would only serve for "fitness for work" (Adorno) and for the adaptations towards a technicalized world. It would always reside "within the empire of unfreedom, wherever it is organized" (Adorno). These critics notoriously overlooked, however, that athletes and sporting people are characteristically identifying themselves emotionally and personally with their own achievement at training, in exercising as well as competitions and that they conceive of their activities and the respective results as their own personal accomplishments, because sporting activity – like any artistic one, too – is explicitly and exclusively conducted according to the principle of self-motivation and *eigen*achievement and not just according to alien compulsion.

portunities for (self-)distinction in a rather conformist society, nevertheless stressing individual values and distinctions. They symbolize ideals of a cultural highly valued achievement not required by day to day sustenance – an accomplishment which however really makes the human being the acting one, the cultural being it is, symbolically figuring and reaching beyond everyday necessities by, e.g., an outstanding symbolic achievement. Thus the athlete, like the artist, would symbolize even a certain "herculean" or "promethean" "myth" (see my 1972, 1976a, 1985) of a cultural exceptional achievement and a symbolically highly valued excellent accomplishment stemming from personal engagement, devotion towards a task, aspiring goals and aims. Indeed, and again, man does not live on bread alone, but would need meaningful tasks and sense-engendering goals. Without such cravings, strivings and achievements of any creative activity whatsoever, there would not be any challenge or instigation for a rather personal and autonomous development of the personality. Any strong active engagement of a voluntary form is an achievement in the mentioned wider sense and should be honoured as a creative expression of the personality.

Personal acting, *eigen*achievement, authentic personal engagement, self-responsibility are amongst others essential criteria of personal development, an expression of individual freedom. Regarding the fashionable *baisse* of any self-motivated aspiration for achievement in many branches of the public opinion lasting for some decades before the last one, we would and should postulate the revitalisation of a positive treatment of achievement, a rather new cultivation of the creative concept of *eigen*-achievement and self-acting. Indeed, it is especially democratic societies which are dependant on these dynamics and presuppositions of self-motivation and readiness for personal actions and achievements. These latter premises and the very conditions should be particularly fostered in our educational institutions.

To be sure, achievement is not everything and achievement as such, taken just in the abstract or by formal and external evaluation (e.g., pure athletic records as such), barring social meaningful objectives, would not be recommendable as a panacea for education and behaviour in general. But *without* authentic personal striving for accomplishments and achieving, without the strong will for particular achievements, for personal improvement, for creative activities, higher civilisation would not be possible at all. The cultural being is the *eigenachieving being*. This ideal comprises as mentioned a value and ideal expressing the human striving for the better. Personal authentic action, *eigen*achievement is an important expression of creative life.

It has to be stressed, that *primary* motivation should go in front of secondary (indirect) motivation characterised by just being assigned gratifications, opportunities, chances, etc. We need object-orientation, enthusiasm for tasks and work to be done *("Sachbegeisterung")* instead of only secondarily looking for indirect gratifications. There is a danger within the over-administrated society and even its formalized institutions of education that primary motivation is played down instead of or by secondary motivation, checks and controls and the perfection of curricula and administration as well as over-sophisticated differences in grading. Over-administration tends to produce a narrow job mentality and would almost kill personal initiative deriving from enthusiasm for real tasks and challenges. This would exacerbate a social dilemma in education (see already my 1976): Society is dependant on the mobilisation of enthusiasm for tasks and objectives as well as personal devotion which by itself cannot possibly be engendered but may in turn more easily – all too easily! – be destroyed or, at least, emasculated by over-administration, red tape and bureaucracy. Personality and particularly the creative capacities are not the products of administration. Here initiative, inspiration and trust as well as freedom are much better than perfect control and checks. Young aspiring personalities and co-workers should not lose their enthusiasm and autonomous initiative as well as primary motivation in difficult job situations as well as intensified job competitions. The more one identifies with his self-chosen task, the more one can achieve and accomplish in fulfilling this. Perhaps this rather educational perspective may open a way of saying farewell to exaggerated self-indulging thoughts of safety and complacency and to give us a chance for coming back to really authentic striving and *eigen*initiative.

VI. SUMMARIZING THESES REGARDING *EIGEN*ACHIEVEMENT, PERSONAL INITIATIVE AND ENTHUSIASM

1. Only the human being can personally act, "*eigen*act" in the authentic sense of the expression. Acting however is not specific enough: Humans frequently and characteristically try to improve in their acting, according to precise gauges or standards of goodness, amelioration, proficiency, efficiency and comparative achievements. They would like to act better and better. They would like to achieve something, to distinguish themselves by the results of one's own acting and accomplishments. The human being is not only the acting being as tradi-

tional philosophical anthropology would have it, but also and characteristically *the achieving being*, i.e. the authentically achieving, *eigen*achieving being. Only authentically engaged achievement can be creative. One could talk of a "principle of creative *eigen*achievement". This kind of achievement principle is not outdated or useless as many social critics thought some decades ago. Achieving and achievement orientation as well as the pertinent motivation is necessary now and in the future. Society is even existentially dependant on them.

2. Education towards meaningful authentic achievement-orientation is indispensable. Since and insofar *eigen*achievement is creative, many opportunities of any kinds should be offered to youngsters and be made accessible to them. *Eigen*achievement should be considered and fostered as a personality developing activity of great pedagogical and social significance. It has to be learned and exercised time and again. This is true for any of its multiple sorts: Any creative form of *eigen*-activity has to be re-commended, developed and exercised again and again – in arts, music, writing, sciences, adventurous enterprises, sports, in symbolic activities like science and technology as well as other "creative ventures" (Weiss 1992) – even in voluntary social services, etc. The chances and opportunities for personal acting and *eigen*achievement should everywhere in society be improved and simplified: Manifold forms of offers and ramifications are necessary – especially for adolescents. *Eigen*activity should be instigated and fostered in a much more multifarious form than hitherto – in particularly for youngsters and adolescents as well as trainees of whatever kind.

3. In strict and harsh competition, the orientation at teamwork, cooperation and even at communal achievement should not be underrated. Even if we need internal competition for raising an increase of achievement levels, primary motivation and enthusiasm for the task as such *("Sachbegeisterung")*, teamwork and group orientation should be equally valued and fostered, respectively. We need motivation for competition, but combined with cooperativeness and real primary task orientation. Team achievement should be especially fostered. Competition should be combined with cooperation and active engagement in real tasks and by primary motivation.

4. Enthusiasm for a task as such *("Sachbegeisterung")* is decisive for the art of *eigen*achieving: Primary motivation is in the last analysis much more important than secondary motivation (this latter one only

being an auxiliary means for instigating the less motivated ones). The essence of enthusiastic achievement-oriented life seems to be: *Only the enthused ones may enthuse others!* (Merely) Enthusiasm carries away. Achievement-enthused (should) lead the way.

5. Moreover, one should not forget about the special attraction of the fascinating challenge provided by prototypes and paragon examples of excellent achievements for activating and instigating achievement motivation. Paragon achievers are much more efficient than just preaching and citing laws and regulations. Extraordinary achievements are not a result of only dressage, drill or compulsion. This is true, even if tension, exhaustion and frequently monotonous repetition are characteristic for sportive or artistic exercising. Without special challenge, without devotion and self-overcoming, if not self-overwhelming, no really extraordinary genuine personal achievement, no autonomous development of the personality would ensue. You cannot command self-superation. Top-level achievements are not just rendered by compulsion, commands or regulations. The same is true for really creative achievements in all realms of autonomous achievements. Top achievers figuring as paragons would fascinate, would thus function in an educational way – and this will also hold true for the future. (However, supporting social and political as well in particular educational measures are necessary.)

6. Of course, society and its development are dependant on proper authentic achievement and the development of achievement motivation. We have to develop a general positive education for self-determined authentic achievement, of self engagement and personal responsibility in that respect. In short, we need a societal fostering of the principle of creative and self-responsible authentic achievement, *eigen*activity and *eigen*achievement. All this needs incentives and a positive instigating training of self-determined creative action – particularly in all institutions of education. We definitely need a new cultivation and support of free and voluntary *eigen*achievements of whatever kind.

7. The principle of authentic achievement should be combined with the idea of humanity and humaneness: The *eigen*achievement principle should be *a humanized principle of achievement*. If and insofar as it is an essential task for the future to conceive of and design *eigen*activity as a *"humanism"* this is true also for the orientation of achievements in sports: In top-level achievement athletics as well as in everyday exercises the orientation at a really "human" performance and at con-

ditions of humaneness should not be forgotten in the situation of often too harsh a competition and orientation at solely the victor and victory (see my 1983, 1998): The one and only orientation just at the victor and/or champion ("Winning is not everything, it's the only thing!", as the American coaches Tatum and Lombardi had said) should in highly competitive areas be downplayed a bit, which might turn out to be very difficult indeed. Achievement and competition should be socially meaningful and be humanized in some form. (This applies in particular to mass media and the over-emphasis of the winner and winning only as well as records in sports and also to the artificial manipulation of winning by doping and other forms of betrayals or unfairness.)

8. Our society, which already now and in the long run will need less and less working force and is more and more confronted with the structurally induced problems of unemployment, should modify the traditional Protestant working ethics only appreciating professional and paid job activity. Voluntary achievements and social activity, free citizen engagement as well as self-active artistic designing, the devotion to an *eigen*achievement just for itself should get assigned much more social value and emphasis than hitherto. In its *eigen*activity only, the human being probes and confirms itself as an individual. The difference and borderline between work and meaningful leisure activity will and should become much more fluid than nowadays. Democracy needs engaged *eigen*achievements, it even lives on these – also and especially some such ones which cannot be rendered in compulsory form. Societally speaking, *eigen*achievement and voluntary authentic activities are absolutely indispensable. They should however also be appreciated from a social perspective. Authentic achievement should be socially honoured as such.

9. For group and team achievements, we may summarize: Motivation psychology has hitherto incorrectly neglected group situations and specific group factors for the development and strengthening of the achievement motive and achievement motivation. It is indeed important for the practice of teamwork and group achievements to study and deal with the interplay of achievement motivation and team conditions because group factors in achievement-oriented teams are considerably influential for achievement motivation, the increase of achievement and (the probability of) success. Barring extensive practical analyses one may transfer experiences from top-level team sports to other sorts of achieving teams. Sport and athletics figure as a

rather extreme paragon example in which the dynamics of achievement and teams would combine with each other rather neatly.
10. According to my own experiences and social-psychological (sociometrical) analyses, the group situation and its feedback seem to be much more influential than any just individualistic exhortations. One may learn from dealing with sports teams: Preaching and verbal appealing is much less conducive or useful (if at all) than the instigating incentive of achievement comparison within the group – according to the appropriate structure of the activity by a sportive or even direct internal competition. Mere verbal summonings go idling.

All this may be generalized to any objectifying procedure of achievement comparison being much more efficient than just verbal admonishing. The same is true for realistic exercises with planning in groups. The systematic exploitation of group dynamical interconnections seems to be much more practice-oriented and realistic than – and is as well as efficient as – just verbal appeals. Generally speaking, in psychological research and philosophical interpretation of achievement motivation, the role of team situations and the feedback onto the shaping of motivations, have not enough been taken into consideration – in particular those group dynamical interconnections and factors which can directly (by their very action structure) be used for incentives and instigation of achievement-orientation. Practical experiences and "rules of thumb" may be transferred from top-level sports to other realms of achieving activities – particularly also in creative and scientific-technical as well as entrepreneurial contexts – as far as the respective personal engagement and authentic achievement motivation is at stake here, too. The dynamics of the achievement process is rather similar everywhere – as already quoted from the world renowned rowing coach Karl Adam in his only slightly overstated insight: "The structure of achievement is equal in all fields".

Generally speaking, within the philosophy of education and the anthropology of the achieving being the insights and results of social psychology, practical experiences with top-level achieving teams as well as philosophical interpretations of the human being as the authentically personal achieving being *(the eigenachieving being)* can be integrated in a particular plea for developing a positive new cultivation and sophistication of the social and psychological factors of achievement orientation – above all in education. Social and philosophical anthropology have thusfar erroneously neglected or downplayed these rather practice-oriented factors and the very dynamics of achievement orientation and personal authentic acting. Indeed, at least for Western societies and world views, *eigen*activity and *eigen*achievement are an essential component of the self-interpretation of the human being. The human being, being not only the rational-cognitive, but also the social and cultural as well as creative being, is *the authentically eigenachieving being* at the same time.

LITERATURE

ADAM K., "Nichtakademische Betrachtungen zu einer Philosophie der Leistung", in LENK H., MOSER S., BEYER E. (eds.), *Philosophie des Sports*, Hofmann, Schorndorf 1973, pp. 22-33.

ADAM K., *Leistungssport als Denkmodell*, Nymphenburger, Munich 1978.

ATKINSON J. W., BIRCH D., "Die Dynamik leistungsorientierter Tätigkeit", in LENK H. (ed.), *Handlungstheorien – interdisziplinär*, Band 3, 1, *Halbband*, Fink, Munich1981, pp. 353-434.

ATKINSON J. W., FEATHER N. T. (eds.), *A Theory of Achievement Motivation*, Wiley, New York u. a. 1966.

ATKINSON J. W., RAYNOR J.O., *Motivation and Achievement*, Washington 1974.

CZIKSZENTMIHALYI M., *Beyond Boredom and Anxiety*, San Francisco 1975.

HECKHAUSEN H., *Hoffnung und Furcht in der Leistungsmotivation*, Hain, Meisenheim 1963.

HECKHAUSEN H., "Leistungsmotivation", in THOMAE H. (ed.), *Handbuch der Psychologie*, Vol. 2, Göttingen 1965, pp. 602-702.

HECKHAUSEN H., *The Anatomy of Achievement Motivation*, New York/London 1967.

HECKHAUSEN H., *Leistung und Chancengleichheit*, Hogrefe, Göttingen 1974.

HECKHAUSEN H., *Motivation und Handeln*, Springer, Berlin/Heidelberg/New York 1980.

HECKHAUSEN H., "Ein kognitves Motivationsmodell und die Verankerung von Motivkonstrukten", in LENK H. (ed.), *Handlungstheorien interdisziplinär*, Bd. 3, 1, Fink, Munich 1981, pp. 283-352.

KROCKOW C. v., *Sport. Eine Soziologie und Philosophie des Leistungsprinzips*, Hoffmann & Campe,Hamburg 1974.

LENK H., *Leistungsmotivation und Mannschaftsdynamik*, Hofmann, Schorndorf 1970, 1977.

LENK H., *Leistungssport: Ideologie oder Mythos? Zur Leistungskritik und Sportphilosophie*, Kohlhammer, Stuttgart/Berlin/Köln/Mainz 1972, 1974.

LENK H., "Leistungssport in der Erfolgsgesellschaft", in GRUBE & RICHTER (eds.), *Leistungssport in der Erfolgsgesellschaft*, Hoffmann & Campe, Hamburg 1973b, pp. 13-39.

LENK H., "Leistungsmotivation als theoretischer Begriff", in LENK H., *Pragmatische Philosophie*, Hoffmann & Campe, Hamburg 1975, pp. 168-183.

LENK H., *Sozialphilosophie des Leistungshandelns*, Kohlhammer, Stuttgart 1976.

LENK H., "Herculean 'Myth' Aspects of Athletics", in *Journal of the Philosophy of Sport* 3, 1976, pp. 11-21.

LENK H., *Team Dynamics*, Stipes, Champaign, IL 1977.

LENK H. (ed.), *Handlungstheorien interdisziplinär*, 4 Vols, Fink, Munich 1977 ff.

LENK H., *Social Philosophy of Athletics*, Stipes, Champaign, IL 1979.

LENK H., *Eigenleistung. Plädoyer für eine positive Leistungskultur*, Fromm-Interfrom, Osnabrück/Zurich 1983.

LENK H., "The Achieving Being and Athletics", in LENK H. (ed.), *Topical Problems of Sport Philosophy*, Hofmann, Schorndorf 1983a, pp. 329-341.
LENK H., *Die achte Kunst: Leistungssport – Breitensport*, Osnabrück/Zurich 1985.
LENK H., *Konkrete Humanität*, Suhrkamp, Frankfurt/M 1998.
LENK H., MOSER S., BEYER E. (eds.), *Philosophie des Sports*, Hofmann, Schorndorf 1973.
MCCLELLAND D. C., *The Achieving Society*, Princeton, NJ, V. Nostrand 1961 (quoted after the German ed., *Die Leistungsgesellschaft*, Kohlhammer, Stuttgart 1966).
MCCLELLAND D. C., ATKINSON J. W., LOWELL E. L., CLARK R. A. (eds.), *The Achievement Motive*, Appleton, New York 1953.
MEYER W.-U., *Leistungsmotiv und Ursachenerklärung von Erfolg und Mißerfolg*, Klett, Stuttgart 1973.
SCHMALT H.-D., MEYER W.-U. (eds.), *Leistungsmotivation und Verhalten*, Klett, Stuttgart 1976.
SCHMIDTCHEN G., *Neue Technik und Arbeitsmoral. Eine sozialpsychologische Untersuchung über die Motivation in der Metallindustrie*, Deutscher Instituts-Verlag, Köln 1984.
SCHMIDTCHEN G., *Menschen im Wandel der Technik. Wie bewältigen die Mitarbeiter in der Metallindustrie die Veränderungen Arbeitswelt?*, Deutscher Instituts-Verlag, Köln 1986.
WEBER M., *Die protestantische Ethik und der Geist des Kapitalismus*, (1920), München/Hamburg 1969.
WEINER B., *Theories of Motivation. From Mechanism to Cognition*, Markham, Chicago 1972.
WEINER B., *Die Wirkung von Erfolg und Misserfolg auf die Leistung*. Klett, Stuttgart 1975.
WEISS P., *Sport – a Philosophic Inquiry*, South. Illinois Univ. Pr., Carbondale/Edwardsville/London/Amsterdam 1969, 1971.
WEISS P., *Creative Ventures*, South. Illinois Univ. Pr., Carbondale, IL 1992.
ZUCKERMAN M., *Sensation Seeking*, Hillsdale, N.J. 1979.

EDUCATION AS CREATIVITY

Vladislav A. LEKTORSKY
(Russian Academy of Sciences, Moscow, Russia)

Contemporary education faces a lot of critical problems. They are the result of those of our civilization.

In many centuries it was clear that the aim of education is to teach a pupil knowledge, skills and habits. The latter ones were understood in different way in different historical contexts. So the notion of an educated person changed historically. The ideal of education in ancient times was *Paideia*. It presupposes the education of reason, the feeling of harmony and civic virtues. The central point in this ideal is cultivating reason, because harmony, and moral and political deeds are impossible without reason. But educating reason was considered possible only with the help of teaching definite kinds of knowledge, in particular mathematics and philosophy. In the Middle Ages the main aim of education was teaching religious knowledge and abilities and skills for reading the Holy Scripture. The system of education that has formed in the most countries of the West for the last two hundred years presupposes teaching the basic elements of scientific knowledge, training some skills. An educated person has been identified with one having a lot of knowledge. According to a common opinion, formed at the time of the Enlightenment, it was the knowledge of natural and social dependencies that enabled a human being to control the environment and become a free person.

But to-day this ideal is being contested. There are several reasons for that.

The first. The development of a civilization based on scientific knowledge and technology has created a lot of problems, beginning from the ecological crisis and finishing with the problem of personal identity and inter-human relations. There is a wide spread opinion that one-sided scientific and technological progress is a deadlock in the human development. So a question has arisen: is it necessary to have as an important aim of education teaching basic elements of scientific knowledge?

The second. Now it is clear that the possibilities of scientific reason have limitations. For example, it is impossible to predict the behavior of the complex organized natural and social systems in certain points of their development (so called the points of bifurcation). So the human being can't be considered as a master of all natural and social processes.

The third. All systems of education in history presupposed that teaching knowledge and skills is in harmony with moral education. But nowadays scientific and technological knowledge is usually used instrumentally and in many cases even for non-moral aims. So teaching scientific knowledge doesn't necessarily lead to moral development.

The fourth. We are living now at the age of interaction of different cultures, of viewpoints, of styles of living, of different norms of assessment and behavior. Is it possible in such a situation to form a common ideal of an educated person?

The fifth. The fast development of science makes a more and more great part of knowledge out of date. So it is not clear what parts of scientific knowledge must be taught at schools and universities.

Traditional systems of education as a rule prefer not to discuss these questions, as they can't give answers to them.

Some contemporary theoreticians of education try to give answers to these questions, but in some cases these answers can't be considered satisfactory. I mean in particular the famous ideas of Ivan Illich about education as not an affair of schools and universities, but as a personal affair of an individual. According to Illich a person acquires knowledge first of all from everyday experience and professional practice, but not from school and special teaching. (I. Illich 1972.)

I think that these recommendations are in contradiction to important features of the contemporary civilization. This civilization, which sometimes is called an informational one or the civilization of knowledge, presupposes production, distribution and use of knowledge as one of its bases. Science is the main producer of this knowledge. Ecological problems can't be solved without science, but only with its help. So it is impossible to avoid teaching elements of scientific knowledge in school and university. The problem is what scientific knowledge should be taught, taking into account the process of its outdating.

The second problem is how to teach knowledge.

As knowledge is embodied in certain statements, one can think that acquiring knowledge is identical to learning these statements and texts consisting of such statements. But the aim of teaching knowledge is creating possibilities to solve problems by means of this knowledge. In such a case a pupil should be able to use this knowledge in different situations and be able to choose those portions of knowledge which are suitable for solving a definite problem. Knowledge doesn't only refer to a certain reality, but is included in contexts of dealing with it, in definite types of activity. The mastering of knowledge presupposes the knowledge of its criteria, the scope of its application, in other words, a reflective, critical attitude. So teaching knowledge can be successful in those cases when it means teaching critical thinking.

The development of informational civilization creates contradictions, which are directly connected with the problems of contemporary education.

The appearance of contemporary information technologies (television, the use of a computer, communication by means of Internet, etc.) affords receiving a lot of information. It is a great achievement, without which our civilization would be impossible. At the same time it doesn't necessarily lead to the development of critical thinking, but in many cases hinders it. The TV images have a special force, which can block not only critical reflection, but also the abilities of imagination. As investigations of Russian specialists show, to-day many schoolchildren during their homework prefer not to make their own texts or to think about something, but to use ready texts from Internet. The acquiring of such information is not identical with the acquiring of knowledge. It doesn't help to develop thinking, but destroys it.

But the development of the contemporary civilization creates another problem.

To-day many social processes are fast acting, and a lot of social and cultural structures are ephemeral. It is a consequence of a special role of producing and distributing new information in our life. Non-standard situations arise very often, and the degree of risk in life is increasing. An individual finds oneself in such situations more and more often. In these cases he or she has to find a creative, non-standard solution of a problem. So nowadays the cultivation of the ability of creative thinking is a necessary condition of living.

One of the main aims of education to-day is teaching creative and critical thinking. Teaching knowledge, skills and habits are derivative from this. A person who has an ability to think creatively and critically can acquire new pieces of knowledge instead of outmoded ones. He/she can apply knowledge successfully in different contexts, as this process is creative.

But how to teach creative and critical thinking? Is it possible?

I would like to formulate problems, which arise in this connection.

1. A pupil should have confidence to knowledge that is taught. Otherwise he/she cannot acquire any knowledge. But if a teacher wants to teach critical and creative thinking it is necessary to teach doubting and questioning. How can it be combined?

There is an opinion, according to which questions in philosophy, science and education are principally different.

Questions in science stimulate research of problems and tasks and indicate directions of research. Each question obtains a definite answer, and this creates a new question, which also obtains an answer as a result of new research. All the history of science can be interpreted as a constant change of questions and answers. Philosophers deal with the so-called eternal questions concerning being, knowledge, consciousness, etc., which have a different meanings in different historical contexts, which they discuss, try to answer.

Questions in philosophy and science presuppose the absence of ready answers and a process of search. Meanwhile in education questions have ready answers. The aim of questions in this case is not finding something unknown, but only testing a pupil's knowledge. H.-G. Gadamer wrote that a pedagogical question is not genuine, because "…it is a question without a questioner" (H.-G. Gadamer 1985).

Usually the aims of questions in education is to inquire what a pupil has learned. A teacher can ask a pupil, for example, when a certain event took place, how to do a sum by means of a method that a pupil must have learned, etc. A teacher knows answers to his questions. Such kind of questions depends on the nature of education that exists now in most schools in the world. In the past many theoreticians of education, beginning from Jan Amos Komenski, said that a genuine education presupposes the activity of a pupil, his ability not only to find ready answers, but also to put questions to others and himself. In this connection they referred to Socrates and his question and answer method of a dialogue. But if the main aim of education is the appropriation of knowledge and skills, as it takes place in the most systems of education now, it is impossible to change the nature of education and, in particular, the type of questions in education.

2. There are norms, paradigms, criteria of correct thinking. At the same time creative thinking means that sometimes some of accepted norms and criteria can be doubted. The teacher should teach norms and criteria of thinking. And he/she should teach doubting and questioning. How is it possible? Teaching is impossible without the authority of a

teacher. Young schoolchildren have an uncritical attitude to a teacher. The destruction of this attitude can lead to destruction of school teaching as a whole. But how a teacher can teach critical and creative thinking in such conditions?

3. Critical thinking presupposes a reflective attitude to own thinking. It is possible if a person can accept a position of another, to look at his/her own ideas, at his/her own thinking from the point of view of another person. At the same time in the case of critical thinking he/she should have critical attitude to positions of another person. If another person is a teacher, it is possible for a pupil to be critical to oneself from the point of view of a teacher, but it is impossible for him/her to be critical to a teacher. What is a solution of this dilemma?

4. Pre-school life of a child is connected with acquiring knowledge, which is in close relation to his/her everyday life, with his/her practical activity, with the solution of problems, which exist in real life context and are interesting for a child. So a child comes to school with a readiness to continue learning and with striving for studying. But after the first or the second years of learning many children don't want to learn any more: their learning motivation drastically decreases. The explanation of this fact is as follows. The aim of the traditional education as giving a pupil knowledge and skills doesn't help to create a striving for understanding, for activity and creativity, for participation in solving problems. So traditional education can't form a learning motivation. Forming motivation that gives sense to study is a special and difficult problem for the existing school. There are different recommendations how to solve this problem. Some theoreticians of education suggest to connect knowledge that is taught with everyday context. But it is impossible to do in relation to many subjects that are taught in school. Others suggest to combine teaching with some kinds of games. But it is not clear, whether motivation for playing can be the same as motivation for learning, as they are very different. So the problem is how to form motivation of a pupil to learn creative and critical thinking?

I will briefly analyze three attempts to solve these problems in the practice of education. These were made in the USA and Russia. These attempts are different, but they have common features. The followers of these pedagogical innovations interpret the latter ones as the future of education.

*
* *

First of all it is a program, which was elaborated by Matthew Lipman and other scholars from the USA and which is called "Philosophy for children" (M. Lipman 1991). The program has been realized in the practice of education for two decades in the USA and many other countries, including Russia. The main thesis of Lipman is that it is necessary to teach creative and critical thinking in school, and that the best way of doing it is teaching philosophy in a special form for many years. Because, according to Lipman, philosophy in more degree than any scientific discipline liberates thinking and affords to doubt statements that are usually considered evident. It is important that pupils should not study philosophical texts and discuss already existing philosophical conceptions, but should be involved in philosophical thinking, should try to give their own answers to some problems that can arise in ordinary life, but which have philosophical nature. Pupils with the help of special texts and a teacher are involved in the discussion of problems that have no generally accepted solutions. A discussion, something like a Socratic dialogue, arises between pupils. The participants of a dialogue put questions to each other, answer to them, formulate arguments against given answers, give counter-arguments, put new questions, etc. The class of pupils becomes the inquiry community (it is a key notion for Lipman). The participants of such a dialogue acquire not only ability to reason, to argue, but also to view analogies, to take into consideration a context, formulate hypotheses, give non-trivial solutions. They are taught ability to ask such questions that presuppose non-trivial answers. Questions of participants to each other help to find such presuppositions in their reasoning which were not clear to them before a dialogue. A teacher organizes a dialogue. He asks such questions that don't suppose a single and known answer, but stimulate a discussion and direct it.

In Russia there are also attempts to develop creative thinking of pupils by means of introducing elements of inquiry into education. One of such attempts is so-called program of "the school of the dialogue of cultures", which was elaborated by a philosopher, a theoretician of culture and education Vladimir Bibler (V. S. Bibler 1998). The followers of the program think that creative thinking can be taught not at special lessons (as it takes place according to Lipman's program), but by the change of teaching all school disciplines, beginning from mathematics and physics and finishing by history and literature. In this connection a teacher can put such questions, including ones about main notions of mathematics, physics, biology, etc., which admit in any case several answers. Pupils become to be involved into a discussion with each other. Certainly, they are inclined to be guided by a teacher's authority. It is natural and important. Without this, education is impossible. But this inclination should be supplemented by a pupil's striving to ask non-trivial questions and answer them. It is possible, if a pupil interacts not only with a teacher, but with other similar pupils. Because in the latter case the equality of positions exists. A pupil can't participate in a dialogue with a teacher as equal to him, to ask and object him. He can do it with his classmates. The realization of the program showed that for it the problem of learning motivation doesn't exist. It turned out that creative thinking motivates itself. A pupil engaged in creative thinking doesn't need an external motivation for learning.

At last the third pedagogical program with aim of developing the creative thinking of a pupil is a program of the so-called developmental teaching, elaborated by the Russian specialist in pedagogical psychology Vasilii Davydov (V. V. Davydov 1996). He and his followers have created, in particular, a method of a playing a special game by a teacher. A teacher plays a part of a pupil and pretends not to understand some questions and answers. A teacher specially makes mistakes and provokes a pupil to doubt and make mistakes. A teacher shows to a pupil possibility not to understand a question, to ask a question again, to ask a proof. A teacher creates "points of amazement" and the condition of a dialogue between pupils. A pupil finds the existence of different points of view and as a result of it he first has a certain discomfort. There is not only his own position, which is self-evident for him, but also there are other ones (of a teacher, of other pupils). A pupil learns to understand a position of another pupil, to assess it, to doubt it, to ask questions to another pupil, and so to begin to realize his own position, to be able to distinguish it from another one, to defend it, to answer question concerning it.

*
* *

So all three systems of teaching creative thinking, although they are different from each other, have some common features. I would like to formulate them.

1. All of these systems proceed from the idea that a critical dialogue is an important means of teaching critical and creative thinking. A dialogue affords to put questions, to formulate doubts, to discover different

points of view. A dialogue is not a simple conversation, as it has an aim (a solution of a problem) and is directed to this aim.

2. The participants of a dialogue are pupils, usually belonging to the same class. All of them are equal in formulating their points of view and criticizing each other. Critical and creative thinking is carried out first as a collective activity. It is an inquiry community, as Lipman calls it. As a result of this activity a reflective position of each individual is formed and a possibility for autonomous and critical thinking arises.

3. A teacher plays a very important part. He/she demonstrates paradigms of a discussion and organizes an interaction of pupils. He/she stimulates the activity of children and teaches them to put questions and to doubt. Critical and creative thinking obeys certain norms and rules. There must be something stable in a dialogue and mutual criticism. Teaching norms and rules of discussion is not indoctrination, not an imposition of a rigid image of reality, it means creating the very conditions of a critical dialogue. Teaching such thinking would be impossible without an authority of a teacher.

4. Creative thinking is such a mode of activity, which has its own inner motivation. So teaching creative thinking can help in solution of the problem of forming learning motivation.

5. All these systems consider the process of education and the process of investigation (in science and philosophy) as not something principally different, but as close to each other. It is possible, if education is considered and practiced as creativity.

*
* *

A dialogue as a means of education can be used not only for teaching creative and critical thinking, but also for moral and aesthetic education.

Moral relations presuppose that I relate to another person as to myself and to myself as to another. Under such understanding moral behavior is not only following a certain system of prescriptions (and not a "moral arithmetic"), but first of all empathy, a feeling of problems and pain of another person, the recognition of him/her, a care of him/her. But it is possible only in a condition of a constant dialogue with another and with myself and presupposes an ability of imagination, of critical self-reflection, and of creative transformation of myself.

Art can be considered as a means of achieving a new experience of the world and joining an experience of other people, social groups, and cultures. In many cases only art can help to understand another experience, to empathize it. But it means a dialogue with other people, cultures, points of view and an ability to creatively change own stereotypes and attitudes. Aesthetic education is unique in that respect.

I think that practicing of dialogical education can be important also in solving some problems created by globalization and multiculturalism.

Globalization is connected with spreading new means of information technology (TV, a computer, Internet, etc.). As a matter of fact it creates two modes of education. The first one is simple teaching means of receiving information. As a rule it doesn't presuppose the development of critical and creative abilities, the development of a responsible person. An individual becomes only a receiver of information. Moreover such mode of education can lead to indifference to cultural values. The second mode of education combines teaching informational technologies with cultivating archaic cultural values. It creates fundamentalists. Dialogical education is a means of forming a critical and creative personality, who not only uses informational technology, but creates new knowledge, solves non-standard problems, respects different cultural values and critically interacts with them.

Multiculturalism is not a conflict (or war) between different cultural values, and it is not a simple co-existence of cultures. It presupposes an interaction between them, their mutual changes.

The current civilization is facing the situation, when it is clear that we cannot be satisfied by present relations of people to the nature and people to each other. The experience accumulated by different cultures in the sphere of these relations is not sufficient to-day. There is necessity of extending this experience. It is possible to fulfill it only by taking into account the experience of each other. It does not mean uncritical acceptance of another experience. It means only that it is possible to see in another position, in another culture, in another system of values not something necessary hostile to my position, but something that can help me in solving problems, which are not only mine, but also the problems of other people and other cultures, other intellectual and value systems.

Contemporary world is facing a dilemma: either the collision of different civilisations (which can lead to a war conflict between them), or the organisation of a dialogue, attempts of mutual understanding, mutual criticism, self-criticism and mutual changes. In this case pluralism is not a hindrance for the development of a certain culture, but the necessary condition of it, and a mechanism of the development of a culture as a whole. Education can play a very important role in that process. Genuine multicultural education is possible only in the context of a critical and creative dialogue.

*
* *

The "school of the dialogue of cultures" of Vladimir Bibler and the theory of the developmental teaching of Vasilii Davydov have used some ideas of the outstanding Russian philosopher and the theoretician of culture Michail Bakhtin (M. M. Bakhtin 1986). Studying the structure of F. Dostoevski's novels, M. Bakhtin discovered that they are polyphonic, in other words, they can be interpreted as a dialogue, as the interaction of different voices, representing different conceptual positions. This dialogue includes questions, answers, arguments and objections, elucidation and the development of a position, new questions and answers, etc. As a result of the analysis of the pre-history of polyphonic novels by F. Dostoevski, M. Bakhtin came to studying a Socratic dialogue as a genuine source of poliphonism. But as it is known, Socrates used a dialogue not only as a means for searching truth, but also as a means for education. Later M. Bakhtin elaborated the dialogical conception of all cultural phenomena, beginning from language. Every statement according to M. Bakhtin can be interpreted as a part of a certain dialogue: a question, an answer, an objection, an elucidation of a position, etc. He suggested similar interpretation for literature, philosophy, science. A certain culture from his point of view can be interpreted as an obvious or a hidden dialogue with other ones. The consciousness of a person can't be understood out of the context of its dialogue, including questions and answers, with consciousness of other people and with itself. M. Bakhtin's ideas has influenced a lot of studies in the theory of literature, art, culture, in philosophy, psychology. Now they are becoming more and more influential in the theory and practice of education.

I think that the idea of a dialogue is a key to education as creativity, in other words to the future of education.

REFERENCES

BAKHTIN M. M., *The Aesthetics of Creativity in Writing*, Iskusstvo publishers, Moscow 1986, pp. 281-307 (in Russian).
BIBLER V. S. (ed.), *Philosophical and Psychological Presuppositions of the School of the Dialogue of Cultures,* Rosspan publishers, Moscow 1998, pp. 13-87 (in Russian).
DAVYDOV V. V., *The Theory of the Developmental Teaching*, Intor publishers, Moscow 1996, pp. 366-393 (in Russian).

GADAMER H.-G., *Truth and Method*, Crossroad Publishing Company, New York 1985, p. 327.
ILLICH I., *Tools for Convivality*, New York 1972.
LIPMAN M., *Thinking in Education*, Cambridge University Press, Cambridge 1991, pp. 7-100.

UNTRADITIONAL EDUCATION

Lars-Henrik SCHMIDT
(Research Centre Gnosis, Aarhus University,
Campus: Copenhagen, Denmark)

The work of the educator is often described as a cross between craft and art. In my view, this is a misunderstanding of both craft and art; but it is impossible to mistake the allotting education this position. In 1762 Rousseau proclaimed that education was 'l'art de former des hommes' – the art of forming people[1], which has nothing to do with the modern conception of either craft or art. If both craft and art are involved we approach the concept of handicraft, as in the arts and crafts movement, and thus proceed to the classical concepts of 'praxis' and 'poiesis'. In my view it is not a matter of 'both-and' but of 'as much- as'. 'The art of …' has dimensions which are as much eternal as contingent, partaking as much of necessity as of freedom.

As educator or teacher, one's doings do something, and they do something to the doings of others, for these doings exhibit many mean or merely stereotyped traits which vary from teacher to teacher and from pupil to pupil. These doings, which do *something* and do something *to* another, make up the learning relationship, which with variations will always be associated with the formative aspect of education. However, this formative aspect is not always a major theme in educational discourse. In periods in which there is predominantly focus on 'instruction', the formative aspect of education is relegated to the practical and artistic dimensions. But this should not lead one to believe that a new interest in education as personal formation is identical with an interest in practical and artistic subjects. Personal formation is not tied to crafts or to art. It is certainly linked to an aesthetic factor, but it is not obvious what this aesthetic factor is in the modern conception of education as personal forma-

---

[1] Jean-Jacques ROUSSEAU, *Émile ou de l'éducation*, Paris 1957 (1762), Préface.

tion. How has it come about that this aspect of education has again become a major theme in the final phase of modernity?

CULTIVATING THE TASTE

To deal with this question we must begin by investigating the traditional conception of education as cultivation (In German: *Bildung*, a concept usually contrasted with vocational training, and referred to in the following as 'cultivation', or more generally as 'education'). In the modern epoch, which saw the rise of this idea (it was unknown in antiquity, when the propensity for elective affinities was dutifully resisted) personal cultivation is quite simply the cultivation of taste. Many modern teachers find this preposterous, because in their work they strive, first, to find something individual but not subjective, and then to find it purged of the influence of trend-setters. The grounds for their disquiet are in my opinion an unjustified prejudice against the category of taste.

As Voltaire puts it[2], in all civilised languages there is a connection between 'having a taste for' and 'the sense of taste'. What is interesting is how the sense abiding in the palette has metamorphosed into the aesthetic sense, the sense of judgement, the power of judgement, in fact. We are accustomed to think that aestheticism is concentrated around good taste – possibly around an attack on good taste – and the history of ideas provides a good basis for this belief. In previous periods it was taken for granted that particular groups were able to pronounce on the ins and outs of taste, and this went for all areas. With the hindsight of democratic culture this approach is condemned; but if one focuses on this aspect of the problem of taste one risks losing the very idea of education. Kant's pronouncement that education is merely the cultivation of taste rests on his typical contemporary belief in good role models; and for the founder of modern philosophy the model is what is old and lasting: the authors of antiquity[3]. Not in order to say that these are good taste, but to debase bad taste, distance oneself from it, by means of the examples of good taste gleaned from classical authors.

It is thus not possible to say precisely what good taste is. It is however clear that cultivation is not the same as opinionated nitpicking. Cultivation is the art of declining the unacceptable; not the art of giving rules of good behaviour but of refusing to authorise unacceptable and unappe-

---

[2] VOLTAIRE, "Goût", *Dictionnaire Philosophique*, Paris 1994 (1769).
[3] I. KANT, *Schriften zur Metaphysik und Logik. Werke in Sechs Bänden,* Band III, 1983 (1800), p. 471.

tising behaviour. Cultivation is not the art of knowing what should be done but rather of allowing something to pass as long as it does not provoke. Many modernistic types of artist have had a hard time with point of view because they feel that without provocation nothing happens. One exercises one's taste in the borderland between too much and too little. One can determine when something is too much or too little, but this does not mean that one can find the exact boundary. As cultivation involves negative rather than positive determinations, it is not a question of taste but of distaste. Decency is the exercise of distaste[4].

The reason why it is so important to connect cultivation with taste, or rather with distaste, is that by doing so we have insisted on the sensory element. The classic definition of aesthetics specifies that it deals with sensory perception, and does not privilege a particular sense or group of senses. However, that is how it is in educational discourse, where the metaphor of the theatre is very prominent as an image of the educational situation.

Senses which operate at a distance carry the most clout. The sense of sight is the one that matters. Therefore drawing and painting are no longer on the curriculum in Danish schools but have been replaced by pictorial studies. Unfortunately, instead of teaching the art of making images we provide training in understanding the images made by others. This is in fact completely at odds with the spirit of the new educationalism, which regards the pupils as collaborative and as partners in creativity. Essentially, aesthetics has nothing to do with art in the modern sense, but it has with the science of image-making and with the properties necessary to reject the image-making of others. The main thing is not to understand other people's images (pictorial studies) or to see an image through another's eyes (discernment). The main thing is to share image-making with others, images which make up virtual realities. Virtual realities are only realities to the extent that they can be shared with others, and they can only be realised, be made actual, if we do not disagree about their reality.

Aesthetics is the struggle for these virtual realities and their realisation, their actualisation. It is therefore about balancing different reality-options, different reality-sketches – for example, different art realities. Art consists of making reality an option and of taking over the reality-options of others, of changing, balancing, defeating the reality-sketches of others. And in a period in which the metaphor for the space in which

---

[4] L.-H. SCHMIDT, *Det sociale selv.* Aarhus Universitetsforlag, 1990, pp. 241 ff.

taste is exercised is changing from that of the theatre to that of the arena, aesthetics does not privilege a particular sense in its dealings with these reality-options. In the theatre our actor is tied to script and choreography, but there is no scriptwriter in the modern arena. Here it is not a case of knowing one's lines but of asserting one's point of view or of affirming one's own personality.

The reason why it is difficult for educational discourse to grasp this transition is because it fixes the educator and the role of education. Now the educator must also assert himself in the arena, not just follow a ready written script. So many practitioners of education have therefore conceived a desire for art, to return to the theatre, the script. And if their longing is not merely for clear scripts and directions but for art, this is probably because art is the least modern thing we have.

Art is the place where the idea of a script, or what in philosophy is called metaphysics, has survived. In the world of education, many are fond of art because art is supposed to be progressive, like the self-image of education. But today it is difficult for art to be provocative and disturbing, and art institutions have their own identity problems. Modern art first spoke out against the banal, then for the banal, and now it merely wants something to happen so it can demonstrate the banality of events. Art has quite simply become the place where, if anything, one is assured that everything is still as it was in the old days; that is, that a reality exists which has a creator and a cause (auteur, maker, artist), a *'Urheber'*. A reality with a meaning and a purpose – in brief, a work – an intention, possibly an intention that others should give meaning to something apparently meaningless, as is the case with much modern art.

The ideology of art assures one that one is the subject of one's actions, exactly as the artist signs his works; that somewhere or other there is a meaning in this madness, or that a meaning can be created, even if it is only that the work must exist, of necessity, or that it creates itself.

FROM ATTITUDES TO VALUES– ONCE AGAIN

There are also many in the world of education, not necessarily different from those mentioned above, who are drawn to the philosophy of Enlightenment, the philosophy of modern Enlightenment, and thus to sociological theses concerning modernity. Their faith in Jürgen Habermas, who has no aesthetic philosophy but speaks of dramaturgic – i.e. theatrical – rationality, is touching, but out of date.

Just as at present we are moving from the theatre to the arena, the centre of gravity of educational discourse is also moving: now knowledge and instruction have been replaced on the agenda by cultivation and learning.

Addressing the question of why we now encounter so much discussion of education, I will put forward my first thesis: *education has become an issue in line with the school's loss of authority in the upbringing of young people.*

This can perhaps be best illustrated by staying with the metaphorical shift from theatre to arena in thinking of the role of education. In the theatre it is in a way easy for the teacher or educator to think of himself as director and maybe even see this as a progressive element since he doesn't claim to be the manager. Under a previous Education Act, the scriptwriter might be the Ministerial Directorate, and the Blue Paper would be the dictate of an actual script to be performed by schools, unlike today's brief delineation of *aims and central areas of skills and proficiencies*. In the transition to the new legislation it has become clear that the script doesn't exist, and there is no longer a Directorate but a Department for Schools, no longer School Inspectors but Educational Consultants. Even the Principal has now become the School Manager, and powerful interests wish to turn teachers into work managers.

Being in an arena rather than a theatre, the individual no longer has a specific role to play or carry out, as with a government post, but must assert himself, must fight to make his mark. The educator must make himself felt to the same extent as the 'inmates' (children, pupils etc). But what is vital is that the educator to make himself felt; no longer with the advantages of former times, even though they are naturally present in any educational situation and in my opinion both will and should remain, but with what could be called a handicap. The teacher has one hand tied behind his back, for in opposition to the pupil modern educational theory demands that he only shows his good side and makes sure that the pupils can learn from this.

The teacher mustn't take advantage of the teaching situation to do missionary work ('indoctrinate') but must service the pupil. This implies that the metaphorical shift from theatre to arena can also be characterised as a transition from attitudes to values. Never have we had so few attitudes and so many values. This change may not appear to be very significant, but it marks an important event: the cessation of discussion.

Attitudes are per definition combative: they aim to convince. When you maintain an attitude it is a matter of principle to regard all diverging viewpoints as wrong, because you are in possession either of what is *true* – i.e. a so-called scientific truth, or what is *correct* – i.e. an ideological truth. But in either case one feels one has a perfect right to reprimand others and try to convince them of the excellence of one's own view.

It is quite otherwise with values. Values are *not* combative; they don't need to be, for the simple reason that values *have the right* to be respected. Values are implicit whilst attitudes are explicit, and can be compared to an overcoat which can be put on and taken off. But these days we demand honesty of each other: we are expected to dwell on the nature of existence, be authentic, and so the opposition between inner and outer no longer functions. We are expected, if not to be transparent at least to maintain consistency between our inner and outer selves, to show the world what 'we' are; in other words, our ethical make-up must appear aesthetic.

Organised attitudes make up what we call *ideologies*; organised values make up what we call *culture*. There has never been so much culture as now; we live in the era of culturalism. This also means that we no longer have ideological critics – or at least those who have survived are very lonely – for an ideological criticism must subscribe to what is true or correct, whilst a cultural analysis is an analysis of cultural values. These days the latter is popular at our institutions of higher education, where humanistic knowledge has largely been replaced by cultural analysis.

The change I am here attempting to clarify is also the change from *authority* to *management* and from *authorisation* to *quality control*. Management is necessary because there is no longer authority, and quality control is needed because the authorisation formerly assured by the examination system can no longer be relied on. Previously, teachers gained their qualifications at a college of education and the quality of their teaching was thereby documented and guaranteed. Such teachers could then provide their pupils with education and some skills which could be measured in a national examination system.

With this, teachers have gone from being or filling the role of a teacher to having to behave as teaching personalities. For good or bad, the teacher has become a key figure. He no longer has a vocation, but neither does he perform the wage labour which replaced the vocation in a period when one only sold one's labour for so many hours per day or per week. Now teachers prefer to call themselves professionals; but theirs is a profession in which one sells oneself 24 hours a day, in which one is sold hair and hide. In this way 'manpower' has been re-feudalised, and thus the post-Enlightenment era becomes reminiscent of the pre-Enlightenment.

FROM CIVILISATION TO CULTURE

In short, enlightening others has become problematic, and therefore so has defending an idea of civilisation which legitimated the connection between enlightenment and universality. The concept of enlightenment implies that some people know (because they are already there!) the direction which others should take; thus like another Messiah, the Enlightener can say 'follow me'. The idea of civilisation is connected with a claim for universality, so the philosophy of the Enlightenment was a one which aimed to disseminate civilisation. One way in which criticism of this paradigm of civilisation and its associated Enlightenment philosophy was conducted was through a Romantic philosophy of education, which advanced the argument that education was not based on universal values but tied to a particular culture and its development. Thus civilisation was replaced by culture, which is not universal but limited – it is not disseminable but edifying.

The point is that the movement from civilisation to culture repeated itself in the post-war period, a new age which regained the idea of civilisation, now understood not as enlightenment but as criticism. It is true that through culturalisation we have understood the limitations, but the culturally embedded critique will at least be able to make its aspirations public, even if it cannot universalise them, and universality has been replaced by public awareness. Through *self-enlightenment* we can examine what is central, and legitimation is found in the democratic endeavour itself. This can be said to be an exemplary form of the combative phase described above. It is possible to exchange viewpoints, and together the united forces will – democratically – determine the proper solution and indicate the correct way to proceed.

In the present age we have witnessed a new culturalistically toned criticism of the claims of civilisation. In other words, we have a new version of the concept of cultivation, which is critical of the critique's limited public, of the organisation. Now the idea is not to appeal to the democratised public but to understand that the private sphere is not mainly concerned with privacy but with the modern *personality* in action. There is simply something that evades the public gaze (or more accurately: evades the distinction between public and private), and which just demands *respect* – without insisting on the right to protection.

The question is no longer one of universality, the public or democracy, but of personality. The vital issue is not so much that I can demand to be heard and consulted but that the matters discussed (or those that I'm expected to listen to) should have significance for me. What does it mean for me?! The issue is not the protection of privacy but the opportunity for personal realisation. Thus commences the *epoch of self-cultivation*.

This is a new version of the opposition between civilisation and culture, between instruction and cultivation. Now the opposition is between self-enlightenment (or self-critique, which expresses how reason relates to itself) and self-cultivation. Cultivation on present-day terms – modern self-cultivation – is linked to personhood. It is not classical education, where individualisation leads to becoming part of a larger whole; in aesthetic terms, *Apollonian education*. In the realm of the new education we do not automatically become a part of something larger than ourselves, we do not experience education as transcendence of self but as an extension of self, i.e. as a *Dionysian education*.

We do not transcend ourselves in relation to great ideas, as was the case in the epoch of edification, but we experience our selves as being part of a greater Self by devolving our egos into the greater Self, for instance in the beat of rhythmic music or at a sports event. Unlike classical edification, this forfeiture can be regarded as a kind of controlled psychosis. Personality develops, but horizontally rather than vertically: it throws itself into situations without being able to put itself aside. In education this gives rise to an overwhelming problem: how is it possible to develop a sense of community in a context of self-cultivation?

It is at least clear that we are not in a position to say 'Follow me'. In our media age we are more inclined to say 'Where do you think we should go?', because it is no longer taken for granted that we educators have the authority or legitimacy to 'elevate' others. We are quite simply not able to 'elevate' others as we could in the days when teachers had authority and with it legitimacy. We have advanced the delinquents, and thereby renounced our right to say which direction they should take. Do we even know any more? We cannot bring people up, so we go back to insisting on cultivation. This gives problems in a country like Denmark, because we cannot but believe that adequate education should mean that those being educated will do the same as we do. If we can't teach them how to behave we must do something else: we must give them role models. Taking an interest in their characters in this way, we get back to education: that is, we believe we can turn the coming generation into reasonable people by bestowing education on them. And in the process, interest in shared values – usage, custom, norms, rights – is always at risk. We would like everyone to go hence and do like us, but how can we get them to? By promoting education; because then they'll do it automatically without feeling that others are pulling them up.

Without our making any effort they follow us because they follow the educated – which is us, isn't it? It can scarcely be anyone else. The problem is merely that in their cultural self-bedazzlement everyone thinks that they are the educated ones. Culturalism privileges education, and we educate as never before, because we can't enlighten, can't influence upbringing – and because we won't or can't give up on socialisation.

How could the idea ever dawn on us that it would happen automatically, that we wouldn't have to do anything special for our offer of education to be received? The explanation should not be sought in the folk high school argument (learning about life through history, literature and songs), claimed by the Danish educator N. F. S. Grundtvig (1783-1872) but in the social-democrat idea of culture. We are in a phase of insistent culture in which we try to promote cultivation by promoting culture. But what is culture to us? It is both art and culture. In Danish one says 'art and culture' in the same way as one says 'ethics and morality', using both terms to ensure that nothing is forgotten or left out. When we say 'art and culture' we've covered the whole field, and that's what we want education to take on. Which kind of education? Aesthetic, of course.

THE DOUBLE CONCEPT OF CULTURE

With this philosophy of education and this aesthetic philosophy two elements are combined which should hardly be mixed together, producing a confusion of two different concepts of culture. The point is that the distinctively Danish view of culture is most at home in this confusion, where an aesthetic concept of culture which refers to *cultural life* and an anthropological concept of culture which refers to *life culture* are mixed together. This confusion is not only evident in a respected Danish newspaper or a graduate programme at the *Centre for Cultural Research* at the University of Aarhus; it is fundamental to Danish aesthetics, education and cultural philosophy.

This can perhaps be best illustrated by a story concerning the former Minister of Culture Jytte Hilden. Asked on the occasion of her unexpected appointment to define Danish culture she gave the prompt reply, "Seagull coffee sets and morning beer". The most important word here is the 'and', simultaneously signifying both identification and distance. The idea is not that we should drink our morning beer from seagull coffee cups. The gold rims are also problematic: seagull coffee cups with gold rims exist, but it won't do to drink too many morning beers from them.

Jytte Hilden's formulation builds a bridge between the Danish petty bourgeoisie and Danish working-class culture. Interestingly, it implies the idea that it is possible to educate oneself out of working-class culture and into the lower middle class. Hartvig Frisch, a Danish Social Democrate and Minister of Education from 1947 to his death in 1950, said that culture is habits[5], but that isn't what is important here: the significant point is that the two forms of culture are connected. When we promote Danish culture we like to talk about Grundtvig, but our practice shows something different: we translate Klaus Rifbjerg into French[6]. It was actually Freud who formulated the cultural philosophy underlying this trait, and he should be given special notice for having thought about this problem at all. Most theoreticians and practitioners merely talk round it. Freud thought it was important that culture (aesthetic culture, with art, science and religion) should be able to compensate for the cultural work of deflecting instinctual drives (anthropological culture). Freud thus presents a theory which at least concerns itself with the connection: most frequently, the slide from life culture to aesthetic culture is merely taken for granted. We believe, quite simply, that when we invest in cultural life, life culture will pull itself up automatically. This is a special Danish idea of cultivation. We believe in a thesis of refinement or representation which ensures continuity and thus cultural homogeneity. Compensation can be made from one register to another, and thus our only concern is how to convince someone who feels insufficiently compensated either that he is wrong or that he can get his share in the redistributed benefits.

My second thesis is that it is *the idea of continuity between the anthropological and the aesthetic concept of culture which gives substance to the project of cultivation as a substitute for the project of enlightenment*.

We conceive of cultural life as a refinement of life culture, and therefore it can seem to us that a literary novel will tell something about our culture, our way of coping with the world. We believe that our socialgrundtvigian heritage will not merely be presented but in this way represented. This self-fulfilling and self-reinforcing thinking belongs to the way we were educated, or it is the idea of refinement held by the leaders of taste. Everyone is pleased that cultivation is again being talked about; not because there is agreement on the subject – but there is not disagreement. And this not-disagreement can end up as a problem for the Danish

---

[5] Hartvig FRISCH, *Europas Kulturhistorie*, Copenhagen 1973 (1928), Vol. 1, p. 9.
[6] Klaus RIFBJERG, *Anna, Moi, Anna*, Stock 1971; *Poèmes*, Seghers 1998.

education system as it implies that certain groups are allowed to promote something, and those groups quite naturally assume that their own cultivation is what should be promoted. Certainly, they cannot instruct the world, they have no right to the world's respect, but by means of the teaching relationship a particular idea of cultivation becomes dominant. However, this also means that, in line with the continuity thesis, the life culture of a particular segment of society is proclaimed as cultural life.

It is more than interesting that the account of the *Aims and central areas of skills and proficiencies* [in Danish: *Formål og centrale kundskabs- og færdighedsområder*] sent out by the Ministry of Education turns out to be an art book, an account of what we can expect of pictorial art. It is thought-provoking that this publication is often referred to as CKF and not as FCKF[7]. The aims *(Formål)* get lost, but we can take comfort from the fact that the recommended curriculum is more dilatory in the contra-intentional sense that it contains elements of painting and self-management. But the tone is unmistakeable. It is clear that all subjects taught in the Danish Public School can be illustrated with pictures; in other words, they can all be aestheticised and culturalised. The most important educational document after the Education Act itself is an aesthetic publication which supports a particular ideal of education, one which in many ways appears antiquated – if it wasn't for the work of the curriculum committee. And aestheticisation chimes in well with the general humanisation of school subjects which we recognise in the leading position of didactics in pedagogic discourse.

THE WILL FOR EDUCATION

As stated, the basic tone implies that everyone wants to educate others and everyone will insist on the significance of education, but there is disagreement about what education is, or wherein it consists.

For the sake of clarity we can draw a *map* of education. In the socio-analytic sense, a map is an attempt to sketch out double relations within which we are forced to orientate ourselves. In continuation of the above we can say, on the one hand, that education stretches between culture ('Danish' values) and civilisation (general European or global norms). This means that the values argued for are at different levels of particularity or universality. But on the other hand one must also take into account how far these values are such as will always be valid (hyper-

---

[7] The Danish Ministry of Education: *Formål og centrale kundskabs- og færdighedsområder*, Copenhagen 1994.

historical) or whether their area of validity, their logical extent can be defined (historical). If we add a second axis to this dichotomy the result is a map with four fields, and these fields can illustrate the contemporary insistence on education, which everyone does not disagree should be cultivated.

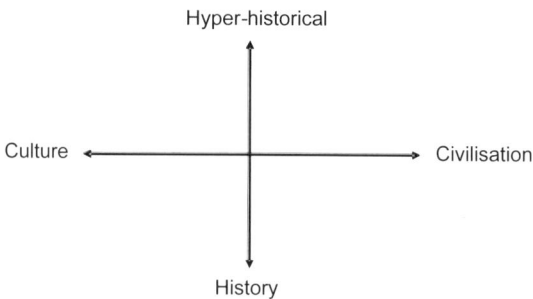

The first field contains cultural values which are thought to be hyper-historical. This is the field of traditional cultivation, symbolically marked in the idea of 'a good home with a piano'. It still exists, with the piano replaced by books on shelves and internet access via a personal computer. Today the educated petty bourgeoisie consists of people who have their internet connection paid for by someone else.

It is these good-tasters who are convinced that the rest of the world will acknowledge their values whenever they come in contact with them. With all their modernity they are classical because they think of themselves and their values as the rightful heirs of classical cultivation.

The second field is a *generalisation* of the first. The values expressed in the first field must be made general not only through cultivation but by the State assuming responsibility for giving the individual a general education to ensure that everyone shares more or less the same taste horizon. The State school system undertakes the task of offering every Danish citizen the knowledge that H. C. Andersen and Søren Kierkegaard were contemporaries, and that Kierkegaard wrote 'Marry and you'll regret it, don't marry and you'll regret it' (under a pseudonym and with a covert reference to Socrates). This is really a matter of the cultivation of taste and of experience, but as a project, not as growing up. Danish young people must learn the difference between Karen Blixen[8] and Susanne Brøgger[9], between Flemming books and comics. We must

---

[8] Karen BLIXEN, *Out of Africa*, 1937.
[9] Susanne BRØGGER, *Deliver Us from Love,* Harvill Press, 1977; *A Fighting Pig's too Tough to Eat*, Norvik Press 1997; *The Jade Cat*, Harvill Press 1999.

therefore form a national canon so that Danish pupils know approximately the same things or hit the same targets when exercising their taste. It is assumed that literacy is still related to literature.

And there are others whose concept of education is what I will call *competence*. In the third field no time is allowed for formative experiences, and what we're left with is a reading list. Here the significance of knowing that Kierkegaard and Andersen were contemporaries and that Kierkegaard said interesting things turns into something else – a curriculum: pragmatic knowledge which it is good to have when you meet your foreign business partners. If it's expedient, let me take a course in dinner-table management and general etiquette. Education becomes a caricature of itself, something acquired programmatically: one has education so that one's labour can be used on the job market. In itself this is a perfectly reasonable aim; but it's a totally different idea of education.

Finally we have the fourth field, which I will call untraditional education. Here it is accepted that self-cultivation is the new conditions for education, that the labour force is made up of individuals and that it is difficult to enforce uniform standards, etc. What the teacher wants and what the pupils want need not be identical: in fact, the teacher will have to teach the pupils something that the teacher does not already know. Unlike the traditional pedantic pedagogue, we realise the importance of not really knowing what we're supposed to teach the young. At the same time, we can only teach them anything at all if they assume that we know what they're supposed to learn. However, this ambivalence means that the education system must be a little more leaned back in its proposals for training programmes.

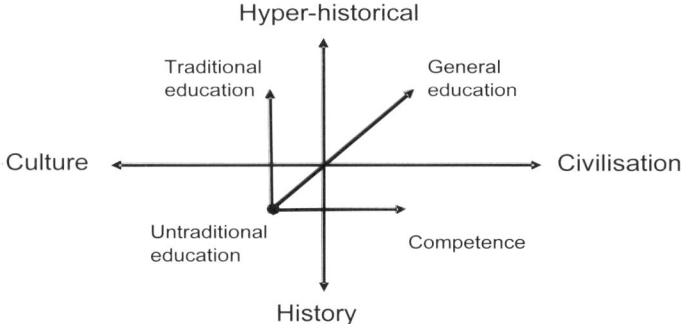

We haven't completely found out what is necessary to satisfy the modern need for education, so all parties attempt to push through their own concept as the one that fits the case. Everyone (i.e. the proponents of traditional education, universal education and competence) wants to translate education to their own familiar concept; but no-one, apparently, makes any attempt to grasp what education should be under contemporary conditions. The consequence is that we are faced with forms of education which correspond to the three first fields: life-form education, literary education and education in market or competitive skills.

But a present-day form of self-cultivation cannot be a traditional education. It cannot be the universal expanding of the education of the traditional cultivated classes, spreading from a group to being a national education and further to a general state education, nor can it be an attempt to live up to the demands of the modern market. All the same, that's the direction that should be taken; and here we must suggest that it is not possible to think about education solely in terms of the practical/artistic dimension.

It is necessary to understand what education for the new age should contain, but at present this will require an effort of translation since we do not possess an education strategy which is in contact and on a level with the educational horizon of the new age – with what we called, above, self-cultivation.

UNTRADITIONAL EDUCATION

In using the category 'untraditional education' I am not aiming at an anti-traditional model, nor at one which is critical of the system, but at one with features which are markedly different to those of traditional education. It is not necessarily of general validity because of its curriculum, the canon it refers to or a prescribed syllabus, nor that it teaches competence. Untraditional education must insist on being educative in accordance with an idea of education. This is not to pay tribute to the idea that in our century education is as blue blood to the aristocracy and money to the bourgeoisie; it represents not nature, not riches, but opportunities for development. It is important that an untraditional education should still be a cultivation of taste, developing the determination to decline what is perceived as unacceptable, which is the same as formative experience.

To get closer to this element we must look for the experiential dimensions which in other contexts we have drawn up as a four-fold figure[10], comprising orientation towards, respectively: the other; the others; my own other; each other (in the sense of general otherness or foreignness as such). And correspondingly, in the history of ideas the great tra-

---

[10] L.-H. SCHMIDT, *Diagnosis I*, DPI, 1999, Chap. 1.

ditions of the western world can be described as historically specific explorations of these speculative systematic dimensions.

The other	Christianity
The others	Humanism
My other	Enlightenment
Each other	Culturalism

In the human experience of abandonment, in powerlessness, one turns to something greater than oneself, perhaps to a Father Creator or a Mother Nature, but in any case to an external power which one knows to be beyond one's control and which marks one's lack of self-reliance. I stand by virtue of the other, not by virtue of myself. This absence of sovereignty is also apparent in the next stage, when I understand that I do not only depend upon the other but also on others, concrete others, and that the other person could in principle be Jesus, in fact actually is Jesus in the shape of our neighbour. With this we have moved from Christianity to humanism, and without creating an opposition, which is important in our tradition. Next we notice that there is something within us over which we are not master but which is in a way master over us. We also experience a dependence on an internal drive, a dependence on 'my other'; a share in the human condition which implies that I am not supreme but must abide by specific laws. Finally there are rules for our dealings with each other, with the general stranger, which give rise to a discussion of values and of cultural differences; my respect for difference is the modern form of reflection we call culturalism. In modern society, culturalism bears the same relation to enlightenment as humanism does to Christianity in classical society; but the accumulation of great traditions cannot be ignored in any education programme of contemporary relevance. Experience is thus experience of one's own powerlessness, the realisation that one is not supreme but that one can strive to be less un-self-reliant.

So where do we find this *modern* experience expressed? In the modern humanities which have taken an interest in this. Access to the other is textual; access to the others is psychological; access to my other is cultural; and access to each other is social.

In the 20th century the humanities have attempted to comprehend anew this experiential horizon, and untraditional education must get to grips with these new ways of reflecting, just as one gets to grips with other fields of knowledge. One compensates for the new learning structure by constructing interdisciplinary subjects and by organising education as teamwork, but the very concept of learning must change so that we do not go on thinking about it as if it were what we are already familiar with – traditional education which reproduces taste.

My third thesis is therefore that *a new professionalism has arisen which must be expressed in a new approach to the content of education.* The figure below shows how this professional approach can be organised:

text	Discourse analysis
psychology	Psychoanalysis
culture	Social anthropology
society	Social philosophy

Through the lens of the new professionalism it becomes apparent that new insights are created by other disciplines than those we usually take into account: discourse analysis, a form of general textual analysis whose object is a generalised concept of text; psychoanalysis, which attempts to understand the way to others by means of an understanding of the psyche; and social anthropology, which appears to be the gateway to my other by studying the outward manifestation which both sets the conditions for it and exhibits it, so that I can relate to my own inner world through the outer world. And finally there is social philosophy, which teaches me how we can relate to relating to each other.

It is necessary for schools today to understand the need to put the great traditional areas of knowledge into a new framework and get them to function as part of a curriculum. The same is the case with all other professional areas, all the areas which schools have left untouched because an antiquated idea of education has been held onto.

First and foremost, this implies a break with the idea that Scripture and Danish – with History as the connecting link – are the essential educating subjects; it implies gaining the insight that *all* subjects are *also* a source of cultivation. Underlying these two dimensions is the idea of the greater general culture (tendentiously, a civilisation) to which we are connected on the one side and our own specific culture on the other. With this, we have succeeded in getting out of the 'mission culture'.

COMMUNITY

By means of untraditional education schools can and must cultivate both the collective and the individual; but primarily it is the schools' obligation to ensure that no opposition is felt between these two dimensions in everyday experience. This federalism is part of a modern professional approach, and should not be entrusted to specific school subjects. It is of course necessary to organise it in terms of the subjects on the curriculum, with an eye to how they should be taught, but federalism – absence of supremacy, the experience of powerlessness – is decisive, because it opens the way for otherness, for everyone to pull together, or whatever phrases are available to express this idea. But in a way all subjects can express it.

This gives rise to my fourth thesis: in schools, as in other places, it is necessary to make use of procedures and subjects, aims, knowledge and skills which can establish a transcendence of individuality guaranteed by individuality and an individuality- transcending guarantee of individuality.

We recognise this from our rituals, of which a meal is the best example. Here it is not enough to focus on gratifying one sense but to orchestrate a medley of sensual input. Domestic science is the most misunderstood subject in the Danish school system. It is no longer (or not primarily) an education in domestic hygiene, training the little ones in the hygienic use of the dishcloth and the wholesome and economical administration of the household budget. It is probably the cultural subject par excellence; because the senses are its gateway.

And this is what sensual experience can achieve: because we can experience the same things, but not in the same way. This is our experience of powerlessness, in which everyone else is also powerless; but in an ensemble of powerlessness each one of us can become less powerless. Powerlessness is simply the gateway to other people. The principle is simple: my enjoyment is the other's enjoyment too, and I have to ask myself: what can I do well for you so I can do better for myself? In other words: the least poor thing I can do is to take responsibility that you are given the opportunity to do your best.

For the same reason I am deeply sceptical about the great amount of focus in modern educational thinking on how much people are capable of. My right to success, elitism at all levels, and other versions of the Danish success pedagogics. As long as power is the educational parameter which weighs heaviest and not the powerlessness which I am opting for here, the gateway to the other will remain elusive, and we will not find the will to invite the other in except on the miserable pretext that I need an extra in my show.

EDUCATING FOR DEMOCRACY:
ADAPTATION OR POLITICAL AWARENESS?

Kurt NIELSEN & Anne-Marie EGGERT OLSEN
(School of Education, Aarhus University,
Campus: Copenhagen, Denmark)

The study of upbringing for democracy is faced with a problem at the outset: to which general category does the issue belong[1]?

'Political upbringing' *('Politische Erziehung')* seems excluded due to its negative associations with the notion of a particular political system being regarded as given and unquestionable. 'Upbringing for democracy' or 'democratic upbringing' seem free of these kinds of associations. On the contrary, they deal with something worth pursuing, a positive regulative norm of educational activity.

But is democracy not political? And is upbringing for democracy not to be regarded as political upbringing? Perhaps the problem is with 'upbringing' *('Erziehung')* and not at all with 'political'? When you can talk about 'democratic upbringing' *('demokratische Erziehung')* without any associations to political indoctrination, the reason may be the positive modification of upbringing *('Erziehung')* by the addition of 'democratic'?

If 'upbringing' is substituted by 'formation' *('Bildung')*, it becomes a different matter entirely. 'Political formation' *('politische Bildung')* is not different from 'democratic formation' in connotative value. The question is rather whether a distinction can be made at all, i.e. whether

---

[1] The conceptual frame of reference of this article is the distinction between *'Bildung'* und *'Erziehung'* which is as fundamental in Danish as it is in German. In order to present our case, we revert to the emergency solution of quoting the German terms in the first paragraph. In the rest of the paper, 'formation' is used as a translation for *'Bildung'* and 'upbringing' for *'Erziehung'*. 'Education', consequently, has to serve the double function of referring to 'upbringing' as well as to 'formation', and the precise significance must be derived from the context. Finally, the term 'pedagogy' is used in the sense of the profession or discipline of education.

political formation – in contradistinction to political knowledge, craft, or flair – can be conceived as anything but 'democratic formation'. Political formation must at least include some experience of participation solely obtainable under democratic conditions[2].

At the same time it might be suspected that it is the concept of formation that has a certain impact on and modifies the term 'political'. Like democracy, formation is basically good; 'undemocratic' and 'uneducated' are indisputably negative terms.

But if 'democratic' in combination with upbringing has a potential that 'political' lacks, what is then the matter with the political? And if 'formation' in combination with the political has a potential that 'upbringing' has not, what is then the matter with upbringing? Or is it rather the case that the very concepts of democracy and formation have become ideological, merely expressing 'All is well!'?

In any case, there are some indications that the connection between politics and formation is as complex – and precarious – as ever and very difficult to articulate impartially. Many therefore choose other terminological solutions to the problem. The concept of formation *('Bildung')* is abandoned in favour of 'learning' and 'competence'; and efforts are made to articulate democracy as common value, ethos, and social structure rather than as a form of state and government.

These solutions to the problem are understandable, but also useless. First of all, the original issue of the relation between education and politics is left unchallenged. Secondly, abandoning this traditional educational-philosophical concept complex hinders reflection upon those parts of reality that actually articulate themselves and their activities within these traditional categories; they become incomprehensible on their own terms – and as such cannot be subjected to immanent critique. Finally, the question arises as to whether renouncing the traditional political and theoretical educational concepts, despite their problematic devaluation, means renouncing the truth content they hold historically?

Another approach is therefore preferable: Addressing rather than evading these traditional categories and asking what upbringing for democracy might be as a specification of political formation *('Bildung')*?

---

[2] From a historical point of view, political formation is of course often obtained through oppositional or directly revolutionary activity, i.e. perhaps not under actual democratic conditions, but at least through the struggle to achieve them.

UPBRINGING OR FORMATION?

In general, talking about political formation is a complicated matter because of the indefiniteness which characterises the very concept of formation. Like any other concept of central historical influence it has absorbed many different meanings. One stable meaning, however, is that formation has to do with development and transgression, but the determination of the form and content of the process has varied throughout history.

The concept of formation itself is a result of interpretations and as such is open to new ones. Also, it must be continually reinterpreted, as it precisely aims at grasping an ongoing and open transformation process. Consequently, the concept of political formation must be understood in the same way if it is viewed as a specific form of formation.

Interpretations of political formation traditionally adopt the following general perspective: Political formation is about a normative orientation in which formation is related to political ideals such as participation, co-determination, and solidarity. These ideals function as regulative ideas, i.e. as norms orientating the process of formation, and as the dynamic force of the process of formation. The aim is to produce a political subject, and formation is therefore viewed as the formation of character or attitude.

Lately, another perspective has entered into the educational discourse. According to this, political formation is conceived of as observation and identification of a given political system. Political formation is consequently determined solely by its function, which may neutrally be defined as 'learning to arrange oneself with others'.

The question of upbringing for democracy as it is viewed from the general perspective will be dealt with first; later on we shall comment critically on the second perspective.

When political formation is examined in a specifically educational context, the impression given is that the educational reflection has been seduced by the democratic project of modernity. This project seems to be grasped in such a way that it automatically points out the direction of democratic formation. An example of this is found in the pamphlet *The School of the Community. The Danish Folkeskole*[3] – *society's most important institution* (The Danish Union of Teachers, 2000), which states the following:

---

[3] The Danish *Folkeskole* (the primary and lower secondary school).

> Among the features of the Danish democracy are:
> that everyone is guaranteed basic knowledge
> that you learn how to acquire knowledge
> that you are able to assess statements and information critically
> that we subscribe to the idea of equal opportunities for all
> that we respect other people and their opinions.

The pamphlet thus expresses normative expectations and a clearly stated connection between the *Folkeskole* and democracy. Standards relating to learning, such as knowledge, acquisition of knowledge and a critical attitude towards statements and information, are directly combined with the political norms of equality and tolerance and are declared to be the essential elements of Danish democracy in particular. Schooling and educating for democracy become two sides of the same coin.

Schooling in democracy is one of the aims of the Danish *Folkeskole*, as stated in the object clause of the Primary Education Act:

> The school shall prepare the pupils for active participation, joint responsibility, rights and duties in a society based on freedom and democracy. The teaching of the school and its daily life must therefore build on intellectual freedom, equality and democracy. (Consolidation Act n° 1195, 30th November 2006, § 1 stk.3.)

It is clearly the aim that a democratic ethos should be developed in the pupil. The goal of "[preparing] the pupils for participation, joint responsibility, rights, and duties in a democratic society" means that a task of political upbringing has been imposed on the school. Upbringing presupposes an authority that is able to legitimise the heteronomy involved in the process of upbringing, just as it is implicit in the concept of upbringing that it is an intentional act oriented by a *telos*, in casu participation, joint responsibility, rights and duties in a society based on freedom and democracy. This is a declaration of a clear objective as far as the development of the pupils is concerned. On this background the process of upbringing can be regarded as a process of political upbringing, aimed at producing a political subject with certain political attitudes.

The task of political upbringing, to prepare the pupils for democracy, may of course be formative, but upbringing and formation are not identical. Formation, first and foremost, is inextricably linked to individual development as something which is acquired *by* the individual himself. Formation cannot be imposed by an external authority; it is indefinite and a process as well as a product: An open-ended transformation process, not a continuous progression towards a specific goal. Formation is a disinterested effort, in so far as it has no object outside itself.

Since the task of upbringing is not only prevalent in the self-understanding of the Folkeskole but is a matter of legislation, a reflection on the concepts of upbringing and formation within a normative context is necessary. It is not easy to evade a closer examination of political upbringing.

DEMOCRATIC UPBRINGING AND POLITICAL FORMATION?

It is therefore necessary to distinguish between upbringing and formation. Political formation is not identical with political upbringing; democratic formation is not identical with democratic upbringing.

This does not mean that these concepts (upbringing vs. formation) are clearly defined beforehand and that it is a matter of course to distinguish. It must always be kept in mind, as expressed by Giesecke, "dass es über eine so wichtige gesellschaftliche praxis wie die Erziehung – und besonders die politische Erziehung – wohl immer dominante, aber keineswegs einheitliche Vorstellungen gibt." (Giesecke 1976, p. 15). The same might certainly be said about political formation. It involves concepts that are not only ambiguous, but which cannot even be defined *per se*, as they cannot be analysed from a privileged and neutral position. The context of our examination, therefore, will be Giesecke's interesting interpretation, *Didaktik der politischen Bildung* (1976).

From the outset a series of conceptual differentiations presents itself. Giesecke speaks of *'politisch-pädagogische Theorie'*, *'politische Erziehung'* and *'politische Bildung'*, *'demokratische Erziehung'* and *'demokratische Schulbildung'* (Giesecke 1976, pp. 15 ff). Among these *'demokratische Erziehung'* and *'demokratische Schulbildung'* at first glance seem most precise, covering democratic upbringing and formation in the specific context of school. In this context, democratic upbringing is a legislative obligation that also defines the intention of upbringing. But upbringing is paradoxical in demanding that the pupil is led to autonomy through heteronomy. The pupil is supposed to be in a 'not yet' position from which he is to be moved by the pedagogical activity of the teacher. Sooner or later the process of upbringing must come to an end.

Contrary to this, formation is a process which cannot be intentionally directed from outside, and political formation *('politische Bildung')* is normally not thought of as oriented by legislation. Traditionally, the educational discourse distinguishes between those two descriptions on the basis of age criteria. Hence, democratic upbringing is understood to concern upbringing in relation to young children and young pupils in schools. Political formation concerns a wider and ongoing project of formation. The political formation of adults is their own concern and takes place both within and outside of institutions, and it is an open question whether it ever stops. However, it is a less open question where political formation begins, and undoubtedly democratic pedagogy *('demokratische Pädagogik')* is a relevant concept.

Even though Giesecke distinguishes in the traditional way mentioned above, he still talks of democratic *formation ('Bildung')* in the context of schools, and it is no simple task to make consistent distinctions between upbringing and formation. This is emphatically clear in relation to the concept of democratic upbringing.

One problem, as noted above, arises from the combination of democracy and upbringing. *Qua upbringing* democratic upbringing must bring something to the pupils, and bring them somewhere; *qua democratic*, however, upbringing cannot claim to realise fixed and unquestionable aims, because democracy presupposes dissent. A democratic upbringing, therefore, cannot insist on and be conceived from a privileged position; it cannot be sustained by referring to a given and accepted truth, but rather by allowing dissent. This must also hold true for democratic upbringing in schools. Democratic pedagogy cannot be a matter of developing competences that tend to abolish dissent; rather, the aim must be to develop competences for handling and living with dissent. The idea of a *democratic* pedagogy challenges precisely the feature which separates upbringing from formation: That it is an intentional, heteronomous, and goal-oriented process within a pedagogical, i.e. asymmetrical relationship.

Another problem is that during the last 10-20 years the concept of upbringing as such has been radically challenged as a relevant educational concept. It is stated that it is no longer possible to act with upbringing authority, and that the teacher neither can nor shall be responsible for actions in relation to the upbringing. This view does not necessarily entail that political formation processes cannot take place in schools. However, they are different from upbringing processes in that they are self-determined processes that cannot be externally regulated or controlled. They must rather be seen as reflective self-transformation processes without predetermined purposes. Formation processes cannot be instrumentalised by or subordinated to the upbringing authority. This, again, does not mean that there is no room for them in schools. But one of the current issues in educational discourse is whether something can still be referred to as an upbringing project and consequently, whether democratic pedagogy still exists.

These problems indicate that democratic upbringing is an interesting, and contradictory, issue. Neither from a political philosophical nor from an educational theoretical point of view is the democratic upbringing project of the *Folkeskole* an indisputable project.

DEMOCRATIC UPBRINGING OR UPBRINGING *FOR* DEMOCRACY?

If we maintain the traditional distinction between upbringing and formation, which is justified in so far as the distinction is of real impact, we might say that the task of schools is democratic *upbringing*, understood as a specification of political upbringing, and that it implies a use of an external authority not immediately compatible with the idea of political *formation*. However, the considerations and problems mentioned above demonstrate the need for conceptual precision and for further differentiations between the terms 'democratic' and 'political'.

Giesecke is inconsistent in his use of democratic upbringing and political formation in the context of schools. The inconsistency continues in his definition of the task of schools in general as *learning* and not as upbringing or formation. The concept of learning is only vaguely defined in educational theory; it has no clear delimitation in relation to upbringing and formation and this lack of clarity also applies in discussion of political formation.

Giesecke does not question democratic upbringing, but neither does he regard upbringing for democracy as a pedagogical task. This may sound surprising but the reason is that pedagogy in general must not be a mediator of particular interests. The aim of pedagogy is not to transfer specific notions to the pupils. Giesecke expresses it this way: "The task of a democratic pedagogy that is committed to the process of emancipation, is the strengthening of the individuals' ego, widening their experiences, assistance in orienting towards the tasks of life, and this is not the transmission of pre-defined opinions, ideas, intentions, and interests." (Giesecke 1967, quoted from Tønnessen 1992, pp. 413-414, our translation.) A superior subject with a determining function in relation to the pupil is downright incompatible with democratic upbringing.

It is obvious how the idea of a democratic upbringing so to speak clashes with the idea of upbringing *for* democracy. A democratic upbringing, in the sense of an upbringing that is in itself democratic, excludes upbringing *for* democracy, in the sense of upbringing for particular political norms and for a particular political system.

At the same time it is obvious how precisely the democratisation of upbringing has been a decisive factor in the rejection of the traditional understanding of upbringing; a 'democratic' upbringing seems to adopt essential features of formation.

But it can also be seen that the concepts 'democratic' and 'political' become obscure. Even if 'democratic' signifies a specification of the political in general, the use of 'democratic' in connection with upbringing expresses almost the opposite: Democratic upbringing signifies precisely an upbringing that is *not* specifically political, while 'political upbringing' signifies an upbringing that *is* specifically political.

POLITICAL OR DEMOCRATIC FORMATION?

What if the point of departure is taken in the concept of political formation? According to Giesecke, formation neither can nor shall be neutral. It must take sides, but it must not become totalitarian. What then could be the foundation of political formation if it is to meet this demand?

Giesecke replies that the foundation of political formation must be the constitution. From here he deduces participation as the most important purpose of political formation. In contrast to the citizenship upbringing of the inter-war period, political formation is not grasped as an exclusive relationship between state and individual. Participation is not restricted to this relationship alone, i.e. formal influence by vote, but includes social conditions in general. Reflecting the democratic-political, the distinction between state and society in its classical form must be abandoned as a delimitation of the political, because politics are no longer to be seen just as affairs of state. Through democratisation as well as through the acknowledgement of the political nature of economy it has become a matter of social affairs. The politicization of society, according to Giesecke, must be included in the conception of political formation.

The constitutional foundation of political formation may thus be understood in the sense that every citizen has the right to participate in the development of society. And this implies that everybody must have the possibility to acquire the knowledge and skills needed for participation. Formally, Giesecke's concept of political formation may be defined as the capacity to fulfil the duties and rights of citizenship. But there is no such thing as political formation in general; it will always vary according to the constitution and social system. Giesecke does not, however, only deal with democratic society in general, but rather a specific one. His thinking is situated within the horizon common to western countries of a national state with a territorially demarcated population. What make up the foundation of political formation are the constitutionally guaranteed personal rights. It is as a consequence of those rights that political formation includes everyone and that the ideal of political formation is constituted by the idea of the citizens' participation in public affairs.

This is almost identical to the idea expressed in the *Education Act* and the self-understanding of the Danish Union of Teachers.

DEMOCRATIC FORMATION OR POLITICAL UPBRINGING?

If political formation is in itself the expression of something political, political formation is not just a question of participation and of participating as much as possible; it also has to deal with the question of the purpose of participation. Giesecke pays attention to this aspect and agrees with Habermas when he criticizes political participation as a political and educational value in itself. (Giesecke 1976)

The emphasis on the need to reflect on the purpose of political participation marks a break with a conception of political formation rooted in the neo-idealistic idea of formation. This regarded formation as based on the idea of the ideal state: political formation meant to understand and orient oneself towards this ideal state. It did not include a critical approach to the empirically existing state, and to an even lesser degree, a perspective of change. The orientation towards the ideal state placed the individual as an object of the interests of the state, and by ignoring the opposition between the ideal and the real the neo-idealistic formation became affirmative of the existing power structure. It has therefore justifiably been criticized for not being formative, but being downright adaptive.

With the accentuation of the constitutionally guaranteed participation as something fundamental to political formation, this situation is changed. In the first place, the individual is no longer seen as merely subordinated by the state, and government is to a higher degree regarded as dependent upon the citizens' political outlooks. In the second place, the focus is no longer one-sidedly on the state and the idea of government embodied in the superior and formal provisions of the constitution, but also on society as a whole. Political formation implies more than constitutional rights and includes therefore the realisation of its ideals of freedom and equality in formation. Even if all citizens have the same constitutional rights, their potential for utilizing them depends upon their socio-economic position. Consequently, Giesecke maintains that political formation has to be joined with an emancipatory perspective and that political conflicts can no longer be excluded from the perspective of political formation.

In this Giesecke confirms the proposition that political formation expresses political activity, and that it has to do with values. From his position within critical theory Giesecke is of course unable to give any positive definition of political formation; critical theory demonstrates its normativity negatively, in reaction to specific, existing power structures. Thus, Adorno writes under the heading *'Fiktion positiver Freiheit'*: *"Freiheit ist einzig in bestimmter Negation zu fassen, gemäss der konkreten Gestalt von Unfreiheit."* (Adorno 1975, p. 230). Political formation in a critical-theoretical perspective must be considered on the basis of a critical and historical examination of what actually furthers or prevents emancipation. By such specific revelation of the democratic potential of different social groups, critical theory revolts against a formal and ideal notion of political formation. This critical focus on specific social conditions means a radically different concept of political formation. The emancipatory perspective makes the citizen a political subject whose actions are directed towards a change in the power structure of existing society, and it becomes clear that the definition of political formation is in itself a political matter.

A DEMOCRATIC STATE OR A DEMOCRATIC SOCIETY?

Taken at face value it would seem that the provisions of the *Education Act* and the Danish Union of Teachers' understanding (to prepare the pupils for a democratic society) are identical with Giesecke's notion of political formation based on constitutional rights. But it would indeed be somewhat peculiar if the Danish legislation and the official statements of the teachers' union were in full agreement with a Marx-inspired critical theory of society.

And the differences are easily singled out. Giesecke distinguishes clearly between, on the one hand, a state or constitution that formally guarantees political participation and, on the other hand, a society which is not only far from realising equal participation but even directly prevents it by its basic proprietary principles. The state may be democratic, but society certainly is not. Against this the *Education Act* stipulates 'a society based on freedom and democracy', and the Union of Teachers declares unconcernedly and indefinitely that 'Danish democracy' comprises a set of democratic conditions and values. The basic premise here is that a democratic society is already in existence. Freedom and participation are awaiting the pupil who just has to be 'prepared' for the use of it.

From a critical-theoretical point of view one of the essential things that political formation comprises is an awareness of the discrepancy between the formal right of participation and the actual lack of freedom in society. This is very far from the idea of a 'preparation' for an already existing, allegedly democratic society through a democratic school based on intellectual freedom and equality. The following critical questions must therefore be raised:

Is the *Act*'s expression 'prepare' merely a sophisticated evasion of the complex problems concerning upbringing and formation, or might it also be seen as a euphemism for the function of schools to adapt the future citizen to the form of society already in existence?

How is the *Folkeskole*, 'society's most important institution', to meet the accusation of exercising political upbringing in the sense of mere adaptation, if it presupposes that democratic society is realised and democracy is indisputable, and hereby excludes political consciousness and criticism of democracy from political formation?

Are we, after all, faced with not politically consciousness-raising democratic formation, but politically guided upbringing for democracy?

While the neo-idealistically inspired theory of formation could be blamed for not taking social conditions into account in the understanding of politics and for focusing on the state aspect, one might question whether the democratic self-understanding of today – for good reason, perhaps – is not somewhat unclear as to the distinction between state and society. This is not just a theoretical source of irritation. It is a problem for democracy that 'democratic' through conceptual – but not least real – mingling of state and society has become applicable to almost every human activity and relationship. If democracy – in its self-understanding – becomes a matter of course, it not only turns repressive and ideological, it also becomes extremely vulnerable.

As a starting point it is obvious and generally acknowledged that democracy signifies two things: A type of constitution and a form of common life, i.e. a type of society or social system. Consequently a distinction must be made between, on the one hand, a democratic *state* that by its constitution guarantees the citizens civic rights such as freedom of speech and assembly, and political participation through universal suffrage, and on the other hand, a democratic *society* in which social conditions are characterised by freedom, equality in welfare, tolerance, solidarity, etc.

This distinction, however, is not just a form-matter distinction. What makes a state democratic is not just something formal, but something material as well. And what makes a society democratic is not just something material, but something formal as well.

Hence political democracy is not guaranteed exclusively by a formally democratic constitution and a general social acceptance of democratic values. A democratic constitution will normally commit itself to observing a series of democratic principles as well as to actively securing and furthering democracy as a social system. This means that in a democratic state there are matters – often as part of commitments to international conventions – which are necessarily subject to legislation.

Likewise, a society is not just democratic by virtue of democratic (life) values. A democratic society is not and cannot be a private initiative or individual enterprise. It must be secured and furthered through governmental rule of civil life. This, in contradistinction, means that in a democratic society there are things that are not subject to legislation.

Still, in common everyday speech 'democracy' and 'democratic' mean something else, namely in general a procedure of decision making. A procedure is democratic when it has comprised information and consulting, open discussion, and a decision by vote. In the ideal of a democratic resolution as an informed majority vote we most clearly see the intermingling of the formal and informal, legislative and social-conventional elements of democracy. The informal or material elements, information, hearing, and discussion must be secured by formal rules or laws. The formal vote must rely on good customs such as respect of knowledge or facts and sympathetic response to objections in order to be informed.

It is to a great extent democracy in this sense that is at work in the case of upbringing for democracy and democratic upbringing. The attitudes and abilities to be developed in the pupil are mainly those that make him capable of partaking in this procedure, the democratic decision process.

It is, however, exactly this understanding of democracy that has been criticised as long as democracy has existed as a form of government. The critique has been twofold: that a decision is not necessarily right just because it is sanctioned by a majority, and that the rule of a majority over a minority is only in practice, not in principle a less dictatorial type of rule. In addition to this more recent critique points out that democracy presupposes a social structure characterised by conflicting interests, and thus as a constitutional form simply sanctions an 'undemocratic' social reality. The possibility of a democratic constitution to implement its own values, e.g. liberty, equality, co-determination, etc., is annulled in advance because of the very preconditions of democracy.

There may of course be much truth in the notion of democracy as the least bad form of rule. The problems arise when the least bad type of rule becomes self-evident as the indisputable basis of political formation, and when democracy in the shape of democratic procedure is postulated as the actual decisive power of society.

Thereby democracy becomes, in the first place, ideological. From the critical-theoretical perspective it is simply not true that society rests on democracy. The decisive, determinative societal mechanisms are not political-democratically constituted and basically they evade political-democratic influence. Democracy rests on society, not the other way around. This is confirmed in so far as the political self-understanding globally as well as locally usually expresses itself cynically and resignedly as 'democratic control of development', 'changing the course of development', etc.

In the second place, democracy becomes fragile and vulnerable when it is universalized and taken for granted. On one hand, it betrays its own ideal of tolerance by not acknowledging non-democratic points of view as political. On the other hand, it becomes inattentive to real, internal as well as external, threats against democracy. If the democratic self-understanding assumes the formal liberty and participation implicit in the democratic constitution as actually and substantially implemented in society, the door is open for the progress of antidemocratic ideals – in a fully legal and democratic way.

The task of political upbringing of the *Folkeskole* is of course committed to the constitution. But this commitment has a double perspective: It has to prepare the pupil for the political conditions of democratic rule and the rights and duties following from legislation. But it also has to make the pupil conscious of the fact that the constitutional ideals are political norms, not automatically societal realities. This will inevitably include making him conscious of the fact that a constitutional, democratic rule and decision process does not automatically lead to actual liberty and participation for the individual. If he belongs to the minority, his democratic prospect is to be outvoted all the time. If there is no awareness of this prospect through a critical understanding of the idea and limitation of democracy, it is no wonder that many make use of their democratic right of non-participation in political life or attack the democratic system directly.

When democracy is understood in the broader sense of a societal ethos rather than as a formalised political system, the task of the school may be regarded as a matter of formation rather than of upbringing. Precisely the democratic perspective seems to guarantee that an adaptation to a specific political object, i.e. a political upbringing, is out of the question, and that the task is one of open-ended democratic opinion formation.

This kind of understanding is clearly expressed within the movement of *Education of Deliberative Democratic Citizens* (Eddemcit), for instance as follows:

> Eddemcit cannot exclusively be identified with specific ends or with the education of children and young people as future citizens, that is educating them for a specific vocation, or developing specific intellectual capacities. Eddemcit cannot be used to transmit specific ethical, social, political, religious knowledge and values in order to teach children and young people certain commitment or loyalty to, or appreciation for, specific narratives, practices and traditions or for specific democratic institutions as currently organised. Such understanding is teleological, strategic, and therefore not open-ended, contingent or oriented towards understanding. (Roth 2000, p. 144.)

It is very hard to establish the concept of democracy at work in this context. At first it is stated that the task of Eddemcit is – albeit not exclusively – to educate children and young people as future citizens. This is seen as an education for a specific profession, and the guarantee that Eddemcit has a broader aim does not alter this. Furthermore it is stated, negatively, that the aim of Eddemcit is not to further specific values, including political values. A consequence of this is the exclusion of democratic values from the perspective of Eddemcit, and it is explicitly stated as well, that Eddemcit has no intention of developing preferences for "specific democratic institutions as currently organized".

The citizen is here seen primarily as member of society rather than as citizen in the strictly political sense of the word, and democracy holds no privileged position, neither normatively nor institutionally. The reason why the movement still claims to stand for democracy is to be found in the almost insignificant first 'd' of the abbreviation Eddemcit: What legitimates the use of 'democratic' is the understanding of democracy as a decision process, as 'deliberative'.

However, if democracy is more than a question of legal citizenship and civil rights, if it is a social matter, too, it does not mean that everything in society must be brought about through democratic procedures. By making democratic decisions the ideal of all political and societal participation, the majority decision is adopted as the one and only respectable one.

POLITICAL FORMATION AND CRITIQUE

Critical theory has been criticised for being founded on a 'superior knowledge'; its emancipatory perspective should allegedly operate with an implicit normativity concerning what is good for society and for the individual. It is not surprising that critical theory's concept of political formation meets with opposition. This is to be expected, because formation and normativity are traditionally connected. There is, however, reason to examine the most important premises of the critique. In this context focus will be placed on the critique that has been stated by systems theory. This critique is particularly interesting as it presents a break with normativity as such as constitutive of political formation.

We find a concentrated expression of this in Lenzen, explaining why critical pedagogy in general has lost its influence. The reason *"lag im Wesentlichen daran, dass innerhalb wie ausserhalb der Wissenschaften der Glaube (!) daran verloren gegangen ist, man könne Welt von einem einzigen Punkt aus sowohl analysieren als auch normativ steuern. Der Verlust hatte nun aber weniger damit zu tun, das dieses für nicht machbar gehalten wurde, sondern vielmehr damit, dass ein solcher Anspruch für nicht mehr legitim gehalten wurde. Denn wer schützt die potentiellen Opfer einer noch so gut gemeinten Weltverbesserungstheorie vor deren Folgen, wie sie an vielen Stellen der Welt in vielen sich selbst gerade als Erziehungsstaaten verstehenden Gesellschaften zu beobachten waren?"* (Lenzen 1999, p. 146).

This criticism may touch on some positions that have passed as critical pedagogy, but is far from challenging the perspective of critical theory. In philosophy the notion that reality could be analysed and judged from a transcendental, Archimedean position outside the world, was abandoned with Kant. In so far as it is upheld in the positivistic understanding of certain sciences, the critique of it has been almost constitutive of *Critical Theory* (cf. Horkheimer, *Traditionelle und kritische Theorie*, 1937).

It is a distinctive mark of critical-theoretical examinations that the theory itself, put simply, is a part of what is to be examined. Thus, critical theory does not only denote thinking that is critical of its subject matter, but also thinking that is conscious of its own conditions and presuppositions, that is, a self-critical theory.

The notion that a pedagogy that understands itself as critical-theoretical should claim to conceive political formation from a theoretically and normatively privileged position is out of the question. Giesecke is an excellent example of this.

Lenzen is right in pointing that the critical-theoretical perspective does not see itself as neutral. There are in general no neutral positions in science and philosophy: This is precisely what makes the self-reflection of theory necessary. As a consequence, critical theory develops the idea of immanent critique, i.e. the demonstration of contradictions in the subject matter, and moreover expresses itself negatively, i.e. in relation to concrete, historical instances of oppression, suffering, and need. Lenzen solves the problem by simply denying the normativity of normativity.

The dissociation from normativity implicit in systems theory marks a clear cut with a traditional understanding of political formation. Traditionally, formation is seen as a superior category of orientation. This implies that political formation in schools has been regarded as a category that could orient the educational process and in this way contribute to the upholding and development of democracy. The aim of political formation may thus be said to be the development of a political subject.

The relation between the normativity of formation and the development of democracy was as early as 1916 expressed markedly in Dewey's *Democracy and Education*. The notion of such a relation is still characteristic of the various concepts of political formation. "I believe that the institution that is perhaps the most crucial in both the formation and maintenance of democratic communities (through the creation of subjects interpellated through the liberal values and norms of the modern nation) is the institution that is often the least studied in academia: the institution of education." (Mitchell 2003)

Systems theory means a change in the way political formation is conceived. The anthropocentric perspective is abandoned. Focus is no longer on the human being to be formed, but on the social system of education. The idea of a subject, which must be said to be essential to most theories of political formation, is therefore not to be found in systems theory. Here political formation is defined solely by its function, which is to learn to arrange oneself with others (Treml 2000). From a systems-theoretical position, political formation has no project of upbringing or formation. It will merely observe politics without any normative expectations. Furthermore, it does not have a concept of *demos*. The educational system as well as the political system is – *qua* socially differentiated – functional systems without any *demos*. A *demos* is inconceivable within systems theory. There are just different kinds of systems. The individual is a psychic system related to an environment, not part of a *demos*. Therefore, self-determination, a central category in non-systems-theoretical concepts of political formation, is not an object of a formative process. On the contrary, it is seen as a *precondition* of being able to function under the contingent conditions characteristic of our modern society. Quite interestingly, Lenzen ends up postulating an observation perspective that is not transcendent, but neither is it situated within reality in the sense of being engaged and normatively affected. In many ways Lenzen is symptomatic of the apparent de-politicisation of society, theoretically as well as practically, within the last decades. While it is common in practice to regret the lack of participation of citizens in political organisations, of voters in the parties, of parents in schools, of students in university politics, etc., despite the fact that real influence does not always follow from formal, the de-politicisation of theoretical activity is seen as a purely theoretical matter. This neo-positivism is markedly present in systems theory. The relation between science and normativity is of course intricate, and the 20th century has a long tradition of reflecting critically on the issue. The entrance of systems theory to educational theory is, however, specifically paradoxical, because pedagogical practice still conceives of itself as normative and intentional and therefore also as political. From Lenzen's point of view the publication of the Danish Union of Teachers, as well as the preamble of the *Education Act*, are simply nonsensical in their formulation of normative intentions. It may certainly be the case that the *Act* and publication are ideological in ignoring an antagonistic reality, but that it should be downright nonsensical to commit oneself to freedom and democracy and strive to realise these ideals in practice, is theoretically as well as practically unacceptable.

LITERATURE

ADORNO Theodor W., *Negative Dialektik*, Suhrkamp Verlag, Frankfurt am Main 1975.
Fællesskabets skole. Folkeskolen – den vigtigste samfundsinstitution, Danmarks Lærerforening, København 2000.
GIESECKE Hermann, *Didaktik der politischen Bildung*, Juventa Verlag, München 1976.
HORKHEIMER Max, 'Traditionelle und kritische Theorie' (1988), I *Gesammelte Schriften 4*, red. Gunzelin Schmied Noerr, Frankfurt/M 1985-96.
LENZEN Dieter, *Orientierung Erziehungswissenschaft. Was sie kann, was sie will*, Rowohlt, Reinbek bei Hamburg 1999.
Lov nr. 509 af 30. juni 1993 med senere ændringer [Primary Education Act].

MITCHELL Katharyne, *Educating the National Citizen in Neoliberal Times: From the Multicultural Self to the Strategic Cosmopolitan*, Royal Geographical Society (with The Institute of British Geographers) 2003.

ROTH Klas, *Democracy, Education and Citizenship: Towards a Theory on the Education of Deliberative Democratic Citizens*, Stockholm Institute of Education Press, Stockholm 2001.

TØNNESSEN Rolf Th., *Demokratisk dannelse i tysk perspektiv: 20 års diskusjon om Hermann Gieseckes syn på den politiske oppdragelsen*, Rådet for Samfunnsvitenskapelig Forskning, NAVF, Universitetsforlaget, Oslo 1992.

TREML Alfred. K., *Allgemeine Pädagogik: Grundlagen, Handlungsfelder und Perspektiven der Erziehung*, Kohlhammer, Stuttgart 2000.

COSMOPOLITAN COMMITMENT IN EDUCATION

Peter KEMP
(School of Education, Aarhus University,
Campus: Copenhagen, Denmark)

The history of mankind is the history of the development of different cultures, i.e. of the formation of communities of languages in which human beings converse and thereby think communally about what to do, how to organize their lives and how to understand their lives from birth to death. These communities of languages originally arose in connection with hunting and farming communities where inhabitants shared in the hunting and farming (culture means cultivation and the cultivated), in the development of things, in the formation of religious symbols and in the protection of the group against wild animals and other hostile groups by sharing the various tasks among themselves. But all this is based on a long and complicated development of language and other skills, and every child therefore needs a long time to develop its skills and learn how to integrate itself into these communities and not only communicate by body language, but master language and other skills on an equal footing with adults, first as a small child in a family or the suchlike, then as a youth whose education and development nowadays take place increasingly outside the family in schools and clubs, and finally, as a young man or woman, who wants to be educated and developed as an independent individual in a society in which he or she is bestowed not only with rights, but also with obligations.

Becoming a grown-up is not easy for someone who has to go through such a long process to be integrated into such a complicated system as a culture. Since the dawn of time, human beings have therefore developed specific educational methods for teaching children language and other skills. These have become integrated as a natural part of life, but have not necessarily been discussed and/or reflected upon. Handbooks on education are a recent phenomenon, and even now many people participate in the upbringing of children and each other without having learnt the least about education or reflected upon it.

In modern times, moreover, one can meet the opinion that every person educates himself, is responsible for his own education, that each person *sets the terms* for his or her own development since the early childhood, has *acquired* the culture needed and has followed the education that he or she has the ability and inclination to follow. But perhaps such a person only holds this opinion because he has been educated by others to believe that "everyone is the architect of their own fortune". The belief that absolute individualization is the key to success is perhaps a direct result of modern education rather than a necessary prerequisite for "complete" human development.

PLATO AND ARISTOTLE

Pedagogy, i.e. the theory of education, is hardly likely to have been conceived if human professional education and cultural formation could be understood to be purely self-education and self-formation. But one can hold the opinion that once a human being has learnt to master a language in conversation with others and has learnt to practice a profession in society, that formation of the person's personality is completely up to himself and that it is up to himself to find the deeper meaning of existence. This was the idea that the first great figure in European philosophy, Plato, expressed in his dialogues when he let Socrates be an educator in the sense that he guided his interlocutors to themselves find answers to the questions they debated. Thus Socrates appeared as the great guide to man's introspection.

But Plato's successor, Aristotle, was of another opinion, at least as far as concerns ethics or wisdom about the good life. Plato could perhaps be right that the human being was able to elucidate logical and geometrical truths, but Aristotle believed that the practical life in communion with others necessitated the existence of "a wise man" to provide guidance about what good actions are, how to find the middle ground between extremes, e.g. courage between recklessness and cowardice, or what could be considered a just society between mob rule and dictatorship, etc. And it is primarily insight into these things that is needed in education aimed at achieving a rich adult life for oneself and with others. Therefore it is perhaps Aristotle's wise man rather than Plato's Socrates that is the model of the true educator or pedagogue – a term derived from the Greek word *"paidagogos"* meaning "a slave who looked after his master's son" from *pais* (boy) and *agogos* (leader).

JEAN-JACQUES ROUSSEAU

It follows therefore that pedagogy is not only the science of education and development that can be thought of as self-education and self-formation, but also the science of how we are educated and formed through others (nursery school teachers, school teachers, tutors, educators, politicians, opinion makers and others). And even though philosophical reflections on education of children were published as early as the 17th Century, pedagogy did not really become the subject of reflection until the 18th Century when, thanks to Jean-Jacques Rousseau (1712-1778), awareness arose that man's long childhood means that human beings only gradually become capable of performing the skills and understanding the things that adults can understand, yet on the other hand have their own way of seeing, thinking and feeling. Rousseau realizes that a child cannot be understood and treated like a small adult or (as John Locke has supposed) as an incomplete adult, but that it develops through different stages and only gradually becomes able to think and act like an adult. He also becomes aware of the fact that education and formation of girls and boys poses different demands if they are to be allowed to develop freely. Generally, Rousseau claims that although a human being's development depends on its skills and organs and the material conditions under which it grows up and on the influence of many other people upon it, one has to let the individual child develop his or her own possibilities according to his or her "receptiveness" at the different stages of development. He writes about the boy Émile in the second book of his 1762 novel *Emile, or on Education*: "Leave him to himself and watch his actions without speaking, consider what he is doing and how he sets about it[1]".

Rousseau did not want human beings to be brought up to be "alone amongst humans" as it has subsequently been said. In the third book of *Emile* he declares that he is well aware that there is a difference between the natural human being who lives a life in nature and the natural human being who lives a life in society, and he states categorically: "Emile is no savage to be banished to the desert, he is a savage who has to live in the town[2]".

---

[1] Jean-Jacques ROUSSEAU, *Émile ou de l'éducation*, Classique Garnier, p. 179; quoted from *Emile,* translated by Barbara Foxley, Ebook, Project Gutenberg, 2004.

[2] *Ibid.*, p. 240; quoted from *Emile*, translated by Barbara Foxley, Ebook, Project Gutenberg, 2004.

In the same year as Rousseau published *Emile*, he also published his work about *The Social Contract*. Here he shows that in order to live in a legitimate cultured society one has to give up the natural freedom to act according to one's wishes in order to obtain freedom at a higher level where one can act as a citizen and benefit from the communal life.

But how is it possible to unite an education as an independent individual with an education as a citizen of society? How can one unite the two goals: personal life and life as a State citizen? This became the major question for the pedagogical philosophy that arose in the wake of Rousseau's new thinking. And – as we shall see – it is still the major question facing pedagogical thinking today.

FREEDOM AND NECESSITY

Since its origin, moreover, philosophy of education has faced another difficult problem that not only concerns the pedagogical relationship, but human action in general. Rousseau is well aware of this problem, declaring that the art of education is "virtually impossible" when one considers everything that influences a person's life. It is the big question of freedom versus necessity that appears here. Isn't everything determined by necessary causes or processes so that any idea of freedom is illusory? One can therefore ask whether it is at all meaningful to speak about education if the goal is to develop free, independent persons? And this is not just a question of education, but of freedom of action in general – both a moral action and artistic creation.

Another 18th Century philosopher, Immanuel Kant (1724-1804), who is also one of the fathers of philosophy of education, understood that he had to find a solution to the relationship between freedom and necessity since a large part of his thinking focused on ethics, politics and artistic creation. If freedom did not exist, this whole part of his philosophy would be meaningless, but on the other hand he had to admit that he could not think of freedom in natural scientific terms, i.e. on the basis of the concept that everything is necessarily determined by what already exists, which becomes causes that strictly result in their effects, such that everything would be calculable and foreseeable if one knew enough.

In his *Critique of Pure Reason,* Kant saw the problem as an antinomy, i.e. a contradiction between two apparently indisputable propositions about causality. One proposition states: "Causality regulated by the laws of nature is not the only causality responsible for all the appearances in the world. To explain these appearances it is necessary to assume the existence of another causality that is determined by freedom." The other proposition states: "Freedom does not exist and everything in the world is solely determined by the laws of nature[3]". Kant's own solution to this antinomy consisted of considering freedom and necessity as two completely different levels of reality. He considered freedom as a purely transcendental idea without any connection to the level of physical appearances, where necessity is assumed to apply. On the other hand he thought that he could conceive of the world of these appearances as being totally dependent on human perceptions of time and space, each of which can be assumed to be both limited and to reach into infinity, such that this inner contradiction in the very nature of their perceptions makes them unsuitable for understanding the whole reality, or what the world is in itself.

Kant claimed, however, that the situation was completely the opposite with freedom. Its idea does not contradict itself. He considered freedom as "an *absolute spontaneity* of causes[4]) that "of its own accord" initiates a series of appearances that subsequently proceed in accordance with the laws of nature. Moreover, he differentiated between a beginning *of* the world and a beginning *in* the world. The first form of beginning has nothing to do with human freedom. Only the idea of a beginning in the world characterizes freedom. But how? Kant is convinced that freedom must be the beginning of a chain of causes that can be ascribed to the action we identify when we ask "who?" or more explicitly "Who is the author of the action?". Such a cause, Kant says, would not exist if everything happened solely in accordance with the laws of nature that physics discovers, because in that case there would always only be a "subordinate" cause and never a primary cause. Consequently one would never be able to identify the primary cause of an action. But since we know from ordinary human experience that we spontaneously make decisions and initiate chains of action, we have to suppose that the spontaneous cause we cannot see when we view the world in the time and space of physics nevertheless has an *indirect effect* in the real world in which we live.

JOHANN FRIEDRICH HERBART

Kant's distinction between a transcendental and a physical world was somewhat unfortunate because it means that our world is split in two. And it was indeed this problem that was the key issue for probably the greatest figure in the history of pedagogical thinking, Johann Friedrich

---

[3] Immanuel KANT, *Kritik der reinen Vernunft,* B., 1787, p. 473, English translation: Norman Kemp Smith, *Critique of Pure Reason*, Macmillan, London 1958, p. 409.
[4] *Ibid.*, B., 474; trans., p. 411.

Herbart, in his 1804 essay: "On Aesthetic Representation of the World as the Principal Function of Education". The relationship between freedom and necessity was a problem for him, not just because human action has no meaning as an activity for which someone is responsible without the assumption of human freedom, but also because the educator takes into account the child's or pupil's naturally determined background and development and therefore has to apply his free influence to the physically and biologically determined causes and effects.

Herbart believed that Kant is right in conceiving of freedom as an action's beginning, but that he thinks too abstractly about freedom. With this criticism Herbart pre-empts what several 20th Century European philosophers (not least Georg Henrik von Wright and Paul Ricœur) have thought about the relationship between freedom and necessity. According to Herbart, freedom in Kant becomes solely freedom from natural inclinations in order to take a position on a moral law that respects other people's independence or autonomy, and not a freedom to take a position on everything another person can imagine of ends and means, and Kant cannot therefore demonstrate anything other than that freedom and necessity do not contradict each other. Kant remains in a counter-position of pure mechanics and pure spontaneity. But in education, Herbart says, the educator must assume that the young man or woman is capable of choosing between good and evil and thereby has the possibility to form his or her own character. And the task of the educator is to make the child or pupil capable of forming his or her own character. Instead of Kant's antinomy between mechanics and spontaneity, Herbart therefore assumes an interaction between natural development and deliberate self-formation such that desires do not directly determine will and action, but are subjected to the judgement of reason. And this judgement judges not only morally, but also aesthetically, by which Herbart means much more than just judging whether something is beautiful. The aesthetic determination of will and action focuses on the whole human being which – as far as education is concerned – means that it will help qualify the human being to participate in all aspects of society and not just specific aspects of society.

Herbart thereby indicates that education has not only a personal, but also a political aim. In his 1806 *General Pedagogy* and later writings, however, he also expresses scepticism about any idea of making the pupil into an uncritical citizen. As professor in Kant's Chair of Philosophy in Königsberg he worked for the implementation of the Prussian school and university reform (the Humboldt reform) that accorded fundamental importance to general education and rendered specialization of secondary importance so that the division of society into classes could be overcome and each individual could be provided with the possibility to develop his own personality. But he was also sceptical about public education as this easily risks becoming solely the training of pupils to become completely uncritical citizens of the State. He considered the private tutor to be a counterbalance to this, but he did not view the private tutor system as a solution to the education issue. He thought that both the public schooling system and the private tutor system could very easily be forms of schooling that adapt the pupils to the specific needs of society without giving them a broader horizon. Even Plato, in his theory of the State, could not desist from imagining citizens being educated to fulfil specific roles and at that time envisaged three main roles: as politicians, as soldiers and as artisans. An education that has only the survival of the State as its end will always be tempted to allow specialization to be the whole aim. The educator who wants to avoid this must therefore demand the greatest possible freedom to strengthen the pupil's personality, even if this means support for criticism of the existing State. The school must not be a factory, says Herbart, but must aim at variety. Thus he ends up prescribing a mixture of family upbringing, public education and free pedagogic education. But he did not manage to overcome the conflict between education aimed at the development of independent individuals and education aimed at the development of citizens.

THEORY AND PRACTICE

Herbart has formulated a pedagogical problem that has remained topical to this very day. But Herbart is also important as the philosopher who has developed a theory about the relationship between theory and practice in education and has thereby focused attention on what must be the core of all pedagogical thinking: reflection on the pedagogical relationship between someone who educates and someone who receives education, for example the relationship between a teacher (or tutor) and a pupil (or child). He presented this theory as early as 1802 during his first lecture on education as young lecturer *(Privatdozent)* in Göttingen.

He distinguishes here between the art of education and pedagogy, with the latter being understood by him to be the science of the former. But at that time "science" was not synonymous with empirical or (as we now refer to it) evidence-based science, but with philosophy as theoretically coherent thinking founded on maxims and principles, and which Herbart consequently calls "philosophical thinking".

He claims that the art of education is a collection of skills that are unified in order to realize a goal. It thus requires action. It may succeed by chance, by sympathy or by the parent's natural love. But it may also succeed due to the ability of the professional educator to take into account ability, gender and age. It is of course the latter form of education for which the theory is relevant, whereas the former can succeed irrespective of whether the educator or teacher has any idea why it succeeds or is aware of any goal. But every human being belongs to a certain nation and a certain epoch and has his own particular ideas, feelings and experiments and the experiences drawn from them. If education is to play a role in this context it must be determined by a philosophy able to provide a general indication of what education is intended to achieve.

However, no educational practice is provided that can logically be deduced from a pedagogical theory. Herbart emphasizes that the professional educator must apply his theory with *tact*, i.e. with delicacy. Tact is expressed in decisions and rulings that are neither carelessly random in practice nor an attempt to draw stringent consequences from the rules developed in the theory. Consequently, while the theory may prepare the ground for the art of education, it cannot predetermine it. It is only the educator's exhibition of tact that determines whether he is a good or bad educator.

But how can this tact be learnt? Herbart is only able to answer that pedagogical theory can render the educator "in favour" of being tactful in educational practice, and that he in any case must learn from his mistakes. And one can fail not only by showing too little interest in the child that is to be educated, but also, like Rousseau, by trying to follow him in every step he makes. Since education should be aimed at developing independent individuals, the perfect educator must be "the wise guide from afar" *(der weisen Lenker von Ferne)*, who "with his earnest words and expressive behaviour trustfully leaves him to his own development in the middle of the game and the competition with his friends."

According to Herbart, all this is based on a conviction about human nature and receptiveness to education *("Bildsamkeit")*, i.e. a view of the human being in which it is presupposed that education is meaningful and that the human being can be developed to lead a good life through education.

KANT'S PHILOSOPHY OF EDUCATION

Herbart represents the peak of philosophy of education in the 18th and the 19th Centuries. The important foundations for his thoughts on general pedagogy naturally include Rousseau, but also the experiment to create The New Elementary School for public education that Johann Heinrich Pestalozzi (1746-1827) performed in Stans and published a paper about in 1799. Just as important for him was Kant, though perhaps more his philosophy in general than his ideas on education, which were first published the year after Herbart presented his epoch-making lecture. But Kant's philosophy of education contained an idea that could be the rudiment of a solution of Herbart's problem concerning the relationship between the individual and the State in education – an outline that the whole troop of early 19th Century pedagogical thinkers did not manage to develop, and which was only taken up and developed 200 years later, i.e. the idea of the world citizen as the highest goal of all education. Using this idea we might today be able to overcome the contradiction between individual and State, because the world citizen or cosmopolitan is the individual who autonomously dares to think beyond the State without ending in anarchistic thinking. The world citizen is on the one hand an extreme individualist, because he or she is the person who defends his or her humanity by thinking beyond the State, and on the other hand is completely political by fighting for a just social order across all State borders.

Kant did not become a famous philosopher because of his lectures on education. While it is true that he held them several times during the period 1776-1787, they were first published by a pupil and friend in 1803 based on notes made by members of the audience. At that time Kant was so old that he is hardly likely to have had any influence on the final text. The lectures are nevertheless clearly inspired by Rousseau. And when Kant according to legend refrained from his usual morning walk in order to be able to read Rousseau's *Emile* without interruption immediately after having received a copy, it was probably because he saw in this work a theory of the art of education that aimed to turn the boy and pupil into an independent individual through the unification of his natural potential with moral and cultural education. In the German word *Erziehung* he saw a parallel to the French word *éducation* in Rousseau, i.e. to the idea of an education that not only consisted of teaching and disciplining children and pupils, but also an art of education and cultural formation (German: *Bildung*) that understands the need to take into account what is appropriate to their age.

He describes the educational process in four stages:

The first stage is the purely negative *disciplining* or eradication of savagery. Unlike Rousseau, Kant did not believe that the human being is naturally good, but rather – as he describes it in his 1793 essay on radical evil (integrated as the 1st chapter in his book on *The Religion Within the Limits of Reason Alone*) – that it is not only predisposed to good, but also has a propensity for evil. In the course of history, however, man has been able to raise himself above his wild nature to become a moral being. In the same way the child, who is born as a wild creature, has to be raised up into culture by suppression of its propensity for evil, thereby enabling development of its disposition for good.

The second stage is *cultivation* through the teaching of skills, i.e. of physical and intelligent competence, and the first scientific teaching is teaching in physical and political geography. In general, the cultivation stage consists of the learning of knowledge that renders the human being able to work. It is of utmost importance that children learn to work, because a human being cannot survive and obtain the necessities of life without labour.

The third stage is *civilization* or formation to a civilized life, i.e. to knowledge of how to interact decently with other people. The child has to learn how to integrate itself into society and become a useful citizen.

The fourth and final stage is *moralization*, which is the development of the moral consciousness that consists of an understanding of and conviction about what not only applies in the case of human beings with the same interests, but what necessarily can be accepted by everybody at any time, i.e. the recognition of a universally applicable ethic.

One can see this as an outline for an authoritarian education, but Kant claims that his pedagogical theory actually entails the opposite: an education to freedom. Like Rousseau, Kant considers education to a political life as the goal since the whole idea is that the human being renounces animal freedom in favour of freedom involving responsibility together with others. According to Kant, education therefore contains an element of care. This care is not purely care of offspring as in the relationships between animals, but also care for cultural, civilized and moral education and formation. Thus, when Kant says: "Man is the only creation that has to be educated", he means "Man is the only creature that has to be taught to be a responsible being".

But as mentioned, Kant also has his eye on another element. He writes that children should not only be educated in accordance with the present state of the world, but with a view to the potentially better state of humanity in the future. And in this respect he distinguishes himself markedly from Rousseau. He declares in his lectures on pedagogy:

> Parents care for the home, rulers for the state. Neither have as their aim the universal good and the perfection to which man is destined and for

> which he has also a natural disposition. But the basis of a scheme of education must be cosmopolitan. And is, then, the idea of the universal good harmful to us as individuals? Never! For though it may appear that something must be sacrificed by this idea, an advance is also made towards what is the best even for the individual under his present conditions. And then what glorious consequences follow! It is through good education that all the good in the world arises. For this the germs which lie hidden in man need only to be more and more developed[5].

Both Rousseau and Kant reject authoritarian education and consider cultivation, civilization and moralization as the essential elements of education, and both place the individual person in the centre of learning. But the difference between them is that Rousseau wanted to educate to individual independence within a particular State and in a particular society and moreover thought that democracy was very difficult to practice in large States, whereas Kant, who thought that democracy could be practiced through elected representatives, wanted to educate to an independence that expressed itself in the capacity to think beyond the State of which one is a citizen.

Thus Kant spoke not only about civil law for the individual society and about international law comprising the acceptance of certain unwritten rules for the conduct of relationships between States, in particular during times of war, but also about a *cosmopolitan law* according to which every human being has the right to freely visit and trade with all others. Moreover, in his 1795 essay on *Perpetual Peace* he assumed unlike in the teachings of Rousseau that human beings cannot only form a State and become citizens of that State as if they had entered into a social contract, but are also able to understand their relation to humanity as a whole as if they had entered into a global social contract. Also he assumed like Christian Wolff (1674–1754) and Rousseau that the mere fact that the social contract was entered into "fictively" in the past does not render it of less importance. The contract becomes a reality simply if one just lives *as if* it had been entered into and thereby assumes that it accords one rights and obligations as a member of the civilization it justifies.

DEVELOPMENT OF THE IDEA OF THE COSMOPOLITAN

The idea of the cosmopolitan was first developed by the Greek-Roman philosophers generally referred to as the Stoics. Around the time of Christ's birth, Cicero, and later the Stoics Seneca, Epictetus, Marcus Au-

---

[5] Immanuel KANT, *On Education* (1803), translated by Annette Churton, Dover Publications, Inc., Mineola, New York (1899) 2003, p. 15.

relius and several others, pondered the idea of the world citizen as a human being who is aware of the humanity he shares with other human beings. This idea, which did not exist in Plato and Aristotle, was of a human nature that has particular dignity as belonging to a sphere of reason that elevates itself above material nature and endows it with awareness of spiritual communion between all human beings. This cosmopolitan of the Antiquity (Greek: *kosmou-polites*) was a humanist and proud of his humanity that made him more than just a citizen of a (city)State *(polites)*.

There was not very much political reality in this idea, however. Marcus Aurelius (121-180), while Emperor of Rome, declared in his *Meditations* (which was written in Greek) that he was a member of the family of rational human beings: as such he considered himself a citizen of the highest city *(polis)* in relation to which other cities are like houses. But this world citizenship was of purely personal character. It was the community of thought with all people, also the scoundrels amongst one's closest and the strangers coming from abroad. In practice this meant being open to everybody and making an effort to understand the other person. The state of the Empire was not changed by this philosophical Emperor, however. The idea was not transposed into practical laws, and it had no influence on the way by which the Empire governed the world.

PRESENT-DAY PROBLEM COMPLEXES

In Kant the idea of the world citizen or cosmopolitan has become more concrete than in the time of the Stoics. But it mainly remains a great, beautiful idea with a glimmer of unreality. And it could not be otherwise at that time, simply because the major transnational problems of today did not exist then. In our age the idea of the cosmopolitan as an ideal of education has become an ideological necessity, however, because unlike in Kant's time, we shall not only have to trade across the borders of countries and need peace to conduct this trade, but we are now also confronted with a number of major problem complexes relating to human life and global survival.

In my book *The Cosmopolitan as Ideal of Education*[6] I examined three such problem complexes:

The first problem complex is that of *financial globalization*. Transnational corporations and international banks have transformed the world into a global market where the power of Nation States is limited. As a

---

[6] Forthcoming in English at Humanity Books, New York. Published in Danish: *Verdensborgeren som pædagogisk ideal*, Hans Reitzel, Copenhagen 2005. Chapters 1-3.

consequence, there is a more or less open fight between this global system and the individual States. Moreover, global financial problems cannot be handled by any single State alone, and States must recognize that they need both economic, cultural and social transnational non-State actors to control globalization in all its aspects.

The second problem complex is that of *intercultural coexistence.* Many prejudices and biases have to be reconsidered if we are to achieve dialogue between cultures. Difficulties have to be overcome not only in the so-called Third World, but also in highly developed countries. And we must recognize that reconciliation between cultures, and especially between Islamic and Judeo-Christian cultures, will never take place unless both parties refrain from trying to solve their differences through humiliation of or violence against the other.

The third problem complex is that of *the physical sustainability of the Earth.* Human beings utilize production methods that may permanently destroy the natural conditions for human life. We may therefore leave future generations with a world that has material conditions inferior to those known to us. We thus need a global democracy that incorporates responsibility towards the other person in a future world whose inhabitants should not have to blame us for the exploitation of the world's physical capital.

These problem complexes are further compounded by the increase in global crime, ranging from financial crime (including Internet crime) to major crimes against humanity, e.g. the war crimes condemned at the Nuremberg and Tokyo tribunals just after the Second World War, and crimes against the future of humanity through the pollution of the planet.

Since these problems cannot be solved by any one political actor alone, but only jointly by them all, we must act as international and transnational world citizens if we want to act in a politically responsible manner. Like Kant, we can say: The basis of a scheme of education must be cosmopolitan. Thus pedagogics cannot just concern the means of education, but must also clarify the goals of education.

Knowledge of the means comes through an insight into what human beings are and are able to do in relation to each other as educators and the educated, i.e. into how they should relate to dissemination of knowledge and convictions. In our culture there has been marked interest in the means since the sophists and Plato. But this knowledge is gradually becoming specialized in psychology, sociology, cultural anthropology and didactics (the art and science of teaching), whereas pedagogics continues to focus on the fundamental aspects of our pedagogical thinking.

The goal is set based on an understanding of what we want to make the world and societies into. This insight cannot solely consist of an acknowledgement of what goals the means enable us to achieve; it must also include knowledge about and understanding of what the world and the societies have become today. Therefore it is first and foremost a question of facing reality.

The reality of today is financial globalization, intercultural differences and environmental crises. That means that we can speak much more concretely about the cosmopolitan than Kant could do in his writings and lectures, but 200 years had to pass before philosophers were obliged to take him seriously on this point. Today, however, philosophy of education cannot limit itself to general fundamental conditions of education, but must concern the world citizen as ideal of education.

In the time after Kant the idea of the cosmopolitan goal rapidly disappeared from most of the debate on education. It is true that J. G. Fichte in his *Speeches to the German Nation* from 1807-08 considered the idea of the cosmopolitan as a precondition for education of the national citizen, but he was nevertheless rapidly interpreted as a pure nationalist. It was therefore Rousseau's teaching that prevailed. This is clear in Herbart and all the pedagogical philosophers that followed him, a development that was undoubtedly due to the fact that national States became the dominant political actors in Europe after the fall of Napoleon in 1814 and the idea of the culturally defined nation concomitantly created the framework for an education that – according to Herbart – should teach the pupil "to swim in the stream of society". The discovery of the importance of languages, literature and history for the richness of a people seems to justify that education should essentially be national and serve the interests of the nation. Furthermore, romantic poets strengthened individualism in contrast to cosmopolitanism (see for instance Ludwig Tieck's 1813 preface to the second edition of his novel *Lovell*).

THE CRISIS IN MODERN PEDAGOGY

The idea that united all European pedagogical thinkers since Rousseau, and which became decisive for the creation of the modern pedagogy that has endured right up to the end of the 20th Century, was that education could not coerce and discipline human beings to particular convictions, but should, in full respect for free self-development of the individual, provide each person with the possibility to think their own thoughts. Modern pedagogy thus aims to educate to freedom. According to Kant the motto of the time of Enlightenment was "Have courage to think your own thoughts". All modern pedagogical philosophers, with Herbart in the lead, agreed that this should be the appeal to every pupil. But we must acknowledge that without the idea of the cosmopolitan, which disappeared from philosophy of education in the 19th Century and remained ousted until the end of the 20th Century, the contradiction between the individual and the State in pedagogical thinking has had little real chance of being solved.

The question of how one can concomitantly educate both to individual freedom and to social citizenship remains the great problem even now. The dilemma is that everyone agrees that the child or the pupil shall develop into an independent being with the responsibility for shaping his or her own life, yet at the same time the individual has to be educated and developed to serve the interests of the State as best possible. Young people shall both decide their own education and satisfy a political desire for early specialization so that society may acquire so many skills and master so many technical skills that the individual State can come out on top in the competition with other States. These persons have to be both individualized and flexible, i.e. they have to be both independent and effective in the scientific-technical State that competes with other States on the global market. They have to both learn to be free and complete human beings and be taught scientific and technical skills. Correspondingly, it is claimed that the tutor and the teacher must on one hand refrain from indoctrinating children and pupils, while concomitantly imbibing empirical knowledge in such a way that it can be proven by tests that the pupils have learnt something in accordance with a ministerially determined curriculum.

One can therefore ask: What does society actually want to achieve through education? Should the aim be to meet the various needs of young people to discover the diversity of life and develop their skills and satisfy their own needs, or to ensure the most efficient differentiation of society into professional and technical functions?

In the latter case the highly praised free choice for the young generation seems rather illusionary. Is there in fact any freedom for the individual to shape his or her life? Isn't freedom today increasingly limited to the free choice of consumer goods? Hasn't freedom in the modern State become like free choice in the supermarket among the multitude of goods that the "little" man or woman can fill into their increasingly large shopping trolleys? Isn't that just the freedom to satisfy disguised economic interests in production and trade, i.e. freedom as an economic necessity?

It is this transformation of freedom to necessity that is the major problem facing pedagogy today. Because what shall we educate our children and pupils and ourselves to be in this educational process, which is no longer limited to the elder generation's education of the younger generation, but has become lifelong learning? In short, how shall we both learn to develop ourselves individually and learn to adapt to the market?

TWO EXTREME SOLUTIONS

As modern national States have undoubtedly become welfare States and their societies have become consumer and service societies, education to individual freedom has to be adapted to these societies. But how can this be achieved? In the public debate it is rare that anyone refutes the right of the individual to be a free human being. But people define freedom differently. And these concepts of freedom appear clearly in two extreme solutions to the dilemma.

According to one solution, freedom can be defined as the freedom to adapt oneself. Freedom here is the possibility to pass all the politically demanded tests and examinations in schools and institutions of higher education. This freedom does not consist of the pupil's or student's participation in decision making, but rather of the possibility to become the cleverest pupil, the most effective technician, the most ingenious and creative director, the most indispensable expert, etc. At the same time the State increasingly attempts to safeguard this development, even if it has to take place at the expense of the classical principles of freedom. Thus the danger of terrorism is increasingly used to justify surveillance of everyone in all public spaces. The aim of education is here to shape human beings who are successful in this adaptation to the societal system and draw others into this educational process.

According to the other solution, freedom is defined as the freedom to have an intimate life in personal relationships and one's own lifestyle in public. This idea can be found among several modern sociologists, e.g. Zygmunt Bauman and Antony Giddens. In his 1989 book *Modernity and Holocaust*, Bauman accuses modern technical culture of lacking a defence against barbarity, i.e. that such a defence does not exist at societal level but must instead be sought in the close relationships between human beings as described by Emmanuel Levinas. Bauman offers no suggestion as to how the problem of relationships between the individual and the State can be solved in our globalized world. Giddens is well aware of the major global problems facing mankind, but he considers in his book *Modernity and Self-Identity* that the individual who has found his own lifestyle thereby acquires new forces for political change. But it is difficult to understand how purely personal emancipation can solve these major problems.

Thus modern pedagogy, the main aim of which is emancipation, has become a problem. It is still praised, but the pedagogical relationship is maintained more as care and personal guidance than as dissemination of knowledge and attitudes. The authority that personal and professional experience formerly endowed upon the pedagog and the teacher is now being replaced by "evidence-based" learning, i.e. impersonally transmitted information. This is an educational relationship that is as far removed as possible from the pedagogical tact referred to by Herbart. And the pedagogical and political "government" from which Herbart wished to free pedagogy is concomitantly rapidly regaining ground in practice, and the possibilities for choosing teaching materials are being restricted if not totally abolished. It could perhaps be said that we are moving towards the teacher-free school unless we can find a way to limit State control of education. Conversely, one may ask if this is not an unavoidable development given that we are so many human beings who have to live together and survive in a very complicated system?

Cosmopolitan Pedagogy

Baumann is surely right that the technical-scientific society in itself cannot provide any solution to our pedagogical dilemma. But can and should we be satisfied with simply cultivating our own intimate self-development and lifestyle? This is the decisive question that determines the aim of education today. During the 1990s a shift in the social paradigm has endowed the debate with a new perspective, however, namely the return of the world citizen to political philosophy and sociology. It is true that the cosmopolitan idea has not returned in the same abstract form it held in stoic philosophy or in the weak form that Kant and the other enlightenment philosophers could give it. But it has returned as the only realistic alternative to the major political ideas of the 19th and the 20th Centuries.

In the preface to his highly important book from 2002, *Macht und Gegenmacht im globalen Zeitalter, Neue weltpolitische Ökonomie* (Suhrkamp, München; English translation: *Power in the Global Age*, Polity Press, London 2006), Ulrich Beck claims that the idea of the cosmopolitan is the next great idea that emerges after the historically worn-out ideas of nationalism, communism, socialism and neo-liberalism, and that this idea *might* make the incredible possible that mankind survives the 21ˢᵗ Century without relapsing into barbarism (*Macht und Gegenmacht,* p. 16). This proclamation of the new era of cosmopolitanism appears in the wake of the above-mentioned paradigm shift in philosophy and sociology in the 1990s. This new thinking was pioneered by the philosophers Jacques Derrida in France, Jürgen Habermas in Germany and Martha C. Nussbaum in the United States, and by the sociologist David Held through his great book *Democracy and the Global Order* (Polity Press, London 1995).

But why precisely in the 1990s? Many of the key global problems of the epoch, and in particular the problem of global pollution, had already begun to manifest themselves and were in people's minds before then. We can therefore assume that the fall of the Berlin wall in 1989 was the decisive political event having an enormous symbolic effect. Indeed, since this event we no longer focus on the East-West divide, but now experience the World's conflicts independently of the former ideological division in two large blocs. Many people therefore see more clearly than before 1989 that we inhabit a "ball", as Kant said, and have common problems that traverse the frontiers.

In addition, the sovereignty of the Nation States is being increasingly undermined, their borders are becoming relativized, not least because they now have strong non-State actors as partners (multinational corporations, NGOs, global scientific networks, international courts, etc.). And Ulrich Beck points out that globalization has a dual effect in that it both weakens the local and national actors and strengthens the alternative actors who operate independently of State borders. Moreover, as the title of the original German book indicates, this creates a paradoxical alliance or fraternization between protest groups and State power, which can unite for instance in demanding international taxes on transnational financial transactions, such as the so-called Tobin tax that has been suggested by the ATTAC-movement, i.e. the *Action for a Tobin Tax to Assist the Citizens* since 1997. This idea was subsequently taken up by the French president Jacques Chirac, thus exemplifying the fraternization between counterpower and power pointed out by Beck.

The anti-globalization movement was only initially strongly against every form of globalization. It quickly became a "movement for alternative globalization" (in French, *une altermondialisation*). Conversely the States increasingly recognize that they need the criticism of the globalization in order to be able to obtain support to survive as relatively independent political powers.

It follows that we today must understand ourselves as citizens of the world having a common destiny. The sociological and philosophical understanding of this situation implies two levels that are inseparable: on one hand an empirical description of the cosmopolitan reality, i.e. as Ulrick Beck puts it, that "life punishes those who remain prisoners of the national look", and on the other hand a normative concept that establishes a cosmopolitan goal for the ethical and political commitment that must prevail today. Thus, the idea of the cosmopolitan has now become both a sociological reality and a philosophical ideal that every education and cultural development must highlight. But this also means that it is necessary to be cosmopolitan if one wants to see the social-political reality face to face, while one is free to renounce world citizenship in the normative sense and may refuse any concrete commitment to solving our major problems.

BETWEEN TWO CITIZENSHIPS

Philosophy of education – which since the time of Rousseau and Herbart has sought an educational goal that serves both the individual and the political life – is now offered a solution. Because an education that has the cosmopolitan as its ideal can set a higher goal than the life of the State without denying the importance of life as a State citizen, it can educate for freedom and personal commitment and at the same time – as in Kant – educate people to act politically in a way that is both best for the individual and the Nation State and best for the world.

And since this education demands that people acquire greater knowledge about the world in which they live and face the challenges it poses, it is no misuse of the educator's action that it becomes an appeal to moral and political responsibility. The attack on the teacher as the master endowed with authority by virtue of knowledge, experience and attitude was a mistake. To hold authority is not the same as to be authoritarian, as Hans-Georg Gadamer shows in his 1960 book *Truth and Method*. Normativity in teaching does not equate with manipulation of the individual person's development if it consists of an appeal to take on board what is taught by the educator in a true *mimesis*. And this mimesis has to be understood in the sense it has in Greek in Aristotle's *Poetics*, where it expresses the creative imitation of the actor when performing the author's text, i.e. not copying, but an actualizing and concretizing interpretation of the thoughts and feelings that are transmitted to the audience.

The Aristotelian idea of mimesis means that the ideas we are free to let our actions be motivated by derive from others. It presupposes that I can only become a responsible person through the other. And the question we have to ask is whether pedagogy can exist without this precondition which – as we have seen – applies in all philosophy of education from Aristotle to Rousseau, Kant and Herbart.

In our epoch the idea of the world citizen has become an idea that we have received from our thought history, but which we naturally cannot take on without modifying our application of it in relation to the global problem complexes we face. In return, this realistic idea about the present global reality could be the ground-breaking creative thought that solves the pedagogical dilemma between education to a free individual and education to a citizen in communion with others.

The idea of the cosmopolitan has always implied the concept of two citizenships: citizenship of the State and citizenship of the world, which it has separated in order to be able to unite them with reason and hope. But precisely because there are two distinct citizenships, the individual who ponders them is not totally integrated in either of them. In the conflict between life as a State citizen and life as a world citizen the individual can – strengthened by his experiences of life with others and their testimony about it – develop and maintain his freedom as to self-education, moral responsibility towards the other person and critical consideration of political issues. And it is therefore in this conflict that pedagogy and pedagogical insight can reveal their justification and indispensability.

ABOUT THE AUTHORS

Evandro AGAZZI: is professor of philosophy at the University of Genoa, and has been teaching at several universities in Europe and America. At present he is President of the International Academy of Philosophy of Science. In the past he was President of the International Federation of Philosophical Societies and of the International Institute of Philosophy (he is now Honorary President of both institutions). His publications (more than 70 authored or edited books and more than 800 papers) deal with topics spanning from philosophy of science to metaphysics, ethics and education.

Anne-Marie EGGERT OLSEN (b. 1956): Ph.D., Associate Professor of Philosophy at the School of Education, Aarhus University (Campus: Copenhagen). Main areas of research are history of ancient philosophy, critical theory, political philosophy, and philosophy of education. Has published (mainly in Danish) a number of books and articles on Plato and on philosophy of education.

Guttorm FLØISTAD (b. 1930): Professor Emeritus of philosophy at the University of Oslo. Member of the Royal Academy of Science, the Society of Oriental Studies, the Institut international de philosophie. Last publications: *Utfordringer. Studier i langsomhetens filosofi* I-II [Challenges. Studies in the Philosophy of Slowness], 2001; *Om å kunne mer enn man kan* [How to achieve yourself more than what you are able to], 1996.

Peter KEMP (b. 1937): Professor Emeritus of Philosophy at the School of Education, Aarhus University (Campus: Copenhagen). President of the XXIInd World Congress of Philosophy, Seoul, 2008. Major works: *Théorie de l'engagement*, I-II, Paris 1973; *Das Unersetzlische – eine Technologieethik*, Berlin 1992. French: *L'irremplaçable*, Paris 1997. *Verdensborgeren som pædagogisk ideal*, København 2005; to be published in English: *The Cosmopolitan*, Prometheus, New York.

Vladislav A. LEKTORSKY (b. 1932): Professor of the Institute of Philosophy, Russian Academy of Sciences, Editor-in-Chief, *Voprosi filosofii*, full member of the Russian Academy of Sciences. Major works:

Das Subject-Object Problem in der klassischen und modernen burgerlich Philosophie, Berlin 1968; *Subject, Object, Cognition*, M. 1983. In English: *Activity: Theories, Methodology, Problems*, Orlando 1990. Editor and author. "Knowledge and Cultural Objects", *The Concept of Knowledge*, ed. by I. Kuçuradi and R. Cohen, Boston Studies in the Philosophy of Science, Vol. 170, The Netherlands, 1995; *Classical and Non-Classical Epistemology*, M. 2007. In Russian.

Hans LENK (b. 1935): Professor of philosophy in Karlsruhe University. President of the Allgemeine Gesellschaft für Philosophie in Deutschland, Honorary President of the Institut international de philosophie (Paris). Last publications: *Grasping Reality*, Singapore 2003; *Bewußtsein als Schemainterpretation*, 2004; *Verantwortung und Gewissen des Forschers*, 2006.

Evanghélos MOUTSOPOULOS (b. 1930, Athens): PhD (1958). Successively Professor at the universities of Aix-Marseille (1958), of Thessalonica (1965) and of Athens (1969). Several times *Honoris causa* Doctor and member of numerous national and international Academies. Has written more than sixty books on ontology, epistemology, axiology, *kairology*, philosophy of art and history of philosophy, mostly published in French and translated into several languages.

Kurt NIELSEN (b. 1945): Associate Professor Emeritus of Philosophy at the School of Education, Aarhus University (Campus: Copenhagen). Main areas of research are values in education and political philosophy. Has published (mainly in Danish) a number of articles on philosophy of education. In particular critical essays on constructivism.

Henrik VASE FRANDSEN (b. 1963): Associate Professor at the School of Education, Aarhus University (Campus: Copenhagen). Major publication: *Emmanuel Levinas og Kærlighedens Visdom* [Emmanuel Levinas and the Wisdom of Love], Odense 2001. Different essays on phenomenology, theology and philosophy of education. Current research project: Experience, Subjectivity and Religon – between Phenomenology and Theology.

Alexander VON OETTINGEN (b.1966): Doctor in Education, Head of the Department for Development and Applied Research, University College South/Denmark, Major works: *Det pædagogiske paradoks* [The Educational Paradox], Klim Aarhus 2001; *Pædagogisk filosofi som reflekteret* *omgang med pædagogiske antinomier* [Educational Philosophy as a Reflected Handling of Educational Antinomies], Klim, Aarhus 2006.

Lars-Henrik SCHMIDT (b. 1953): Professor of Philosophy at Aarhus University, Chancellor of the Danish University of Education (2000-2007). Director of Research at Research Centre Gnosis, Aarhus University (Campus: Copenhagen), regarding the study of mind and thinking from a philosophical and pedagogical perspective. Major works: *Immediacy Lost: Construction of the Social in Rousseau and Nietzsche*, Copenhagen 1988; *Der Wille zur Ordnung*, Århus 1989; *Tragik der Aufklärung – Nietzsches kritik der Metaphysik*, Århus 1989; *The Libertine's Nature*, Copenhagen 2005; *Om respekten*, Copenhagen 2005; to be published in English: *On Respect*, Copenhagen.

Irene SVITZOU (b. in Athens, Greece): She graduated from the University of Athens, Department of Philosophy, Pedagogic and Psychology. She attended post-graduate studies in philosophy at the University of Crete and she is now working on her doctoral dissertation on Plato at the Panteion University of Athens. She works as an Attached Researcher at the Research Centre on Greek Philosophy at the Academy of Athens.

INDEX

A

ADAM Karl, 121, 122, 123, 138, 144, 145
ADORNO Theodor W., 138, 186, 193
AGAZZI Evandro, 9, 12
ANDERSEN H. C., 170, 171
ARCHIMEDES, 84
ARENDT Hannah, 13, 58, 59, 60, 61, 63, 65, 66, 67
ARISTARCHUS, 84
ARISTOTLE, 13, 14, 75, 81, 86, 88, 196, 206, 213, 214
ARONOWITZ Stanley, 98, 117
ATKINSON J. W., 124, 127, 145, 146
AUGUSTINE (St.), 60, 61
AYERS Mary, 104, 117

B

BAKHTIN Michail M., 156
BALLAUFF Theodor, 50
BAUMAN Zygmun, 210
BEAUVOIR Simone de, 105
BECK Ulrich, 46, 211, 212, 213
BEETHOVEN Ludwig von, 123
BENNER Dietrich, 50
BERGSON Henri, 92
BEYER E., 145, 146
BIBLER Vladimir S., 152, 156
BIFULCO Antonia, 117
BIRCH D., 145
BJØRKVOLD Joan-Roar, 102, 118
BLACKINGTON III Frank H., 116, 118
BLIXEN Karen, 170
BLOCK Mary Ann, 101
BOBONICH Christopher, 70
BREEN Dana, 118
BRÈS Yvon, 69, 74
BRISSON L., 69, 73, 74
BRØGGER Susanne, 170
BURDEN Garret, 118
BUUR Hansen N., 46

C

CHIRAC Jacques, 212
CHURTON Annette, 205
CICERO, 205
CLARK R. A., 146
CLEARY J. J., 69, 70, 76
COHEN R., 216
COUSIN Victor, 91
CUMMING John, 118
CZIKSZENTMIHALYI M., 135, 145

D

DALAI LAMA, 64
DALFERTH I. U., 57
DAMGAARD I., 66
DAVYDOV Vasilii V., 153, 156
DERRIDA Jacques, 97, 212
DESCARTES René, 84, 92
DESPOTOPOULOS C., 77
DEWEY John, 192
DILTHEY Wilhelm, 98
DOPPLER, 80
DOSTOEVSKI F. I., 156

E

EDWARDS Richard, 97, 118
EGGERT OLSEN Anne-Marie, 17, 41
EPICTETUS, 205
EPIMENIDES, 36
ETCHEGOYEN Alicia, 118

F

FEATHER N. T., 145
FERRY Luc, 62

FICHTE J. G., 208
FISCHER, 48, 50
FIZEAU, 80
FLEMMING, 170
FLØISTAD Guttorm, 14, 94, 113, 118
FOUCAULT Michel, 97
FOXLEY Barbara, 197
FREDE D., 75
FREUD Sigmund, 105, 168
FRISCH Hartvig, 168
FUREDI Frank, 95, 96, 118

G

GADAMER Hans-Georg, 98, 118, 150, 157, 213
GAUCHET Marcel, 62
GEHLEN, 136
GIDDENS Antony, 46, 210
GIESECKE Hermann, 181, 182, 183, 184, 185, 186, 192, 193
GIROUX Henry A., 98, 117
GRØN A., 66
GRONEMAYER Marianne, 117
GRUBE, 145
GRUE-SØRENSEN Knud, 44, 45, 46, 47, 48, 49, 53
GRUNDTVIG N. F. S., 167, 168

H

HABERMAS Jürgen, 162, 185, 212
HAGELSTANGE R., 121
HALVORSEN William H., 118
HAMMERSHØJ L. G., 36
HANDY Charles, 96, 110, 118
HECKHAUSEN H., 145
HEGEL G. W. F., 87
HEITGER M., 51
HELD David, 212
HERBART Johann Friedrich, 12, 42, 43, 200, 201, 202, 208, 209, 211, 213, 214
HERMANSEN M., 46
HILBERT David, 123
HILDEN Jytte, 167, 168
HOLMES Jeremy, 118
HOMAN, 134
HÖNIGSWALD Richard, 51, 53

HOPPE, 126
HORKHEIMER Max, 191, 193
HUMBOLDT Wilhem von, 12, 41, 42, 200
HUMMEL Charles, 69

I

IBSEN Henrik, 99, 100
ILLICH Ivan, 148, 157

J

JAEGER Werner, 86
JAQUES Martin, 103, 118
JENSEN H. D., 36
JØRSTAD Jarl, 106

K

KANT Immanuel, 13, 23, 45, 50, 59, 86, 92, 160, 191, 198, 199, 200, 202, 203, 204, 205, 206, 207, 208, 211, 212, 213, 214
KAPLAN Abraham, 96, 118
KEMP Peter, 10, 11, 35, 36
KEMP SMITH Norman, 199
KIERKEGAARD Søren, 170, 171
KILBOURNE Jean, 112, 118
KINDLON Dan, 102, 118
KOHEN Dora, 105, 118
KOMENSKI Jan Amos, 150
KOOLHAS Rem, 107
KROCKOW C. v., 145
KUCHARSKI P., 73
KUÇURADI Ioanna, 216

L

LACAN Jacques, 97
LAKS A., 75
LAMBRELLIS D., 75
LANDSBERG Paul-Louis, 11
LASCH Christopher, 96
LASH S., 46
LAURENT J., 71
LEKTORSKY Vladislav A., 16
LENK Hans, 15, 145, 146
LENZEN Dieter, 191, 192, 193
LEVINAS Emmanuel, 63, 66, 210

LEWIN, 126
LIPMAN Matthew, 152, 154, 157
LITT Theodor, 50
LOCKE John, 112, 197
LOMBARDI, 143
LOWELL E. L., 146
LUHMANN Niklas, 46
LYOTARD J., 97, 98, 118

M

MACKINLAY Shane, 67
MARCEL Gabriel, 11
MARCUS AURELIUS, 206
MARION Jean-Luc, 63, 66
MARX Karl, 186
MATTHEW (St.), 110
MATURANA Humberto, 46
MCCLELLAND D. C., 123, 124, 127, 138, 146
MEYER W.-U., 146
MILL J. S., 112
MITCHELL Katharyne, 192, 194
MONTESQUIEU Charles (de SECONDAT), 86
MOORE A., 76
MORAN Patricia, 117
MOSER S., 145, 146
MOUNIER Emmanuel, 11
MOUTSOPOULOS Evanghélos, 14, 77, 79, 84, 87

N

NAPOLEON, 208
NATORP Paul, 50
NELSON Leonard, 45, 50
NIELSEN Kurt, 17
NIETZSCHE Friedrich, 90
NORBERG-SCHULZ Christian, 108, 118
NORDLIEN Svein Olav, 102
NUSSBAUM Martha C., 212

O

OCCAM William (of OCKHAM), 22
OETTINGEN Alexander von, 12, 13, 41, 42, 44
ORTEGA Y GASSET José, 122, 136

OVERGAARD S., 66

P

PASCAL Blaise, 10
PATTERSON Robert S., 116, 118
PAUL (St.), 60
PERELMAN Lewis, 118
PESTALOZZI Johann Heinrich, 203
PETZELT A., 48
PINKOLA ESTÈS Clarissa, 106
PIPHER Mary, 118
PLATO, 13, 14, 69, 70, 71, 72, 73, 74, 75, 76, 77, 78, 80, 88, 115, 196, 201, 206, 207
PYTHAGORAS, 32

R

RANKE, 98
RAYNOR J. O., 145
RICH Adrienne, 105
RICHTER, 145
RICKERT, 98
RICŒUR Paul, 200
RIFBJERG Klaus, 168
ROTH Klas, 190, 194
ROUSSEAU Jean-Jacques, 12, 40, 41, 159, 197, 198, 202, 203, 204, 205, 208, 213, 214
ROWE, 75
RUHLOFF, 50

S

SARTRE Jean-Paul, 11, 98, 105
SCHILLER, 122
SCHLEIERMACHER Friedrich, 51
SCHMALT H. D., 126, 146
SCHMIDT Lars-Henrik, 16, 18, 161, 172
SCHMIDTCHEN G., 131, 146
SCHOFIELD M., 75
SCHÜTZ, 136
SCOLNICOV S., 69, 74
SCOTT Catherine, 95
SENECA, 205
SHAKESPEARE William, 99, 100, 112
SOCRATES, 14, 88, 91, 92, 103, 150, 156, 170, 196

SPENCER H., 122
STENBAK LARSEN C., 36
STERN D., 46
STRAUSS L., 73
STRUCK Peter, 95, 106, 107, 114, 117, 118
SVITZOU Irene, 13, 77

T

TAINE Hippolyte, 86
TATUM, 143
TAYLOR A. E., 72, 73
THOMAE H., 145
THOMPSON Michael, 102, 118
TIECK Ludwig, 208
TJELTVEIT Alan C., 113
TØNNESSEN Rolf Th., 183, 194
TRANØY Joar, 101
TREML Alfred K., 192, 194
TROWELL Judith, 118

U

USHER Robin, 97, 118

V

VASE FRANDSEN Henrik, 13, 66
VOEGELIN E., 72
VOLTAIRE François Marie (AROUET), 160

W

WALKER Sydney, 101
WARDEN, 70
WATERS Roger, 97
WEBER Max, 26, 27, 146
WEINER B., 146
WEISS P., 141, 146
WHITE F. C., 75
WHITE Merry, 94, 119
WIEDEMANN Finn, 44
WINNICOTT Donald W., 104
WOLFF Christian, 205
WRIGHT Georg Henrik von, 200

Z

ZOJA Luigi, 105, 106, 119
ZUCKERMAN M., 146

Philosophie und Bildung

hrsg. von Prof. Dr. Ekkehard Martens (Hamburg), Dr. Christian Gefert (Hamburg) und Prof. Dr. Volker Steenblock (Bochum)

Sven Rohm
Objektiver Geist und Ontologie der Sprache
Nicolai Hartmann und Hans-Georg Gadamer
Das vorliegende Buch versucht anhand der interpretierenden Darstellung und des kritischen Vergleichs bestimmter Aspekte der Philosophien von *Nicolai Hartmann* und *Hans-Georg Gadamer* nach der Relevanz metaphysischer und ontologischer Orientierung in unserer Gegenwart zu fragen, insbesondere nach der Möglichkeit einer ontologisch fundierten Erkenntnislehre und nach ihrem Verhältnis zur modernen Wissenschaftlichkeit. Hier sind neben aufschlussreichen Differenzen auch auffällige Übereinstimmungen festzustellen. Ein Vergleich beider Denker bietet sich schon biographisch an, da der junge Gadamer bei Hartmann in Marburg studiert hat.
Bd. 9, 2008, 256 S., 29,90 €, br., ISBN 978-3-8258-1170-9

Markus Bartsch
Gesellschaftlicher Dialog im Klassenzimmer
Didaktische Implikationen interkultureller Hermeneutik im Fach Praktische Philosophie
Der gesellschaftliche Dialog über Wertefragen im Unterricht mit Schülerinnen und Schülern von kulturell, religiös und ethnisch divergierendem Selbstverständnis macht es notwendig, Pluralismus jenseits von Relativismus lehr- und lernbar zu machen. Das Prinzip des interkulturellen Polylogs im Klassenzimmer macht Didaktik zu einem Verfahren angewandter Hermeneutik. Auf der Grundlage einer qualitativen Analyse interkultureller Wirklichkeitsbedingungen in deutschen Klassenzimmern wird ein unterrichtspraktisch übertragbares Rahmenkonzept präsentiert, das nicht nur zur erweiternden Neuorientierung der Philosophiedidaktik herangezogen werden sollte, sondern auch die Rolle des Lehrers als Pädagoge neu zu definieren hilft.
Bd. 10, 2009, 320 S., 34,90 €, br., ISBN 978-3-8258-1697-1

Chang-Ho Jeong
Philosophieunterricht als eine Orientierungshilfe in der kulturellen Identitätskrise Südkoreas
Die kulturelle Identitätskrise Südkoreas ist auf den exogenen Modernisierungsprozess zurückzuführen. Aber Südkorea ist nicht das einzige Land, das ein Identitätsproblem hat. Kein Land ist in dieser globalisierten Welt vor einer kulturellen Identitätskrise gefeit. Mein Versuch, eine kollektive Identitätssuche der südkoreanischen Kultur u. a. durch die philosophische Bildung zu unterstützen und dadurch mit der Interkulturalität und mit dem vernünftigen Denken verträglich zu machen, kann in diesem Sinne hoffentlich einen Hinweis für Deutschland und andere Länder geben.
Bd. 11, 2009, 248 S., 24,90 €, br.,
ISBN 978-3-8258-1971-2

Ethik und Pädagogik im Dialog

hrsg. von Prof. Dr. Holger Burckhart (Universität zu Köln), PD Dr. Timo Hoyer (Universität Kassel) und Dr. Jürgen Sikora (Universität zu Köln)

Maria Maiss
Ethisch-moralische Propädeutik
Erziehungsethische Überlegungen zur Psycho- und Soziogenese prämoralischer und moralischer Fähigkeiten
Die Autorin widmet sich der Frage, inwiefern zentrale Inhalte der kantischen Ethik, welche primär den Standpunkt selbstbestimmungsfähiger Menschen fokussiert, für die Erziehungsethik fruchtbar gemacht werden können. Um das Verhältnis zwischen menschlichem „Können" und „Sollen" bestimmbar zu machen, werden unter Rekurs auf einschlägige Theoriemodelle unterschiedlicher Disziplinen zentrale ontogenetische und psychosoziale Bedingungen der (Re-)Konstitutionsprozesse (prä-)moralischer Fähigkeiten dargestellt und mit der kantischen Frage „wie Freiheit bei dem Zwange möglich sei" konfrontiert.
Bd. 3, 2006, 280 S., 19,90 €, br., ISBN 3-8258-8726-x

Heinz Eidam; Timo Hoyer (Hg.)
Erziehung und Mündigkeit
Bildungsphilosophische Studien
Das Buch versammelt Studien, in denen die Beziehung zwischen Mündigkeit und Erziehung bildungsphilosophisch untersucht wird. Neben Überblicksdarstellungen enthält der Band Aufsätze, in denen Aspekte der Mündigkeitsproblematik bei Rousseau, Kant, Marx, Nietzsche und den Autoren der Frankfurter Schule (Adorno, Marcuse, Benjamin) zur Sprache kommen. Zudem werden Fragen der Gerechtigkeitserziehung und der Sozialen Arbeit aufgegriffen. Die Beiträge sind Ergebnisse einer deutsch-brasilianischen Wissenschaftskooperation.
Bd. 4, 2006, 240 S., 19,90 €, br., ISBN 3-8258-9867-9

LIT Verlag Berlin – Münster – Wien – Zürich – London
Auslieferung Deutschland / Österreich / Schweiz: siehe Impressumsseite

Philosophy in International Context/Philosophie im internationalen Kontext
edited by/hg Hans Lenk (Karlsruhe)

Hans Lenk
Global TechnoScience and Responsibility
Schemes Applied to Human Values, Technology, Creativity and Globalisation
Bd. 3, 2007, 432 S., 39,90 €, br., ISBN 978-3-8258-0392-6

Wissenschaftliche Paperbacks

Hans-Georg Gadamer
Die Lektion des Jahrhunderts
Ein philosophischer Dialog mit Riccardo Dottori
Gadamers Hermeneutik des suchenden Gesprächs ermöglicht vielen Disziplinen der Geistes- und Sozialwissenschaften, Wege des fachlichen Erkennens mit historischen Sichtweisen zu verknüpfen. Seit "Wahrheit und Methode" (1960) rühmt man die von ihm geleistete "Urbanisierung der Heideggerschen Provinz" (Habermas). Versteht Gadamer jede Aussage als Antwort auf eine Frage, so ist Leben als Dialog neu zu verstehen.
Bd. 2, 2. Aufl. 2003, 168 S., 15,90 €, br.,
ISBN 3-8258-5049-8; 34,90€, gb., ISBN 3-8258-5768-9

Hans Jonas
Fatalismus wäre Todsünde
Gespräche über Ethik und Mitverantwortung im dritten Jahrtausend. Herausgegeben von Dietrich Böhler im Auftrag des Hans Jonas-Zentrums e. V.
Hans Jonas konnte 1979, als Europa sich die Augen rieb und zu räsonieren begann, ob der technologisch industrielle Fortschritt eine "ökologische Krise" verursache, schon seine tiefdringende „Ethik der technologischen Zivilisation" vorlegen. Deren Grundgedanken und ihre Orientierung für das 21. Jahrhundert – das erste einer technologisch und wirtschaftlich "globalisierten" Menschheit – hat er in eindringlichen Gesprächen vor Augen geführt und im Blick auf künftige Entwicklungen zugespitzt. Gegen den Pessimismus macht er Mut zur Mitverantwortung, gegen die Augenblicksversessenheit erschließt er Orientierungssinn aus der jüdisch-christlichen Tradition. Der Berliner Ethiker Dietrich Böhler, der auch die LIT-Reihe „Ethik und Wirtschaft im Dialog" mitherausgibt, hat besonders aussagekräftige, aber kaum mehr greifbare, Gespräche zusammengestellt. Einführend gibt er einen Einblick in die Stationen von Jonas' Denken; zum aktuellen Schluß kontrastiert er PID und Embryonen 'verbrauchende' Forschung mit den Prinzipien Verantwortung und Menschenwürde.
Bd. 19, 2005, 224 S., 17,90 €, br., ISBN 3-8258-7573-3

Hans Albert
In Kontroversen verstrickt
Vom Kulturpessimismus zum kritischen Rationalismus
Kontroversen machten einen wesentlichen Aspekt von Hans Alberts Leben aus. Daß er in seiner Jugend Anhänger der Geschichtsphilosophie Oswald Spenglers wurde, verwickelte ihn in Diskussionen mit Verfechtern der herrschenden Weltanschauung. Nach dem zweiten Weltkrieg, an dem er als Soldat und Offizier teilgenommen hatte, studierte er Wirtschafts- und Sozialwissenschaften in Köln und wurde 1963 Ordinarius für Soziologie und Wissenschaftslehre in Mannheim. Als Verfechter einer an der Soziologie Max Webers und der Philosophie Karl Poppers orientierten Auffassung geriet er in Kontroversen mit Verfechtern anderer Anschauungen im Bereich der Philosophie, der Soziologie, der Ökonomik, der Theologie und anderer Disziplinen, auf die er in diesem Buch eingeht.
Bd. 28, 2007, 264 S., 19,90 €, br.,
ISBN 978-3-8258-0433-6

L<small>IT</small> Verlag Berlin – Münster – Wien – Zürich – London
Auslieferung Deutschland / Österreich / Schweiz: siehe Impressumsseite